Czesław Miłosz and Joseph Brodsky

Czesław Miłosz

and

Joseph Brodsky

FELLOWSHIP OF POETS

Irena Grudzinska Gross

Foreword by TOMAS VENCLOVA

YALE UNIVERSITY PRESS   NEW HAVEN AND LONDON

A previous version of this book was published under the title *Miłosz i Brodski: pole
magnetyczne,* by Irena Grudzińska-Gross (Krakow: Wydawnictwo Znak, 2007).
Copyright © 2007 by Irena Grudzińska-Gross.

Quotations from the published and unpublished works of Joseph Brodsky are
copyright © by Joseph Brodsky and reprinted by permission of the estate of
Joseph Brodsky. Quotations from the works of Czesław Miłosz are copyright © by the
estate of Czesław Miłosz and reprinted by permission. The quotation from Anna
Akhmatova's poem "The Muse," from *Selected Poems,* ed. and intro. Walter Arndt (New
York: Ardis/Overlook, 1976), is reprinted by permission of the publisher. The quotations
from Derek Walcott's poem "Dedication" are reprinted by permission of Derek Walcott.

Designed by Mary Valencia.
Set in Adobe Caslon type by Westchester Book Group, Danbury, Connecticut.
Printed in the United States of America.

Library of Congress Cataloging-in-Publication Data

Grudzinska-Gross, Irena.
    Czeslaw Milosz and Joseph Brodsky : fellowship of poets / Irena Grudzinska Gross ;
foreword by Thomas Venclova.
        p. cm.
    Mostly a translation of: Miłosz i Brodski.
    Includes bibliographical references and index.
    ISBN 978-0-300-14937-1 (cloth : alk. paper)   1. Milosz, Czeslaw—Criticism and
interpretation.   2. Brodsky, Joseph, 1940–1996—Criticism and interpretation.
3. Milosz, Czeslaw—Friends and associates.   4. Brodsky, Joseph, 1940–1996—Friends
and associates.   I. Venclova, Tomas, 1937–   II. Grudzinska-Gross, Irena. Miłosz i
Brodski.   English   III. Title.
    PG7158.M5532G77 2010
    891.8'58709—dc22
                                                                      2009015993

A catalogue record for this book is available from the British Library.

This paper meets the requirements of ANSI/NISO Z39.48-1992 (Permanence of Paper).

10   9   8   7   6   5   4   3   2   1

For Anna and Stanisław Barańczak, with friendship

Only spiritual matters are truly interesting. But it is almost impossible to talk about them—they are transparent like gauze. One can talk only about people and things, so that they throw shadows.

—Adam Zagajewski

Contents

Contents

Foreword

TOMAS VENCLOVA

The present book reminds me somewhat of Plutarch. It consists of two parallel lives of outstanding personalities with similar but strongly contrasting fates. As the author says, Czesław Miłosz and Joseph Brodsky are patrons of all émigré writers of the second part of the twentieth century. They accomplished what seemed to be impossible, or at least very improbable: not only did they not cease to write poetry in a foreign country (this is, in fact, rather a rule than an exception, as proven by Juliusz Słowacki, Cyprian Norwid, Marina Tsvetaeva, Vladislav Khodasevich, and tens if not hundreds of other poets), but in the end they turned out to be two of the most important creators of that country's poetry, while all the time sticking to their native tongue. They were also known to the admirers of poetic art in their second fatherland, mostly, if not totally, through translations of their work. They helped each other in attaining that unusual goal. Not in the sense of mutual promotion—which was beneath them—but in that each measured himself by using the other as a standard. Miłosz, together with Anna Akhmatova and W. H. Auden, was for Brodsky one of a very few poetic authorities. The older Miłosz looked at the younger Brodsky with admiration and was strengthened by the fact of his existence. That is why this book speaks about friendship. The poets were successful in what their predecessors from the nineteenth century were not able to accomplish. The friendship of Adam Mickiewicz and Aleksander Pushkin—a worn-out topic of not-so-distant celebrations of Polish-Soviet friendship—began, perhaps, in the times of Mickiewicz's Petersburg exile, but was blocked and totally destroyed by the November Insurrection of 1830–31. Miłosz and Brodsky differed from their precursors in that their attitudes toward "the Polish question" were rather the same. Of course, they diverged in particulars, but Brodsky, like many other Russians in his times, considered the independence of Poland, and of Lithuania, as a necessary condition of the freedom of his own country.

Like Irena Grudzinska Gross, I was privileged to know both poets for many years, and I could see that their characters were not very easy on those around them. The author of this book mentions the "distance, stubbornness, and egoism" of Miłosz, which protected him against Marxist orthodoxy (and, I should add, against many other dangers). In the case of Brodsky, a similar role was played by his arrogance, nervous irritation, and his idiosyncratic but flawless taste. These differences in character, accompanied by similarity of attitudes and fates, are only the beginning of what separates the two poets.

Miłosz was, most of all, a person of the word *yes*, Brodsky, a person of the word *no*. For Miłosz, the main value in life was rootedness—genealogy, religion, language, landscape. Brodsky existed as if in the air, without roots, contrarian toward everything that surrounded him, always beginning from point zero. Even language, which he considered the most important thing and about which he said a lot, was for him not so much the Russian language or the English language, as simply a human capacity to position within the frame of grammar and diction the chaos of space and the flow of time toward death. Irena Grudzinska Gross has superbly grasped this contrast between the two poets, which was reflected in their lives and even their posthumous fates. Miłosz returned to his fatherland—although after some hesitation, and not to the Lithuania of his birth (which he visited several times) but to Kraków. Brodsky might have repeated the experience of Aleksander Solzhenitsyn—by returning from exile like Napoleon during his "hundred days" (Solzhenitsyn was not totally successful in that attempt). He did not do it, and this, too, was a matter of taste. He used to say that he was not the wind from the Book of Ecclesiastes, so he should not return; that the trajectory of a man does not consist of a circle but of a straight line. He did not visit his Petersburg and was not buried there; his funerals took place twice, in New York and in Venice, foreign cities, which he was able somehow to transform into Petersburgs.

This difference did not annul the similarities. They were both centaurs—they existed contemporaneously in two orders, two countries, two languages, two times. Their work is composed of two clearly distinct parts, before emigration and after emigration. They profoundly reformed the poetry of their countries, basing their work in great part on English-language models. The poetic tradition was their Muse, Tradition with a capital T, which is not a frequent attitude in our modernist and postmodernist, and therefore nihilistic, times. They shared a weakness for ages when ode coexisted with satire—what's more, when satire was hard to differentiate from ode. They were devoted to the management of the estate of poetry, to tending its garden, which meant a loyalty toward other poets, care of them and help in case of need. Although for Miłosz, Szetejnie meant a lot, and for Brodsky so did the village in which he spent his exile, both were the poets of the cities, and of those cities that formed Mickiewicz and Pushkin. Here I should say that the city of Mickiewicz, Vilnius, was loved not only by Miłosz but also by Brodsky. He saw in Lithuania the same spirit of independence and revolt that he found in Poland, and, of course, he was right. In Miłosz's first letter to Brodsky he wrote that they will have long conversations. Just like the author of this book, I witnessed some of them. I can say that they were not only about poems; the words of Mickiewicz: "compatriots' long nightly conversations" would be more adequate, though they were not compatriots *sensu stricto.* But in the end all those who come from that part of Europe are compatriots because such was the decree of history.

The book of Irena Grudzinska Gross is the first and very successful approach to one of the most important topics of the Polish and Russian literature of the twentieth century. This topic does not belong to the past, although we are living already in the next century and the next millennium.

Acknowledgments

A book about friendship could not come about without the help of many friends. This one is therefore dedicated to Anna and Stanisław Barańczak, whose friendship I was lucky to share with that of both Miłosz and Brodsky. I need also to mention right away the support and help of Maria Sozzani Brodsky and Ann Kjellberg. Copies of several unpublished Brodsky documents and drafts were sent to me by Ann Kjellberg while she was readying them for the Beinecke Rare Book and Manuscript Library at Yale University, where they are now located. I thank both Ann and Maria for their permission to quote from Brodsky's works. Thanks, as well, to Anthony Miłosz, the poet's son and his translator.

The shape of this book owes a lot to Joanna Szczęsna, who followed this project right from the beginning. Jonathan Schell read it through, as did Jessie Labov, and I thank them very much for their help. At various stages of writing the manuscript was read by Anna Bikont, Jan T. Gross, Adam Michnik, and Tomas Venclova. Their comments were very useful. I also had long and extremely illuminating conversations about the two poets with Maria Sozzani Brodsky, Ann Kjellberg, Zofia Ratajczakowa, Anatoly Nayman, Robert Faggen, Mark Strand, Nina Perlina, Ludmilla Shtern, Liam McCarthy, and Tomas Venclova.

I would also like to thank for their friendly support Wacława Grudzińska, Marek Edelman, Barbara Toruńczyk, Clare Cavanagh, Adam Zagajewski, Jerzy Illg, Paula and Mirosław Sawicki, Halina and Roman Frydman, Lucyna Gebert, Elżbieta Matynia, Piotr Kłoczowski, Krzysztof Czyżewski, Marek Zaleski, Bożena Shallcross, Marta Petrusewicz, and Michael Kott.

Introduction

The idea to write about the friendship between Czesław Miłosz and Joseph Brodsky came to me several years ago, while Miłosz was still alive. He was very supportive of the project—he valued highly his relationship with the Russian poet, who had already died. I shared with the two poets the experience of exile, as well as a love, approaching obsession, of literature. I first met Joseph Brodsky in 1965—he had just returned to Moscow after his sentence for "parasitism" had been cut in half. I already knew some of his poems and had heard about his trial and other travails in the Soviet system. It was ten years later that I met Miłosz, who was then teaching Russian literature at Berkeley. In the two poets' works I've continuously found thoughts, doubts, and emotions about life that corresponded to what pained or enchanted me. They were a source of strength and wisdom for my entire generation. Now, since their deaths, I feel for them what Jacques Derrida has called "the friendship of thought." With this book I would like to pay back some of the debt I owe them.

The friendship between the two poets was not a result of blind chance: it was the very history of their two nations that forced the greatest contemporary poet of Poland and the greatest contemporary poet of Russia to react to one another. They met in 1972 in the United States and were joined by common goals and beliefs; their principal concern was the frailty and persistence of human life. That commonality allows me to look at their parallel lives, the history of their families, their emigration, their Americanization, and their deaths. I place side by side their attitudes toward religion, history, memory, and language because these two great minds illuminate one another and—especially important—shed new light on the upheavals of the twentieth century. The hidden protagonists of the book are the two empires, Russia and the United States, and the main hero is poetry. I describe the politics of poetry—the confraternity, the fellowship of poets—at home and in the United States. Together with Derek Walcott, Seamus Heaney, Mark Strand, and others, they formed an international group that turned the United States into what could be called an empire of poets.

The book's center is the poetic work of Brodsky and Miłosz—their poems, their thinking about the nature of poetry, and the changes in their poetic languages. Following Osip Mandelstam, Brodsky was convinced that the real biography of a poet is in that poet's works, and that his poetic choices better reflect a life than awards, passports, health problems, or love affairs. So I treat their poetry as a record of their convictions and lives.

I have based the book on materials I started to collect many years ago. I quote their poems, essays, letters, interviews, speeches, lectures, and meetings with students. Their commentaries on each other's works, and their exchanges of opinions, jokes, and humorous asides, unveil their similarities and, more often, their differences, showing how they lived and worked in their home countries and the United States. Their way of formulating a thought, an intonation, their expression of contentment when the phrasing came out well—all of this seemed important to me. This is why I describe scenes that I sometimes witnessed, characteristic moments, conversations, special occasions. It is difficult to accept that the contagious laughter of Miłosz and the electric conversation of Brodsky have been silenced forever. In these pages I have tried to hold steady, if only for a moment, their fleeting shadows.

Abbreviations

ABC   Czesław Miłosz. *Miłosz's ABC's.* Trans. Madeline G. Levine. New York: Farrar, Straus and Giroux, 2001.

CCM   Ewa Czarnecka and Aleksander Fiut. *Conversations with Czesław Miłosz.* Trans. Richard Lourie. New York: Harcourt Brace Jovanovich, 1987.

CJB   Solomon Volkov. *Conversations with Joseph Brodsky.* Trans. Marian Schwartz. New York: Free Press, 1998.

CPE   Joseph Brodsky. *Collected Poems in English.* Ed. Ann Kjellberg. New York: Farrar, Straus and Giroux, 2000.

JT   Czesław Miłosz. *Jakiegoż to gościa mieliśmy: O Annie Świrszczyńskiej* [What a Guest We Had: About Anna Świrszczyńska]. Kraków: Znak, 1996.

LL   Lev Loseff. *Iosif Brodskij: Opit Literaturnoy Biografii* [Joseph Brodsky: A Literary Biography]. Moscow: Mołodaya Gvardia, 2006.

LTO   Joseph Brodsky. *Less Than One: Selected Essays.* New York: Farrar, Straus and Giroux, 1986.

NCP   Czesław Miłosz. *New and Collected Poems.* New York: Ecco, 2001.

NR   Czesław Miłosz. *Native Realm: A Search for Self-Definition.* Berkeley: University of California Press, 1981.

OGR   Joseph Brodsky. *On Grief and Reason, Selected Essays.* New York: Farrar, Straus and Giroux, 1995.

PŚ   Renata Gorczyńska [Ewa Czarnecka]. *Podróżny świata: Rozmowy z Czesławem Miłoszem* [World Traveler: Conversations with Czesław Miłosz]. Kraków: Wydawnictwo Literackie, 2002.

PŚ1   *Podróżny świata: Rozmowy z Czesławem Miłoszem* [World Traveler: Conversations with Czesław Miłosz]. 1st ed., with commentaries. New York: Bicentennial Publishing, 1983.

SL   Czesław Miłosz. *Spiżarnia Literacka* [Literary Bounty]. Kraków: Wydawnictwo Literackie, 2004.

StS Elżbieta Tosza. *Stan serca: Trzy dni z Josifem Brodskim*
[The State of the Heart: Three Days with Joseph Brodsky].
Katowice: Książnica, 1993.

TB Czesław Miłosz. *To Begin Where I Am: Selected Essays*. Ed.
and intro. Bogdana Carpenter and Madeline G. Levine.
New York: Farrar, Straus and Giroux, 2001.

VF Czesław Miłosz. *Visions from San Francisco Bay*. Trans.
Richard Lourie. New York: Farrar, Straus and Giroux, 1975.

YH Czesław Miłosz. *A Year of the Hunter*. Trans. Madeline G.
Levine. New York: Farrar, Straus and Giroux, 1994.

WP Czesław Miłosz. *The Witness of Poetry*. Cambridge, MA:
Harvard University Press, 1983.

Prologue:

"A Consolatory Letter"

On July 12, 1972, Czesław Miłosz sent a letter to Ann Arbor, Michigan, addressed to Joseph Brodsky, the recently exiled Russian poet who was starting his academic career there. "Dear Brodsky!" wrote Miłosz,

> I received your address from the editor of Paris *Kultura*. Certainly you are not capable right now of starting any new work, because you have to absorb quite a few impressions. It is a matter of internal rhythm and of its clashing with the rhythm of the life around you. But, since what happened happened, it is much better, and not only from a practical point of view, that you came to America and did not remain in Western Europe. I think that you are very worried, like all

1

of us from our part of Europe—brought up on the myth that the life of a writer ends if he abandons his native country. But it is only a myth, understandable in the countries where the civilization long remained a rural civilization and "the soil" played a great role. Everything depends on the man and on his internal health.

I would be very happy if you would translate my poems, but first you should acquaint yourself with them and decide if they suit you. I know that you translated Gałczyński, but my poetry is just the opposite of his—it does not strive to have anything in common with "prettiness," as in Gałczyński.

I hope that we will meet and have long conversations.

I don't know yet what kind of funds for lectures we will have in the fall semester, but I will try to do something about this matter.

What else can I say? The first months of exile are very hard. They shouldn't be taken as a measure of what is to come. With time you will see that perspective changes.

I wish you to live through these first months as well as possible.

Czesław Miłosz

P.S. I am sending you a book of my poems. Perhaps you will find interesting the poems or cycles of poems on the pages: 31, 83, 92, 103, 108, 110, 136, 138, 139, 142, 210, 257, 258, 259, 264, 267, 268, 272, 293, 302, 311, 317, 320.

The letter appears to have been the only text Miłosz ever produced in Russian. He dictated it to Mrs. Szebeko, a secretary in the Slavic Languages and Literatures Department at the University of California, Berkeley. Mrs. Szebeko had a Cyrillic typewriter. Miłosz was teaching in the department and knew Russian very well, but all his future correspondence with Brodsky was in English. The letter's tone is direct and cordial—obviously Miłosz was favorably predisposed to the younger poet. And the advice is the same that he applied to his own difficulties and heartaches: work. When unable to write poetry, he was saying, translate. Things will become easier, you will see. And he immediately proposed a concrete task.

He was not without self-interest. Living in exile in the United States, he did not forget Russia and he was looking for a good Russian translator. Brodsky was known as a persecuted Russian poet and translator of poetry, especially of Polish poets Gałczyński and Harasymowicz. Miłosz's main émigré publisher, Jerzy Giedroyć, himself invested in promoting Polish-Russian relations, suggested this newly arrived translator to Miłosz. It turned out to have been an inspired idea.

The letter, as Miłosz declared later on, brought great profit in the form of a long-lasting friendship. When he was dictating it, he already knew a lot about Brodsky's 1964 trial for "parasitism," his banishment to the north of Russia, and his exile. He may also have known some of his poems, in Polish or English translation—or at least, in a conversation with me, he did not exclude that possibility. Brodsky did not know much about Miłosz. Early in the year 1972, right before leaving his native Leningrad for his exile in the West, he had a conversation with the Lithuanian poet Tomas Venclova. "We met in one of the Leningrad restaurants," said Venclova in 1982, "and Brodsky asked me: tell me, he said, who is the best Polish poet, because I believe it is Herbert." Zbigniew Herbert was not an émigré and his poems were published in Poland and in the Soviet Union. "Well, Herbert is good, I said"—Venclova continued—"but there is also Miłosz. And who is he? asked Brodsky. Then I told him a lot about Miłosz, and he asked: but what kind of poet is he, which poet does he resemble? It is difficult to say, I replied, because each great poet resembles most of all himself. Partially perhaps Auden, partially you, Iosif. If so, then he is a good poet, he said, and left for the West knowing only that much about Miłosz."[1] Venclova was one of the very few people in the Soviet Union who knew about Miłosz. The Polish poet went into exile in 1951, and, until his Nobel Prize in 1980, his poetry was not published in Poland and therefore was not translated into Russian. The conversation reported by Venclova is a poignant reminder of the difficulties of poetry spread under conditions of censorship and isolation.

When Brodsky received Miłosz's letter he did not know any of his poems, but had heard his name. He replied nearly three weeks later, on July 31, 1972. "Dear Miłosz," he started, and then excused himself for writing in Russian, because "in Polish or English it would come out much worse." He translated, he continued, not only Gałczyński, but also Norwid, Staff, Herbert, Szymborska, Harasymowicz, Kubiak, and "it seems somebody else, but I do not remember anymore. And now to the main issue. I am very happy you proposed such a task to me." He will not be able to get to it right away, though, because of some obligations. Only at the end of the letter does he respond to the main message of Miłosz's letter: "As for the first part of your letter, my own comes out so short because of what you wrote in yours." The sentence has three crossed-out fragments, as if written with a lot of effort. It seems to be saying: I understand and I am already working; let's not talk about emigration and suffering. The letter ends: "Thank you. Yours, Iosif Brodsky."[2]

Miłosz's letter proved to be an important event in the lives of both poets. They often referred to it, and with time it took on an almost symbolic meaning for both of them. Their recollections were not refreshed by the existing text, as the letter was found in Brodsky's papers only after his death. Since its content was rather complex, they remembered it sometimes as a gesture of welcome, sometimes as an austere challenge, and sometimes as an encouragement to devote oneself to work. Miłosz recalled it later as "a consolatory letter— remember that the beginnings of the exile are the most difficult" (*YH*, 97). After Brodsky's death, Miłosz said in an interview with me: "I wrote this letter from the feeling of solidarity. . . . It was a *priwiet* ['welcome' in Russian], reaching out, as I wanted to tell him that you may perish, but if you don't, then you will be stronger." He also said: "I orient myself like the ants with their feelers. Poets know who belongs to their class."[3] And in his *Roadside Dog*, he wrote about himself: "I had a gift of recognizing in people this high quality in which the virtues of mind and character are joined."[4]

On October 26, 1988, sixteen years after receiving the letter, Brodsky interpreted it as a warning. Only a few writers are able to continue their work in exile, he said during a meeting with his readers in Paris. "If this is what will happen to you"—he was quoting Miłosz's words, "you will know your rank." "I remember that letter," Miłosz clarified. "He did not quote it in its entirety. I was talking there about the first, most difficult period of exile, a period that one has to withstand so that later everything will be easier. It was also my way of greeting him and expressing my support."[5]

The difference in their memory of the letter was quite characteristic. For Miłosz it was an expression of solidarity—he wanted to help. He also looked to further his own work, to have his poetry translated. Brodsky understood both points very well, but took it also as a challenge. In an interview he said:

> [Miłosz] helped me enormously. He sent me a short letter just at the moment of my arrival to America, a letter that immediately helped me to overcome the hesitations that were tormenting me at the time. In that letter, he wrote, among other things (for example translation), that he understands that I am worried whether or not I will be able to write in a foreign country. If you do not succeed, he wrote, if you meet with disappointment, there is nothing bad about that. I did see many people to whom this happened. This is simply human, very normal—a person usually writes within the four walls of his home, in a well-known context. If this, he wrote, is what happens to you, it will show your true value, that you are a good writer [but only] on domestic matters. So when I read these words, I said: No. And this is what I am so grateful to him for.[6]

Although Miłosz wrote that everything depends on the man and his "internal health," I don't believe his letter was intended as a challenge; Brodsky's reading of it reflected his own emotional cast. But why does he (mis)remember it with such gratitude? It was certainly not the only letter he received then, and Miłosz was not the only poet who greeted him in the West. In Vienna, W. H. Auden took him under his wing; in England, it was Stephen Spender. Almost immediately after Brodsky landed in the Viennese airport, Auden brought him to London, to the International Poetry Festival, where he was treated as a member of the guild. At that time, he was also befriended by Robert Lowell. Yet Miłosz's letter touched on the greatest anxiety that tormented the Russian émigré: would he be able to write? It was such an overwhelming fear that he remembered it years later, during one of his last public readings. "At the beginning [of my emigration] I was in a state of real panic and trepidation. For instance, on the third or fourth day after I landed in Vienna [the first stop of his exile], I was trying to find a rhyme for some word. I didn't succeed and was really shocked. That had never happened before. I could get a rhyme to any Russian word, or so I thought. I got scared that something horrible was happening. I started forgetting Russian. The next day I found that damned rhyme."[7] Miłosz was a person from "there," from, as he wrote in his letter, "our part of Europe"; he was an exile who continued to write poems, and therefore a person who overcame the separation from the native land and language. He was a proof of the "portability" of poetry.

Remembering the painful beginnings of his own emigration, Miłosz could easily imagine the sufferings of Brodsky. He wrote about it later in the personal anthology of poetry *A Book of Luminous Things* (1996): "For a newly arrived immigrant, Russian poet Joseph

Brodsky, the American Midwest was a completely exotic land." These words were part of a short introduction to Brodsky's poem "In the Lake District." The poem ends with one of the few complaints Brodsky uttered about those initial, difficult days:

> *Whatever I wrote then was incomplete:*
>
> *my lines expired in strings of dots. Collapsing,*
>
> *I dropped, still fully dressed, upon my bed.*
>
> *At night I stared up at the darkened ceiling*
>
> *until I saw a shooting star, which then,*
>
> *conforming to the laws of self-combustion,*
>
> *would flash—before I'd even made a wish—*
>
> *across my cheek and down onto my pillow.*[8]

PART ONE

Republic of Poets

ONE

Pan Czesław and Iosif

The feeling of friendship is often expressed through a ritualized, private style of address—an intimate formality, so to speak. Miłosz and Brodsky conversed in English and addressed each other as "Czesław" and "Joseph." Brodsky's style of address with Miłosz was always formal. He explained to the Polish writer Wiktor Woroszylski that he would never speak to Miłosz with an informal *you;* and he liked to address the older poet sometimes with the Polish formal "Pan Czesław"—Mister Czesław.[1] It was a slightly humorous way of showing respect to the age and noble origin of the Polish poet. *Pan*—mister, sir, or lord—is the formal *you* in modern Polish, a common way of addressing any person who is not a close acquaintance, but in Russia it was a symbol of the formality of Polish society. A Russian joke about Poles went that everybody in Poland was a "Pan"; even shoes were addressed in this way (the Russian *tufli*, shoes, was *pantofle* in Polish). And Miłosz's origin, not only his bearing, was literally noble. He was born in 1911 to a family of small nobility in Szetejnie, today part of Lithuania, then a province of the Russian empire. He frequented schools in Vilnius, where he also completed his law studies at the university. Since 1918, Vilnius had belonged to Poland, and Miłosz's schooling and home life was all in Polish. He started to write poetry at fifteen years old. In 1937, he moved to Warsaw, and remained there until the end of World War II. After the war, Warsaw was totally ruined, so he lived for a short time in Kraków, but he spent the years 1946 to 1950 in diplomatic service in New York, Washington, and Paris. When, in January of 1951, he asked the French authorities for political asylum, he had already been outside of Poland for five years. He and his family passed the next decade in France, and at the beginning of the 1960s they moved to Berkeley, California, where he became professor of Slavic literatures. In 1980, his poetry was awarded the Nobel Prize in literature. After the Cold War had ended, he started to spend longer periods in Kraków, where he finally moved, and where he died on August 14, 2004. He was buried with national honors in a crypt of a monastery in Kraków.

Almost thirty years younger than Miłosz, Iosif Aleksandrovich Brodsky was born in Leningrad, on May 24, 1940. In his essay "In a Room and a Half," he writes that he was born before the war, but in Poland the war was already in full swing. Leningrad was Brodsky's home for the first thirty-two years of his life, although he traveled frequently within the spacious borders of the Soviet empire. He, too, started to write poetry at fifteen, but was not published at first.

Arrested, interrogated, and "observed" in psychiatric institutions, he was accused of "parasitism," or avoidance of work, sentenced in 1964 to five years of forced labor, and banished to the Archangielsk region. Thanks to the courage of a woman journalist, Frida Vigdorova, who took notes during his trial, the transcript of his "parasitism" case became available in the West. It provoked outrage and dismay, many Western and Russian celebrities rallied to his defense and he was released from exile after a year and a half. His stay in the north had been marked not only by hard physical work and isolation, but also by the blooming of his creative powers. In 1972, he was pressured to emigrate, and after a short stay in Austria and England, he settled in the United States. When he received his Nobel Prize in literature, in 1987, he was already an American citizen. He died in Brooklyn, New York, January 28, 1996, and was buried in Venice.

At the time Miłosz wrote his letter—in 1972—Brodsky was thirty-two years old. His poetry was little known in the West, he was a political case rather than a literary one. Surprisingly, the same can be said of Miłosz, even though he had already resided in the West for more than twenty years. He was known as the author of *The Captive Mind,* and as a translator of Polish poetry into English. The iron curtain cut him off from his natural readership, and he had not as yet found a new one. He wrote often about his place of birth, which is not within the political boundaries of today's Poland. He named the land of his birth sometimes as the Baltic lands, sometimes as the "Grand Duchy of Lithuania," "on the very borderline between Rome and Byzantium.... On my side of the border everything came from Rome: Latin as the language of the Church and of literature, the theological quarrels of the Middle Ages, Latin poetry as a model for the Renaissance poets, white churches in the baroque style." On the other side were Eastern Christianity and Russia. "I certainly felt a sense of menace from the East very early," he declared, "and not from Eastern Christianity, of course, but from what had arisen as a result of its defeat" (*WP*, 4–5).

All of Miłosz's youth was spent in and around Vilnius, and his move to Warsaw in 1937 was his first emigration. Although he grew up in an ethnically and linguistically mixed territory, his culture and language were Polish. He learned to read and write from his mother, who ran a small school for the children of peasants working on their estate. His father was a railroad construction engineer, which involved a lot of traveling within the Russian empire: it was on these trips that the young Miłosz learned his Russian. He often declared that his early and strong attachment to Polish, as well as his family's Catholic piety, formed a solid foundation for his further life and work. Yet, his Polishness was sui generis, and this was the case also of the Polishness of his great predecessor Adam Mickiewicz (1798–1855). The greatest Polish romantic poet, Mickiewicz too was born "on the borderline between Rome and Byzantium," studied in Vilnius, and spent his life in exile. Like every Polish poet, especially those coming from the eastern part of Poland, Miłosz necessarily had Mickiewicz as his point of reference.

In his book *Native Realm*, Miłosz describes the way his national and poetic consciousness developed. In many of his other works he returns to the issue of what Polishness is, and how Polish he is. In fact, Miłosz's poetry and essays are characterized by creative repetitions and returns to the same topics and motives. He wrote *Native Realm* with an astonishing directness—astonishing, because each of the topics he addressed was and continues to be a real mine field—about the land that gave birth to him, about his ancestors, and about Catholicism, Jews, communism, and emigration. This directness in approaching the themes that are merely alluded to or hinted at in most Polish writing constitutes a great strength of Miłosz's texts. He approached these themes with wisdom and analyzed them from multiple points of view. In describing his youth, he paints a black picture of the then-growing myths of racial purity, national exclusivity, the eternal link between soil, blood, language, and religion. His criticism is not directed only against Polish prejudices. Miłosz wrote the *Native Realm* in 1958 in exile in France, addressing Western readers as well as Polish ones, combating Polish and Western stereotypes. Forty-seven years old at the time, he looked at his Europe like an old sage: cold and trenchant toward the West, bitter and sorrowful toward the East—from which, it seemed, he was to be separated forever.

Native Realm, Miłosz writes in the introduction to that book, is about "an East European, born more or less when crowds in London and Paris were cheering the first aviators; about a man who cannot be fitted into stereotypes like the German *Ordnung* or the Russian *âme slave*" (*NR*, 3). Here he is objecting to categories used by the West to classify the people like himself. In the chapter "Ancestry" he declares: "The mélange of Polish, Lithuanian, and German blood, of which I myself am an example, was so common that admirers of racial purity could find little to boast of" (*NR*, 24). He does not fit himself into the corset of linear pedigree, and underlines the diversity of ethnic linkages, delighting in *bizarreries* and *mésalliances* in his family—a river with many confluents. He refers repeatedly to Oskar Miłosz, a cousin of his father and a relative to whom he feels indebted. Oskar Miłosz was a Lithuanian poet writing in French; on his father's side, he continued the long line of Miłoszes, but he was a grandson of an Italian opera singer, Natalia Tassistro, and a son of Miriam Rozenthal, daughter of a Jewish teacher. Czesław Miłosz embraced Oskar's pedigree, because his attitude to his own and his uncle's nationality is preromantic: the history of family is not only that of blood but of multiple loyalties and connections. Hence the strength he draws from the variety and profusion of his family relations. "One should appreciate," he wrote, "the advantages of one's origin. Its worth lies in the power it gives one to detach oneself from the present moment" (*NR*, 35).

Miłosz himself named as preromantic the "antiquity" of his convictions about national and ethnic issues. "My roots were nurtured by a soil that was inhospitable to new plantings, a great many precepts advocating tolerance had penetrated me, and they were out of step with my century. But what finally tipped the scales was my distrust of 'trueborn' Poles. My family practices a cult of separatism—much as the Scots, the Welsh, or the Bretons did. Our Grand Duchy of Lithuania was 'better' and Poland was 'worse.' . . . Poles 'from over there' (that is, from the ethnic center) had a reputation for being shallow, irresponsible, and, what is more, impostors. . . . The more or less unfavorable tone in which Poles were spoken of could hardly have awakened in me any response to the Polish ideology of the divine nation" (*NR*, 96–97). He cited his childhood environment as an explanation for his later rejection of nationalism and right-wing politics. Polish nationalism repulsed him intellectually and physically, as if it were a matter of taste. "My allergy to everything that smacks of the 'national' and an almost physical disgust for people who transmit such signals have weighed heavily upon my destiny" (*NR*, 95).

Although he was born in a home where Polish was spoken, Yiddish and Lithuanian could be heard in the surrounding areas. "The little town, where crops were brought to market, used Polish and Yiddish for everyday. But all the officials imported for administrative purposes—the military gendarme trailing his long, clumsy saber behind him, the tax collector, the train conductor—addressed the local population in Russian" (*NR*, 16). The languages were signs not only of ethnic, cultural, and religious difference, but also of class structure. When he was young, Miłosz's friendships were only with fellow Poles. Writing about his youth in Vilnius, he regrets his lack of interest in the then-blossoming Jewish culture. Only many years later, in New York, does he start to learn about the Jewish culture of Vilnius and the Polish borderlands. "I had to learn English in order to make contact with something that had been only an arm's reach away" (*NR*, 98).

The reasons for this reciprocal Jewish-Polish self-isolation were very complex: we are, after all, in the first half of the twentieth century, the period of the growth of nationalisms, of acute conflicts of classes and generations. The left-leaning or "progressive" Jews were cutting their own roots, abandoning the religion and culture of their ancestors in the name of freedom and progress. Miłosz described their choices with the distance of a historian. He understood the sociological reasons which made young Jews open to Marxist utopias and friendly toward large state organisms like Russia or Germany: they seemed to offer more protection, more options, and greater freedom of movement. He collaborated with many Polish writers of Jewish origin and felt distant from the "Polish racial and national *misterium*." His "position of an outsider" permitted him "to enter the mentality of writers of Jewish extraction who also stood in front of closed gates. We had a common fatherland: the Polish language" (*NR*, 102).

His language was a source of both his grounding and his alienation. He was very proud that he never needed to "add to it." Such grounding in the language could come only from childhood. In his poem "Not This Way" he says: "language is my measure. / A bucolic, childish language that transforms the sublime into the cordial" (*NCP,* 273). The language was his "native land" because he "lacked any other" (*NCP,* 245). Yet he often said that since he was born outside of Poland proper, his Polish was not "central": this was the reason, he asserted, for his conservative attitude to language. The literary critic Ryszard Matuszewski quotes a characteristic conversation he witnessed in 1981 between Miłosz and another Polish writer, Miron Białoszewski, whose treatment of language was free and experimental. "Miłosz underlined in this conversation his admiration for Miron's stubborn attack on linguistic conventions. . . . In a dedication, which he penned on a volume of his poems, there was a mention of his place of birth 'outside of Poland.' Miron took note of it: 'Why 'outside of Poland'? Miłosz: 'The district of Kiejdany, where I was born, it was not Poland, and perhaps this is why my attitude toward the Polish language is different from yours. You were born here, in the center [the conversation takes place in Warsaw]. Perhaps this is why you treat Polish so much more freely. You are more rooted here.' "[2]

In *A Year of the Hunter* he further develops this affinity between himself and Polish Jewish writers. "There is no lack of similarities," he writes, "between my alienation and Isaac Bashevis Singer's. . . . He has the same attitude toward Hassidic orthodoxy that I have toward orthodox Catholicism. That is the source of my true kinship with Singer, which is stronger than with any other living prose writer, Polish or American. Nobel Prizes for two alienated men" (*YH*, 6–7).

At the same time that similarity with the Polish writers of Jewish extraction was irritating because together they strove to "give to their works an ultra-Slavic flavor" instead of "baring their [own] dichotomy. . . . As they repudiated the ghetto, so I hid away the Grand Duchy of Lithuania among dusty souvenirs. But I was more proud than they, if only of my [rooted Polish] ear. . . . It was only proper that a great poet like Mickiewicz had found his medium in our region" (*NR*, 102–3).

Even though for him the language was a kind of sacrum, he never absolutized it, as did, according to him, his fellow writers of Jewish extraction. He strove for a complicated balance of distancing and adoration. Writers of Jewish origin irritated him, not only by their frequent extremism, radical leftism, and fanatical theoretical debates, but also by their ardent devotion to the Polish language, their (for him) excessive linguistic virtuosity. His directness in writing about Jews and his expression of a variety of feelings are quite remarkable and worthy of admiration. "It is hard for me to write about the Jews because no small effort is demanded if one is to distinguish these prewar tensions from one of the greatest tragedies of history: the slaughter of some three million 'non-Aryan' Polish citizens by the Nazis" (*NR*, 105). Jews constitute a topic which is always verging on taboo. The heroine of Polish writer Tadeusz Konwicki's novel *Bohiń* utters the following sentence: "What a strange word—Jew. Before pronouncing it there is always a short moment of fear."[3] This reluctance or rather difficulty in talking about Jews is not a Polish specialty. Joseph Brodsky recalls the first lie he told when he had to fill out in a library card the entry for "nationality." "I was seven years old and knew very well that I was a Jew, but I told the attendant that I didn't know. . . . I wasn't ashamed of being a Jew, nor was I scared of admitting it. I was ashamed of the word 'Jew' itself. In printed Russian the word appeared very rarely" (*LTO*, 8).

Miłosz considered prewar Polish anti-Semitism a kind of psychosis, which limited Poles' understanding of contemporary events, especially the approaching war. He also wrote about the incompleteness of Jewish assimilation, about the resentments it produced even among nonnationalists, about the loyalty of Jewish intelligentsia toward Russian rather than Polish culture, and about the feeling of otherness in the relations between Polish writers and those who wrote in Polish but were of Jewish origin. Although they wrote in the same language, they were different, and that caused tension. He touched on these subjects, for example in *Native Realm*, at a time when, in Poland, nobody wrote about it—when even the Polish emigration, free of Communist censorship and able to choose any topic, didn't know how to do it.[4] Miłosz did not fit into the nationalistic and nostalgic part of the émigré community; he was alone, and spoke about these difficult and sore issues in a way which was very much his own. It was not a matter of politics, but of taboos enshrined in the language itself. Breaking them exposed him to attacks from every side.

Miłosz's attention to Jewish issues (and mine in writing about them in the context of his biography) is not coincidental: there was a similarity between the existential situation of Miłosz and that of the Jewish writers. The social position of their ancestors and parents had been undermined by the processes of modernization, of which the 1917 Russian Revolution was one manifestation. Miłosz felt a certain discomfort in connection with his noble origin and upbringing, while his fellow writers who were Jewish were dissociating themselves from the way of life of their original social milieus. This cutting off, this undermining of the nobility and of traditional Jewry, created a new social stratum: the intelligentsia. Both the nobility and the Jews were subject to the same push toward the cities, the same transformation into a meritocratic layer of society. Miłosz was very conscious of these changes. "Born without security that comes with inherited money, I had to make my own way in the world. The pressure was somewhat mitigated by the care that my parents, who belonged to the intelligentsia, took to prepare me for a profession" (*NR*, 31).

The novelty of this social stratum made both the nobility and the Jews feel a lack of continuity, and they became absorbed with questions of identity and belonging. Hence Miłosz's sentence about the common fatherland of the Polish language. It was language, not religion or blood, that indicated social belonging—and, perhaps, national belonging as well. This is how the issue is summarized by a Miłosz scholar, Aleksander Fiut: Miłosz was marked by "a feeling of an internal split, originating in social alienation (a member of the intelligentsia of noble origin), a consciousness of coming from a multicultural and multiethnic region (hence an almost allergic aversion toward any manifestation and shade of nationalism and chauvinism), the inability to define himself in terms of nineteenth-century categories of national belonging (the poet is a holder of the Polish language and culture, but at the same time declares his attachment toward Lithuania, where he was born), and finally the need to overcome the limitation of living in the worst part of Europe."[5]

The same difficulties with self-identification apply to the family of Brodsky and the changes it went through. During the nineteenth and twentieth centuries there were three large-scale migrations of Jews from Russia, Lithuania, Latvia, Ukraine, Belarus, and Poland. One of these migrations led to Palestine, and it ended with the creation of the state of Israel. The second migration was directed toward the Americas, so that the United States is now home to the largest Jewish diaspora. In the third migration, masses of Jews moved from the European countryside to the cities, and contributed to the creation of a strong urban intelligentsia. In post-1917 Russia, the new intelligentsia was predominantly of Jewish origin.[6] Brodsky, his parents and his literary milieu were a typical product of that last migration. The members of the Russian intelligentsia of Jewish origin were brought up in the cult of intellect and culture, becoming the most devoted readers, the greatest admirers of Pushkin, the most prolific poets and prose writers. The same process took place in Poland, with the appearance of such poets, prose writers, critics, and editors as Julian Tuwim, Antoni Słonimski, Aleksander Wat, Zuzanna Ginczanka,

Mieczysław Grydzewski, Bruno Schulz, Bolesław Leśmian, Irena Krzywicka, or Ludwik Fryde. Miłosz felt a sense of community with these fellow writers. They worked with the same material; they were interested in the same issues; they disliked and were disliked by the same right-wing majority.

The 1917 Russian Revolution—a symbolic sum and result of the processes of modernization—brought the destruction of dynasties, governments, and class privileges; it abolished old family and clan hierarchies, and, with them, the orderly succession of generations. The authority of the traditional groups and the older generation had been weakened: their accumulated knowledge of the world became useless because that world did not exist anymore. That weakening of the authority of the older generation can be found in the ways in which Miłosz and Brodsky wrote about their parents, especially about their fathers who should have been the embodiment of that authority. Both fathers were named Aleksander and neither left behind an image of strength; their sons thought they were weak, averse to conflict, bent on survival. Both Miłosz and Brodsky express more warmth toward their mothers, to whom they owe the learning of language, of reading and writing. Perhaps their fathers disappointed them by failing to be "bedrocks"—a common fate of those who live in times of war and persecution. A different kind of heroism was required from women, a domestic heroism, not directly turned against power and authority, but rather stretched like an umbrella over the heads of those in need of protection. Their authority is not as easily lost as that of men.

There is, however, another possible explanation of why Miłosz and Brodsky were more attached to their mothers than to their fathers.

Politicians build their authority on the commandments of Fathers, but the sensibility of poets is more attuned toward Mothers, who convey words and magic, empathy and forgiveness. In *The Land of Ulro,* Miłosz expressed his gratitude that he was brought up in the Roman-Catholic rite, because it liberated the feminine side of men, a passivity ready to accept Jesus Christ or poetic inspiration. He believed that it is the poetic imagination that makes the acceptance of religious dogma possible. Perhaps this is also the meaning of the sentence repeated so often by Brodsky that aesthetics is prior to ethics.

Aleksander Miłosz, the father of Czesław, was born in 1883 and died in 1952. He was buried in Kraków. In *Native Realm,* his son wrote that Aleksander "had no talent for 'getting ahead' or for making money. He lacked the necessary weapons for fighting people." He could struggle only with the nature that he loved. As a young man he worked on construction projects in the interior of Russia, where he felt truly free while wandering the endless expanses. After the revolution and his return to Poland, he felt constrained and limited; he "constantly complained of the lack of breadth, of the smallness of everything, of stagnation." He even emigrated to Brazil, but soon returned because "he never recovered the same kind of room to breathe in that he had had in the East. . . . Siberia, which had engulfed so many of our compatriots, was not [for him] a land of exile. Having certain literary interests, he filled thick black notebooks, bound in cerated cloth, with hymns in honor of the wild north" (*NR,* 37–39). "Certain literary interests": One can hear a tone of tolerant superiority in the words of the poet-son.

Miłosz's mother, Weronika née Kunat, died right after the war as a result of selflessness: chased away from her native Lithuania, she found herself in Gdańsk and contracted typhus taking care of an older German woman to whose house she was assigned. Miłosz celebrated his mother often in his poems, following Polish literary and even religious traditions. The poems expressed as well a kind of pre-Freudian gratefulness. Nineteen years after her death he used quasi-biblical phrasing:

Born of a foolhardy woman with whom I am united, and whom
I, an old man, pity in my dreams.
Her funny dresses, her dances, so utterly lost yet so close again.

. . .

Through what meadows burned brown does she run with me
in her arms
carrying me to safety, away from the teeth of a beast?
And she, who offered me to Our Lady of Ostrabrama,
How and why was she granted what she asked for in her prayer?

. . .

. . . we are alone in the trial in the dark
And hear her steps nearby, and think she has forgiven.
(NCP, *312–13*)

Another poem about her, written in 1985, is also full of religious images and comparisons:

Those poor, arthritically swollen knees
Of my mother in an absent country.

I think of them on my seventy-fourth birthday
As I attend early Mass at St. Mary Magdalen in Berkeley.

. . .

A reading from the Gospel according to Mark
About a little girl to whom He said: "Talitha, cumi!"
This is for me. To make me rise from the dead
And repeat the hope of those who lived before me,
In a fearful unity with her, with her pain of dying,
In a village near Danzig, in a dark November,
When both the mournful Germans, old men and women,
And the evacuees from Lithuania would fall ill with typhus.
Be with me, I say to her, my time has been short.
Your words are now mine, deep inside me:
*"It all seems now to have been a dream." (*NCP, *463)*

He evokes the memory of her when he himself was very old, describing his return to the place of his birth in the poem "In Szetejnie," which opens with the words: "You were my beginning and again I am with you, here, where I learned the four quarters of the globe." The poem ends with an invocation similar to another celebration of his mother, a 1949 poem called "The Tomb of My Mother," which I will not reproduce here as it is not translated into English. I mention it to show the stability of the image of his mother, which is repeated in "In Szetejnie," written forty-six years later:

If only my work were of use to people and of more weight than
* is my evil.*

You alone, wise and just, would know how to calm me,

explaining that I did as much as I could.

That the gate of the Black Garden closes, peace, peace, what is

finished is finished. (NCP, *640–42*)

Miłosz's family originated in territories not so distant from those that Brodsky's family came from. The Russian poet said, "After all, my ancestors, they were all from there, from Brody, hence the last name."[7] They also had common Baltic connections: Miłosz's mother spoke Lithuanian, Brodsky's Latvian. Miłosz remembered, just like Brodsky, that Russian Jews used to "belong" to Poland, only to be absorbed into the Russian empire after the Russian annexation of formerly Polish territories. Iosif's parents, Aleksander Ivanovich Brodsky and Maria Moysieyevna Volpert, survived the Russian Revolution, the terror of the 1930s, and World War II. "I guess they considered themselves lucky, although they never said as much," Brodsky wrote in his autobiographical essay "In a Room and a Half" (*LTO*, 449). From that text the history of Aleksander Ivanovich and his wife can be reconstructed, though it is given only "obliquely." The father faced many difficulties owing to his doubly "bad" origin, that is his bourgeois and Jewish roots: before the revolution his family owned a printing shop. Iosif's grandfather, one of the few Jews named Ivan, had been baptized and had permission to reside in the city. Little Iosif did meet his grandfather as a child in postwar Leningrad, but we don't learn anything about him and are not sure if it was his paternal grandfather or his maternal one. Before the war, Aleksander must have lived in Leningrad, because Brodsky writes that when his father was fighting to break the Nazi blockade of that city, he lost his home to a bombardment and his only sister to hunger. After the war, he continued his military service, only to be fired because of his Jewish origin; then he became "a newspaper photographer," who also wrote articles. Similar to Miłosz, Brodsky gently laughs at his father's writings: "Most of his articles would start with 'Heavy, storm-laden clouds hang over the Baltic'" (*LTO*, 461). He was a devoted photographer, and every year on Iosif's birthday he photographed his son on the balcony of their Leningrad apartment. Iosif inherited his passion for photography; his archive at Beinecke Library contains thousands of snapshots.

During the first eight years of Iosif's life, his father was away, first at war and then serving in China. Brodsky does not describe the military experiences of his father: certainly it was not a topic of family conversation. Maria Moysieyevna survived the hunger and horror of the blockade of Leningrad with her little son. She taught him to read when he was four years old. Although Brodsky recalls both of his parents as very kind and good people, he underlines the warmth of his mother. She grew up in a Latvian-speaking family and worked all her life as a secretary or accountant, with the exception of a short period right after the war, when, because of her knowledge of German, she became a translator in the camp for German prisoners of war. We don't know what she witnessed there or how she reacted to that task. Her father "was a Singer sewing machine salesman in the Baltic provinces of the empire (Lithuania, Latvia, Poland)" (*LTO*, 482). It is meaningful that Brodsky calls Poland one of the "Baltic provinces of the empire," since it is an expression that no Pole would use. Maria Moysieyevna had a brother who was an engineer and a member of the Communist Party; we learn about his existence in another autobiographical essay of Brodsky's, "Less Than One," only because of the library he possessed. In the previously quoted essay Brodsky mentions as well his mother's sisters, and gives the ages of his parents, but obliquely, in a way that forces the reader to calculate the numbers. "On October 25, 1917 [the outbreak of Russian Revolution], my father was already fourteen; my mother, twelve" (*LTO*, 483). His parents, he wrote, "never told me about their childhood, about the families they were from, about their parents or grandparents. . . . This reticence had less to do with amnesia than with the necessity of concealing their class origins during that potent era in order to survive." When he was thinking about it, he felt like a tributary of "a deflected river" (*LTO*, 482). This was a quotation from his great poetic predecessor Anna Akhmatova.

The term *reticence* is not accidental: it is related, in Brodsky's work, to the word *restraint*, which appears in relation to Akhmatova. "The reason why a good poet speaks of his own grief with restraint is that, as regards grief, he is a Wandering Jew," he wrote in "The Keening Muse," an essay devoted to Akhmatova's work and life. (*LTO*, 39). In the case of both Akhmatova and his family, the reticence and restraint had to do with the horrors of survived experiences. So perhaps the tributary of the deflected river is Brodsky's family's Jewishness? And is he reticent not only as a poet but also as a Jew? The fact that he was radically cut off from the history of his family had to influence his writings. And the reticence that his parents exhibited might have had less to do with the caution related to class origin and more to do with being Jewish. Svetlana Boym has observed that the figure of the Jew resembles a spirit wandering through all of Brodsky's work. It was a spirit that visited several generations of assimilated Soviet Jews.[8]

The fact that his parents form a tributary of a deflected river is clearly visible in the poems Brodsky wrote about them. These poems express no family continuity, they have no religious dimension, and they contain none of the idyllic childhood landscapes against which Miłosz so beautifully placed his mother. The Brodskys constitute a three-person family without any past and without tributaries of their own. Brodsky even chooses not to mention his young son that remained in Russia. The poem "In Memory of My Father: Australia" (1989) is a rough summary of a dream in which his father had appeared. The son and the father are talking on the phone—his parents never received permission to travel abroad and see him. The father in the dream is not a patriarchal figure but a defenseless, complaining old man, on the phone from Australia where he has somehow gone after his death. The conversation seems to reflect the regular telephone conversations the Brodskys had over the years, hence "the triple echo" of the voice in the receiver and complaints about "ankles [that] keep swelling." Although it must have been their own choice, Brodsky seems shocked by the fact that his parents were burned in a crematorium, that the father became "the silky powder" and "formed a cloud above a chimney" (*CPE*, 360). For a Jewish son who could not accompany his parents at their death that must have been especially hard, though no association of crematorium and Jewish history is alluded to.

His mother is commemorated in the poem "In Memoriam" (1985), opening with the surprising image: "The thought of you is receding like a chambermaid given notice." In fact, the mother is shown in the poem in a domestic situation, "with all her saucepans," not suited "for the status of statues. Probably our blood vessels / lacked in hardening lime." The poem ends with something akin to an explosion of despair: "She has died, she has died" (*CPE,* 341). It is full of bitter irony, or perhaps simply of bitterness, as in the poem "In Italy," in which he states about his parents: "those who have loved me more than themselves are no / longer alive" (*CPE,* 340).

In both of these poems the narrator turns directly to his mother or father, saying "you." The "I" appears here only obliquely: it is the mother and father who are subjects of these poems, and not the grieving son—"you" is here more alive than "I." Such a discreet putting aside of the narrating I expresses restraint, the tempering of despair. Perhaps it is a stylistic sign of the lack of continuity between the succeeding generations: dead parents are more real than the child who is commemorating them. It is an atypical narrative decision in an elegy: the genre tends to foreground the poet rather than those who are mourned, as Brodsky observes in "The Keening Muse." In his prose, the lives of his parents are presented in a fragmentary way due to the nature of his memory; in his poems, it is they who are put forward, not their mourner. Brodsky often uses an inverted perspective, which allows him to see things in a new, unexpected way. Here that reversal makes the lost parents live again. The father, silky ash, and the mother, snowy marble, are made permanent in engraved words.

Their memory is preserved in poetry, for Brodsky the highest and the most resilient of human activities.[9]

In his essay "In a Room and a Half" Brodsky writes that his parents have no objective existence outside of him, that after their death he is all that remains of their family. He is "their only afterlife," and he decides to liberate them from the language of the state that enslaved them—he "house[es] them in . . . English" (*LTO*, 461). Perhaps he is right when he says that his parents' reticence about their ancestors was not a result of a lack of memory but a deliberate choice. Yet, when we try to reconstruct the history of his family, we see that whatever its reason, the reticence did lead to amnesia. It is striking how differently Miłosz speaks about his ancestors, not only in *Native Realm* but also in many other writings. He starts the history of his family in 1580; its members, close as well as distant, are presented against a historical background, with many details and with panache. Miłosz sees himself immersed in history; for him history is built out of individual lives. Brodsky is not interested in the past of his family; rather, he continues the reticence of his parents. But, unlike Miłosz, he describes and pays attention to the physical characteristics of his parents. We can see them, we know their height, the color of their hair, their favorite sayings, and their habits. This is his entire family, so he paints it very thoroughly because "the poor tend to utilize everything" (*LTO*, 479). Miłosz, on the other hand, says more about his distant relations than about his mother or father. Having such riches to choose from, he can afford to be wasteful.

This difference between them—the profound rootedness of Miłosz and the shallowness of Brodsky's genealogy—are not accidental; they illustrate the historical processes that governed their lives.

Miłosz felt pride in his family, a pride that was inherited together with the memory entrusted to his safekeeping. His insistent remembering of the past, of people and events, his will to record the disappearing world, came from that sense of continuity, contained in and renewed by memory. It is thanks to his ancestors that he believed in remembering, in memory's power to restore life. Brodsky was taught how not to remember. The tradition of his ancestors was not transmitted to him; it functioned only as a lack, an empty trace of difference, of otherness; it was a stigma and a burden. He never denied being Jewish, and he did not convert to Orthodox Christianity as did many Russian writers of Jewish origin. He did not identify with religion but with culture. Miłosz said many times that he admired Brodsky because he reconstructed the broken continuity of Russian culture. Brodsky did not search for this continuity in the history of his family or of his country, but reached out to the classics, to the culture of Rome and Athens. And in his Nobel lecture, he mentioned with gratitude his real forebears: Osip Mandelstam, Marina Tsvetaeva, Robert Frost, Anna Akhmatova, and Wystan Hugh Auden. This was his adopted family, his roots, the only ancestors he cared to remember.

TWO

Poetry, Youth, and Friendship

The biography of Joseph Brodsky began to turn into a legend while he was still alive. One of the main ingredients of that legend was his early circle of friends. Growing up in Leningrad, where Pushkin, Dostoyevsky, and Mandelstam used to live and write, he was aware of the poetic tradition of that city and of the links between poetry and friendship. He knew that the poems written by the romantics were born, not only of books they read together, of shared beliefs and dreams, but also of hours spent in each others' company, of card games, evenings passed at the theater, exchanges of letters, love affairs.[1] Being together helps to create the language of friendship, which is very difficult to speak well, because, as W. H. Auden wrote, unless it is spoken often, it "soon goes rusty."[2]

Early friendships were the most stable part of Aleksander Pushkin's life, and each year, on October 19, he celebrated with his friends the day of the founding of their school, the Imperial Lyceum at Tsarskoe Selo, near St. Petersburg. Each year he tried to write an occasional poem for that day, devoted mostly to friendship. Nothing was more serious for him and his circle than poetry, which also involved playfulness and competition. Poetry was intrinsically linked with friendship. That attitude toward poetry was revived by Brodsky and his Leningrad circle. For his generation, Brodsky said in a conversation with Solomon Volkov, the most important matter was "everything that happened in this city in the first quarter of the nineteenth century, when Pushkin, Krylov, Vyazemsky, and Delvig lived there. When Baratynsky used to visit" (*CJB*, 273).[3] Brodsky's friend and fellow poet Anatoly Nayman summarized it: "Pushkin set the tone with which friendship is approached in Russia."[4]

In the conversation with Volkov, recollecting poetic friendships of his youth, Brodsky said: "There were four of us: Rein, Nayman, Bobyshev, and me. Akhmatova used to call us the 'magic choir.'" It was a group, he continued, "that in many respects was similar to Pushkin's Pleiad. That is, there were approximately the same number of figures: an acknowledged leader, an acknowledged idler, and an acknowledged wit. Each of us repeated a certain role. Rein was Pushkin. Delvig, I think, that was probably Bobyshev. Nayman, with his caustic wit, was Vyazemsky. I, with my melancholy, evidently took the part of Baratynsky. Like any parallel, this one shouldn't be made too much of, though" (*CJB*, 210–11). This playful reconstruction of poetic history threw a literary gloss on the everyday life of young Leningrad poets and imparted additional importance to their poems. They were looking for models and they shaped their lives to fit literature. Romanticism, as is well known, tried to turn the quotidian into the artistic. In the 1950s and 1960s, young Russian poets were truly romantic.

Romanticism, especially in its later incarnation, implies irony: the "magic choir" collected itself around Anna Akhmatova, and after her death its members were called "Akhmatova's orphans." Yevgeny Rein met her first, when he was still a child, thanks to his aunt and Akhmatova's friend, Valeria Poznanska. Much later, Anatoly Nayman became her secretary, but, according to Bobyshev, he was not eager to introduce his friends to her. Rein and Bobyshev decided to visit her themselves, and it was Rein who, in August 1961, brought Brodsky to meet her. Anna Andreyevna Akhmatova was a great admirer of Pushkin, and she immediately saw an echo of the Pleiad in the group of young poets. They only needed, according to her, a young poetess, and she proposed Natalia Gorbanevskaya. Nayman thought this suggestion totally unwarranted. Akhmatova was for the group a link to another, already nonexistent world, to poets and manners destroyed by the revolution and Stalinism. Miraculously, she was able to convey that Atlantis. "Akhmatova," said Brodsky, "transformed you into *Homo sapiens* with just the tone of her voice or the turn of her head. . . . In conversation with her, or simply drinking tea or vodka with her, you became a Christian, a human being in the Christian sense of that word, faster than by reading the appropriate texts or attending church. The poet's role in society largely comes down to just this" (*CJB*, 207).

Many of Brodsky's ideas about poetry were taken from Akhmatova or shared with her. She impressed on the then young poet the sense of duty that poetic talent imposes on its bearer. A poem has to be remembered; its real existence is in human memory. Mnemosyne-memory is the mother of all the Muses, and therefore the basis of poetry. It is the rhyme that shelters poems from oblivion. The poet "keeps company" with his predecessors, toward whom he has grave obligations. Akhmatova and Brodsky were convinced that in poems not only words but also sound, rhythm, and rhyme are bearers of meaning. It was from her that he learned how Mandelstam, the poet who died in the Gulag two years before his birth, had recited his poems. Brodsky did not modify his attitude to poetry even later, when his Anglophone critics expressed their reservations. Like Akhmatova and Mandelstam, he was a poetic extremist.

Akhmatova's generosity, wisdom, and independence of character cemented the friendship and convictions of the young poets: friendship needs an external binding factor, be it an idea or a person. Rein, Bobyshev, and Nayman were older than Brodsky. They met as students and, according to Nayman, were considered a poetic group as early as 1957. Brodsky joined them a year or two later, like d'Artagnan, ruining their triangular symmetry. "Iosif appeared when he was eighteen years old, I was already twenty-two," said Nayman in his conversation with me. "I cannot say that I was eager for this friendship or even acquaintance. We were surrounded by enough poets." Indeed, there were many poets at that time in Moscow and Leningrad; poetry was part of a definite counterculture. Meeting in private homes, young people wrote, recited, and sang poetry, accompanying themselves on guitars. They competed over who wrote better, whose memory was best. The majority of them studied hard sciences, so as to escape the ideological pressure present in humanities departments. They rarely published their poems, though some of them were very well known. In their poetry they used all registers of language, from the highest to prison slang. They did not abide by censorship rules, yet their nonconformity had to be expressed indirectly. The very fact of writing and performing was rebellious enough. It was an act of resistance against the "thin diet," as Brodsky later said, of the official literary life. In the kitchens and common rooms of Leningrad, Moscow, and other Soviet cities, young poets created their own polis. I had a glimpse of that world much later, in June 1997, when I witnessed a poetic duel between Rein and Tomas Venclova. The scene of that duel was not a Soviet common room, but a restaurant in Venice, during a meal after Brodsky's funeral. "Remember? Remember?" Rein asked Venclova and Venclova asked Rein in return, while reciting poems, Rein at full throttle and spattering his food, Venclova in a trance, sotto voce. They did remember, and the recitation lasted a while.

Poetic counterculture was linked to the cult of friendship, and both expressed resistance against the control imposed by the all-powerful state. In the Soviet Union everything was nationalized, including human relationships. The 1930s was the period of greatest terror, but the friendships I am writing about were formed after the death of Stalin.[5] The invasion into everyone's privacy did not end after Stalin; it only weakened. The Soviet state promoted friendship because, like a caterpillar eating every leaf it sits on, it occupied the concepts dear to its citizens. It was to be a group friendship, a state-building activity, modeled on a maimed version of Pushkin's relations with his friends. In the official history of literature, the friendships of the Pushkin circle were anticzarist, while contemporary relations among friends were to be supported and furthered by the state. The post-Stalinist generation reacted with a cautious subversion. To the nationalization of feelings, they replied with their own privatization. Hence the role of the poetic discussions around the kitchen table, the consigning of poems to memory, the cult of forbidden poets. It was a self-defense and a revival of a culture that had gone through the ordeal of terror.

The Soviet state attempted to rule over friendship, poetry, and language, but none of these domains is easily nationalized. Soviet power used language to subordinate its society and unify its empire. The state's language was full of brutal, unmasked coercion. It was not used to inform, to convince, or even to censure, but to undermine all intimate relations and civic solidarity. The stolen concepts functioned within a sphere of a language emptied of meaning, put into the service of bureaucracy.[6] The most flagrant instances of such nationalized language were slogans like "Stalin—father of nations." It was not a report on reality, nor even a project for the future. It was simply a vague threat. You had to agree with it, or expect some adverse consequences. Poetic creativity was a reply to such use of language. It took language back, made it one's own. The individual challenged the state on the field where theoretically one was permitted to go, since language and literature were encouraged. The poet (or the reader of poetry) privatized language and that activity had civic consequences. Poetry undermined the state's newspeak, and recitations of poems were acts of civil disobedience. They created a community, united the group, formed a basis of friendship.

Like his contemporaries, Brodsky committed his own poems to memory, as well as the poems of many fellow poets, dead and alive. He was almost compulsive about reciting them, some of his friends remembered. His poetry became popular rather early; his poems were set to music and they were sung in the apartments of Leningrad and Moscow. But they were not highly respected among other poets, including his friends Nayman, Venclova, Lev Losiev. Brodsky himself was not very happy with them, and recited them, Nayman said in our conversation, "as if contracting—he did not like these words, but could not find any better." Later in his life he read his prose that way, "contracting" as if he did not like it. He called these early poems his "kindergarten" and never wanted to translate or reprint them.[7] His literary "kindergarten" ended when he wrote "The Great Elegy for John Donne" (1963). He then called Nayman, whom he was meeting daily, and, informed of his whereabouts, found him in a ticket line at a train station. To the astonishment of the queue, he "sang-out screamed-out" his poem. Never again did he write a similar poem, but it was a moment of finding his own voice.[8]

That voice, though totally apolitical, had of course a different tone than the official language, a tone that marked its creator as "antisocial." Even before writing "The Great Elegy" Brodsky did not fit into the tightly regulated society. He had dropped out of school when he was fifteen years old, did not belong to any organization, had no steady job, did not follow any officially sanctioned course of study. He was reading voraciously, and he translated and wrote poetry. Soon he became an object of the interest of the state and of the attacks in the press. From a youngster who joined the group of "older" poets, he turned into its main character. Eventually, his arrest, the psychiatric "observations," and his trial would make his name well known even outside of the "empire." Norenskaya, to which he was exiled, was even more isolated than Mikhaylovskoye, from which the exiled Pushkin had sent his poems about friendship. Anna Akhmatova commented on Brodsky's experience with a famous phrase: "A good biography is being prepared for our redhead."

His trial constituted an attack against the entire artistic community of Leningrad, and mobilized many people, including Akhmatova and Dmitry Shostakovich, to defend the twenty-four-year-old poet. Even Jean-Paul Sartre wrote to the Soviet authorities asking for his release. The trial was a show of total lawlessness, though Soviet standards were quite lax to begin with. The extreme stupidity of the presiding judge and of the entire proceedings prevented Brodsky from claiming the status of a victim—it would have been too embarrassing. And at that time something else occupied him: he was passing through a serious love crisis. Shortly before his arrest, Marina Basmanova, the woman he loved, had a brief affair with "Delwig"-Bobyshev. There was no final separation, and she visited Brodsky in exile, although the trip was long and politically compromising. Nayman, Rein, and other friends visited him there as well, but it was the beginning of the end of the "magic choir." "Iosif then started to turn into Brodsky, into a different persona," Nayman said in our conversation. The cloudless period of "the magic choir" had lasted for almost five years. In the history of literary friendships, it will endure forever.

The dissolution of the "magic choir" did not undermine the myth of youthful friendship between poets. Czesław Miłosz was one of the supporters of that myth when he wrote: "The example of the group of Leningrad poets, friends of Brodsky, proves the existence of a touching fraternal solidarity, of the concern about the entirety of Russian poetry and the respect for the hierarchy of talents and achievements."[9] Miłosz understood that the role of these friendships in the model biography of a poet did not depend on their stability or duration. "When the poet becomes older, his need for such friendly affiliations lessens, their ways are parting. The young are very similar to each other, because they move as one herd. . . . But later these boars separate and each has a kingdom of his own."[10] In fact, the most important factor in the dissolution of that group was the emergence of a poetic hierarchy. Almost thirty years later—in 1991—Bobyshev wrote a poem about it. His romance with Basmanova is alluded to with the words: "Forgive me, Joseph, the then-victim of my vanity." He pays more attention to their poetic competition. "You, I know it, the first; and I always the second, / that means 45th, 104th." Anatoly Nayman had a similar reaction. Asked when he had realized that Iosif was a genius, he would often reply: We were all geniuses. Indeed, they were all gifted poets, though some more gifted than others.

The Pleiad-magic choir was also undermined by life, and especially by marital entanglements: the first wife of Nayman married Tomas Venclova, the first wife of Rein became Mrs. Nayman. In 1969, Marina Basmanova gave birth to Andrei, the son of Brodsky, but the couple did not remain together. In truth, Brodsky was never comfortable in any group; all of "Akhmatova's orphans" were very individualistic. They had been brought together by youth, literary tradition, and the pressure of the Soviet state, and by a very happy coincidence—the survival of Anna Akhmatova through wars, purges, and revolutions. But the "magic choir" had already dissolved shortly before Akhmatova's death in 1966. She united them one more time during her funeral, a moment immortalized by a dramatic photograph. At the center-bottom of the photo, we see in an open casket the face of the dead poetess. On the left, Nayman is bending over her; on the right, Brodsky with a look of despair covers his mouth with his hand. Behind them stands a despondent Rein; and behind him are Era Korobova, Nayman's wife at the time, and a pale Bobyshev. They are all turned toward and looking at Akhmatova. It was their last common meeting.[11]

When Brodsky found himself in exile, his youthful friendships were already gone. He wrote a Pushkinian, ironic poem of farewell to his friends, but it is just as much a poem about aging—about the fear of approaching death, of loneliness. Friendship here clearly is linked to belonging to a nation, with its solidarity, togetherness, and, especially, its community of language. Paraphrasing Prince Igor's address to his warriors in the old Russian epic *The Lay of Igor's Campaign*, Brodsky writes:

> *Listen, my boon brethren and my enemies!*
> *What I've done, I've done not for fame or memories*
> *in this era of radio waves and cinemas,*
> *but for the sake of my native tongue and letters.*
> *For which sort of devotion, of a zealous bent*
> *("Heal thyself, doctor," as the saying went),*

> *denied a chalice at the feast of the fatherland,*
> *now I stand in a strange place. The name hardly matters.*
> *(*CPE, *69)*

"Denied a chalice at the feast of the fatherland"—here is a tone, even if somewhat ironic, that Brodsky will rarely use in the future. And the name of the place to which he came soon started to matter.

Very few friendships accompanied him across that border between the fatherland and the new place. One was his poetic and personal affiliation with Tomas Venclova, to whom he dedicated two musically entitled poems: "Lithuanian Divertissement" and "Lithuanian Nocturne." After finding himself in the West, Brodsky tried to help Venclova, who was at that time in danger as one of the founder-members of a Lithuanian human rights organization. In 1976, Brodsky published a letter in his defense, calling Venclova "*the best* poet living on the territory of that empire of which Lithuania is a small province."[12] Czesław Miłosz joined in these efforts. In the second of the preserved letters to Brodsky, dated February 4, 1974, Miłosz wrote: "I have translated and published in *Kultura* one poem of Tomas Venclova. He has seen it and I have received from him a message of friendship and gratitude. So you see the results of our conversation in Berkeley."[13] Three years later the Soviet authorities felt forced to permit Venclova's departure from the Soviet Union. "Without the help of Miłosz and Brodsky I would have certainly perished. Due to their efforts, my case became a *cause célèbre* and I was able to leave. I am not imprisoned as my friend Petkus, or Orlov or Scharansky," Venclova said in the already quoted conversation.[14] And the solidarity of poets did not end with Venclova's emigration. Miłosz and Brodsky translated his poems and helped him look for a job. Miłosz was proud of their triple friendship and often repeated that it meant more for Polish-Russian-Lithuanian relations than all the work of the politicians.

Venclova is a poet, but also a literary historian, and he has deciphered for us allusions and obscure passages in Brodsky's works that were dedicated to him. It was, by the way, a reciprocal relation: Venclova's own poetic work is in constant dialogue with what the Russian poet wrote. In the "Lithuanian Divertissement" Venclova is mentioned only in the dedication; the poem itself is a cycle of almost baroque variation on Lithuanian themes.[15] In the second poem, "Lithuanian Nocturne," Venclova is ubiquitous—it is a work of friendship. The narrator shows himself as an apparition, a specter "tearing [himself] from the New World" to visit Tomas "in a destitute province of the Empire." Their separateness soon transforms into oneness, like "Castor looming through Pollux." "My pohoži; / my w suszcznosti, Tomas, odno," writes Brodsky in the Russian original, which he translates into English:

> *Tomas, we are alike;*
> *we are, frankly, a double:*
> *your breath*
> *dims the same windowpane that my features befuddle.*
> (CPE, *218*)

The poets are linked not only by "our inkpot alliance," but also by the Muse. Venclova interprets this motif as a continuation of the traditional literary topos of the encounter of two poets; he believes that Brodsky develops here the theme known especially from the "Kishiniev poems" of Pushkin, which refer to Ovid and empire.[16] This is, therefore, a poem that contains the most important motifs of Brodsky's poetics: exile, loneliness, the brotherhood of poets, the horror of empire. But, though the tone of the poem is, as often with Brodsky, ironic and rough, the "Lithuanian Nocturne" is also lyrical, declaring faithfulness in friendship. This last feeling or rather character trait—faithfulness in friendship—is what Venclova underlined in his remembrance of Brodsky after his untimely death.[17]

That faithfulness was very selective. From the remembrances of his Leningrad friends, as well as from his own writings, one could conclude that Brodsky felt burdened by his old relationships. Friendship thrives on mutual support in difficulties and adverse circumstances, but friends also need to be able to enjoy each other's successes, honors, and awards. For many of his old acquaintances, Brodsky remained part of the reality he had long left behind. They considered his literary output written in exile inferior to his early writings, did not understand his new literary choices, and felt sorrow at his moving into English, in which he wrote not only essays but also poems. With his own daughter he spoke in English! They did not approve of his ambition, new friendships, attitude toward religion. He did not evolve in accordance with those who remained in Russia or with those who emigrated. He went his own way. He did not break off with most of his friends, but he often rebelled against their possessiveness and then apologized. He frequented Russian New York; he liked especially the restaurant Russian Samovar, on Fifty-second Street and Eighth Avenue, started by his Leningrad friend Roman Kaplan, an enterprise to which he contributed money. He often met with friends at that restaurant, where he liked to eat herring with potatoes, drink vodka, and sing along to piano accompaniment. His musical repertoire came from the Russian 1960s, consisting of unabashedly sentimental Soviet songs. It also included a Polish patriotic ballad "The Red Poppies at Monte Casino," popular in the Soviet Union of his youth thanks to a film of Andrzej Wajda, *Ashes and Diamonds.* A book about this restaurant has been written by Anatoly Nayman, and a big part of the book is devoted to Brodsky.[18]

His health declining, he nevertheless helped his compatriots as much as he was able to. He wrote numerous book reviews, letters of recommendation, book prefaces; he organized poetry readings, meetings with publishers. In his archive there remain voluminous files full of copies of letters, appeals, petitions, and articles written on behalf of people in need of help, held in arrests, or not permitted to emigrate. However, these efforts did not fulfill the requirements of his milieu: new or unlucky immigrants expect unlimited solidarity on the part of their more successful compatriots. The recriminations were proportional to the beliefs about the reach and potential of his power. When he wrote a negative review for his publisher of a manuscript of a novel by Vassili Aksyonov, it caused a miniscandal. For the Russian émigré community, loyalty toward a fellow émigré was more important than free literary judgment. Brodsky helped another writer and his Leningrad acquaintance, Sergey Dovlatov, to publish his excellent stories in English translation. I've heard that Dovlatov used to say: "Iosif helps, but he likes to humiliate you a bit on such an occasion."

The early friendships of Brodsky impressed Miłosz so much because they fitted well into the remembrances of his own youth. In the years 1931–34, Miłosz had belonged to "Żagary," a Vilnius literary group, and published his works in a periodical of that name. Besides Miłosz, the group included future writers, such as the poet-critics Henryk Dembiński, Stefan Jędrychowski, Teodor Bujnicki, Jerzy Zagórski, Tadeusz Byrski, and Jerzy Putrament, all of whom are often recalled by Miłosz in his musings about the past and the nature of memory. When I asked Miłosz about the contrast between his individualism and belonging to associations bound by the feelings of friendship, he replied (referring to the Leningrad Pleiad): "Yes, great value was attached to the camaraderie. Young poets need poetic friendship. They are not self-assured, they read their poems to each other. The classical example is the confraternity of the poets of Petersburg, 'the angelic choir' around Anna Akhmatova, of which Iosif Brodsky was a part. The entire history of Iosif in Petersburg is, in fact, the history of the affiliations between friends, very needed. For me it was similar, the Żagary group and all my youth in Vilnius consisted of the same things. It is a certain pattern."[19]

The members of Żagary were not so close as those of the "magical" or, as Miłosz said, "angelic" choir, and Żagary was not the only group to which Miłosz belonged when young. His membership in various associations was more formalized and diversified than Brodsky's. While a student, he belonged to at least three organizations: the Vagabonds' Club, the Circle of Students of Polish Philology, and the Club of Intellectuals. But already before his studies, in the school year 1928–29, he became a member of the "conspiratorial group 'Pet,'" which meant for him "friendship, discussions, books, and brotherhood"

(*TB*, 159). Unlike the Leningrad group, Miłosz and his friends were not united by a figure of one master, but they too read prose and poems together, and shared everything they wrote. Living in a democracy, however imperfect, they did not have to commit as much poetry to memory. "Usually I would wait patiently while Dorek Bujnicki attended to his students, after which we showed each other our poems and dreamed up literary pranks." These "pranks" consisted most probably of the poems they wrote together and published in *Żagary* under the pseudonym Aron Pirmas. Although their poems often were catastrophic in tone, they remained "unaware of the devilish traps that History had already set for [them]" (*TB*, 37, 34).

The literary friendships of Leningrad were doubly transgressive: they reached back to the prerevolutionary cultural tradition and they created a space for autonomous, uncontrolled affiliations between the young. In comparison to Leningrad, Vilnius of the 1930s was a city of freedom. Miłosz's writings show that the atmosphere of his youth was less emotionally intense than that of postwar Leningrad. But the groups to which Miłosz belonged continued the tradition of conspiratorial, illegal organizations, some of them Masonic, some irredentist, that existed in the city before Poland regained independence in 1918 (with Vilnius incorporated into that new Poland). About one of these groups—"Pet"—he wrote: " 'Lodge' is an exaggeration, but I cannot think of our group or of the Vagabonds' Club, which I joined shortly afterward, other than as the peculiar creations of Wilno, the city of Freemasonry. Just as during the period of Wilno University's preeminence, prior to 1830, when many of our city's luminaries belonged to the Masonic lodges and rumors about this circulated freely, although I found out how numerous were the Masons among us only many years later" (*TB*, 42).

Friendship is one of the virtues of Masonry, and, like marriage, it combines an intimate rapport with social duties. Friends share the idea of service, of participation in and responsibility for public life; they are united by an external value, be it God, country, honor, or art. The social, institutional character of friendship was described long ago by Aristotle, as well as by Plato, Cicero, and Montaigne, and transmitted in classical studies in most European schools. The Enlightenment and romanticism transformed the idea of friendship between a couple of "brothers" into that of friendship of a group of like-minded men, linked by loyalty and united by the pursuit of justice. The Masonic lodges, secret student circles, and university associations formed the Polish romantic poet Adam Mickiewicz and his contemporaries. Vilnius-Wilno was then a Polish-speaking city within the borders of the Russian empire. A hundred years later, in newly independent Poland, the city maintained its memory. Miłosz's groups and circles continued that associational tradition. It did not die even after World War II, when Wilno became Vilnius—a capital of the Lithuanian Soviet Republic. Tomas Venclova has attested to the fact that young people "remembered" the city's conspiratorial past, although—as in the times of czarist Russia—they had to be extremely cautious when implementing that remembrance through unofficial meetings or poetry readings. The new empire was even more unforgiving than the old one.

For Miłosz and Brodsky, youthful friendship had a similar value: it was the only social institution they could depend on. The history of their native cities preordained a linking of poetry with the virtue of friendship. Pushkin worshiped friendship, as we have already seen. The same has to be said of Adam Mickiewicz.[20] Both Miłosz and Brodsky used their great predecessors as models. "All creation comes from the encounter of the human soul with another soul," wrote Miłosz in his essay about "Dorek" Bujnicki, where he credits his Vilnius friendships with steering him toward literature (*TB,* 166). Żagary and "the magical choir" belong to the same romantic tradition. That tradition was long preserved and reenacted in Warsaw, Petersburg, Vilnius, and other cities of the region.

I have already mentioned the first "emigration" of Miłosz, his leaving Vilnius (Wilno, as it was then called by its Polish name) for Warsaw in 1937; the brutality of the political atmosphere forced him to change his place of work. The coming of war two years later cut him off from Vilnius and transformed that city into a memory. As he wrote in the poem "City without a Name":

> *Who will honor the city without a name*
> *If so many are dead and others pan gold*
> *Or sell arms in faraway countries?*

The twelfth part of this poem opens with a dramatic question:

> *Why should that city, defenseless and pure as the wedding*
> *necklace of a forgotten tribe, keep offering itself to me?*
> *(*NCP, *214, 219)*

Until the end of his life, Miłosz would remember the "nameless" city in poems and essays. In his eighties, he returns to it in *ABC.* Vilnius is present in this book right from the first entry: "Abramowicz, Ludwik. Wilno always was a city verging on a fairy tale."[21] That fairy-tale character of the city was due to the existence of secret societies and Masonic lodges. This is also the content of several other entries, many of which are concerned with Miłosz's friends and friendly associations he knew about. Symbolically, the first and last entries are about Wilno, so the book is devoted to that city from *A* to *Z*. And, since it is a matter of youthful friendships, the story of Teodor Bujnicki runs throughout.

Bujnicki used to be called Dorek-Amorek (Dorek being a diminutive of Teodor). A few years older than Miłosz, he was a faithful and cordial companion, the most promising young poet of Wilno, very successful in writing satirical cabaret poems. But his life was far from a series of "literary pranks," and he did not escape the traps of History. Miłosz wrote about his friend's life as early as 1954, forty years before the creation of the *ABC's*. The essay "Teodor Bujnicki" is one of the many biographical-autobiographical texts in which the city of Wilno is also an important protagonist. Czesław was seventeen years old when he approached the twenty-one-year-old Bujnicki "with love and respect" and with admiration for his literary achievement, talent, and joyful character. Miłosz does not forget how wonderful "Dorek" was, even though later, during Soviet occupation of Wilno in the years 1939–41, Bujnicki published pro-Soviet poems in the Soviet newspaper *Prawda* (Truth); and when Russians returned to the city three years later, he joined them again, this time as a member of their government-in-progress, the Association of Polish Patriots. As was true of all of the bodies that the Soviets imposed on conquered Poland, the name of the organization was a hundred percent false: it was neither an association nor was it composed of Polish patriots. The Polish underground, it seems, condemned Bujnicki for his unpatriotic acts and he was executed. It was 1944 and he was thirty-seven years old.

Miłosz deeply regrets Bujnicki's death, while at the same time he dissects Dorek's character, looking for the reasons that led him to join the occupiers. Bujnicki always felt a need to belong to a community, and he always sought agreement, adjustment to people and circumstances. Also, he was frustrated in his literary work and was looking for new impulses. He lacked distance, coolness, and wisdom. Miłosz describes these characteristics with hesitation, asking: how have I avoided a similar fate? He feels a great sense of compassion toward his dead friend—a compassion that moves his pen—and a feeling of responsibility: "To me belongs the power of bringing him back from oblivion," writes Miłosz (*TB*, 182). Death kills twice, because it also erases the dead from memory—friends have a duty to remember. Those who outlive their friends have a task to ensure that the dead are not forgotten. Hamlet, while dying, says to Horatio:

> *Horatio, I am dead;*
> *Thou livest; report me and my cause aright*
> *To the unsatisfied.*
>
> . . .
>
> *. . . tell my story. (5.2.279–80)*

Miłosz's late writings are in a large part a fulfillment of the friend's duty to remember.

The narrative drive of Miłosz always coexisted with his lyrical impulse. The portrait of Teodor Bujnicki is only one of many fragments of an extensive autobiography, or even an autobiographical novel that Miłosz never completed. During the 1998 Claremont McKenna College festival celebrating the Polish poet, Madeline Levine spoke about the novelistic momentum of his autobiographical texts. Miłosz expressed his surprise and agreement at this diagnosis, saying that he always believed his prose to be "a kind of a novel of the XX century,"[22] or "an autobiography of our century."[23] That portrait is very similar to several others in which Miłosz analyzes and describes ideological choices of his friends, former friends, or contemporaries. His renowned book *The Captive Mind* is a collection of portraits. Interpreted mostly as an ideological work, it is also part of his autobiography, which is why it survived its topic: communism. The book consists of portraits of concrete and recognizable persons in which we follow their entanglement with History. And, even though the book harshly criticizes the people it describes, writing it was an act of friendship.

In a letter to Thomas Merton, Miłosz said of *The Captive Mind:* "That book was written [in 1953] *in extremis* by a poet who could not address foreign language readers in verse and hesitated between two aims: to convey the meaning of the 'Eastern' experience to those not acquainted with it, and *to tell the truth* [my emphasis] to his colleagues in Poland."[24] The book was an explanation not so much of communism itself as of why certain Eastern European writers and intellectuals felt attracted to it. It was also a farewell message of one choosing exile and rupturing his relations with his country. He addressed the West but also spoke to the people he left behind. His book was a summation, an accusation, a self-revelation. It was not the first text Miłosz had written after choosing exile. In May 1951, in the émigré monthly *Kultura*, he published a fifteen-page article entitled "Nie" (No). In it, he expressed the themes he developed later in *The Captive Mind:* "What I'm going to tell now could well be called a story of a suicide," he began. The suicide in question was his decision to emigrate, which Miłosz feared would prevent him from writing poetry. He shared the then-common belief that in order to create, the poet had to be with his people. Thus, the dramatic effect of this opening sentence should be taken seriously: the gamble was real. But the word *suicide* had a larger meaning. Miłosz was worried about "the vulnerability of the twentieth-century mind to seduction by socio-political doctrines and its readiness to accept totalitarian terror for the sake of a hypothetical future."[25] *The Captive Mind* explores the deep causes of longing for even "the most illusory certainty."

The book's structure is unusual. It speaks about "the history of the last decades in Central and Eastern Europe which abounds in situations in regard to which all epithets and theoretical considerations lose meaning." The opening chapters present the history and nature of communism and the book ends with a defense of the Baltic peoples. But its core is composed of case studies that analyze and describe concrete lives and persons who succumbed to the Hegelian—that is, Marxist—temptation. The identity of four men is hidden behind Greek letters and the fifth person is nicknamed Ketman, an Arabic term borrowed from Gobineau. The concept of Ketman was "developed by Miłosz to describe citizens engaged in the so-called people's democracies in a conscious mass play to deceive their rulers. It is not a mechanism of enslavement but of resistance, " said Andrzej Walicki when *The Captive Mind* was discussed during the International Czesław Miłosz Festival in 1998.[26] The character of Ketman was somehow related to Miłosz's friend and mentor Tadeusz Kroński, who remained in Poland. But Kroński was a "Hegelian Ketman," and Miłosz wrote about him directly in an important chapter of his *Native Realm* that underlined this friend's influence on his two treatises, moral and poetical.[27]

The Greek letters hiding the identity of four main protagonists suggest a certain universality of the cases and a moral lesson that could be drawn from them. Yet these were concrete life stories and the case studies avoid clear-cut moral recommendations. Miłosz abhorred anonymity and general rules; he often repeated that man had no greater foe than generalization. In *The Captive Mind* his is an angry voice weaving accusations, but with elements of compassion and justification. All four people, like Dorek Bujnicki, are flawed characters facing the unprecedented ravages of triumphant totalitarianism. Miłosz exposes and condemns them, but without finality. This is why moralistic writers, like Gustaw Herling-Grudziński, rejected *The Captive Mind.* For them the "Hegelian temptation" was a self-justification of the weak and fearful, and Miłosz's book nothing but a sleek self-absolution. But the Polish poet had a very different kind of temperament and talent. He felt not only compassion but also the commonality of guilt. He was interested in nuance, not in sentencing. He feared the "traps of History" and never stopped wondering about the reasons that helped him to avoid them, even if only partially.

The Polish reader had no trouble in decoding these four portraits. Beta was Tadeusz Borowski, well known in the United States for his collection of short stories *This Way for the Gas, Ladies and Gentlemen,* written right after World War II. When Miłosz was writing about him at the beginning of the 1950s he was already dead by suicide. Gamma stood for the failed writer, Jerzy Putrament, in his youth a member of the group Żagary but now a party *apparatchik.* The poet Konstanty Ildefons Gałczyński is described in the chapter about Delta. But the most important portrait is that of Alpha, or Jerzy Andrzejewski, best known as the author of *Ashes and Diamonds* (on which Andrzej Wajda's film was based). Miłosz knew them all—they were writers, his "brothers-in-trade." But his relationship with Alpha was extraordinary and special.

Miłosz, his wife Janka, and Alpha-Andrzejewski passed the war years together. It was a wonderful friendship which must have saved all three from total despair. They traveled, conspired, and drank together: Polish history of male friendship would necessarily have to include a long chapter devoted to vodka. Also, vodka was very much in use during World War II; it softened, I believe, the harshness of reality. Miłosz and Andrzejewski read, wrote, conspired, and laughed, allowed themselves practical jokes and daring provocations. In reading both Miłosz's and Andrzejewski's reminiscences of the period, and the letters they exchanged during and after the war, one is struck by an aura of happiness that seems almost impossible in such bleak times.

They found joy in their friendship, their literary collaboration, their challenges to the occupiers, funny and unnecessarily risky, or perhaps necessarily so, as they served to maintain dignity in the face of humiliating oppression. Miłosz's postwar disappointment in his friend was severe. In *The Captive Mind* his bitterest words are about Alpha. "The man I call Alpha is one of the best-known prose writers east of the Elbe. He was [!] a close friend of mine, and memories of many difficult moments that we went through together tie us to each other. I find it hard to remain unmoved when I recall him. I even ask myself if I should subject him to this analysis. But I shall do so because friendship would not prevent me from writing an article on his books in which I would say more or less what I shall say here."[28]

What Miłosz had to say about his friend, or his former friend, was very critical. Both Miłosz and Andrzejewski understood that postwar Poland needed a renewal, but Miłosz saw very quickly that his place was on the outside. He joined the Polish diplomatic corps so as to reside abroad. This joining is sometimes understood as gaining access to the regime, but Miłosz never committed any act that would be shameful, never declared his allegiance to the new regime, never wrote anything supporting the communists. I am not aware of a single activity of his that would have to be censored today. And very quickly he abandoned the diplomatic service.[29] Andrzejewski, however, was courted by the new authorities, as many writers were, and could not resist a chance to become a moral authority. Thus resulted the postwar difference in attitude of the two friends toward the communist regime, a difference, according to Miłosz, not due to divergent political worldviews so much as to dissimilarities of character. Andrzejewski had a weakness for moral extremes. During the war, both writers, but especially Alpha, were involved in dangerous underground work. Loyalty was necessary during wartime, and Andrzejewski wrote about loyalty to the nation and loyalty to friends in his wartime fiction. Of course, where there's need for loyalty, there's also betrayal. Alpha was bitterly disappointed with the Polish government in exile. Then history came to Poland in the shape of the Red Army, and all loyalties were broken. It was not unreasonable to be convinced that the war demanded dramatic payback in the form of social revolution. War's devastations warranted a new beginning and radical change. Alpha embraced that change without the cool distance that characterized Miłosz and saved him from total immersion in communism. After a few years, the ways of the friends parted.

But the memory of friendship and its duties remained. In another letter to Merton, Miłosz wrote that *The Captive Mind* was both an explosion of long-contained fury and an act of cold vengeance. The high tenor of emotions was due to the despair at the suffering caused by that war. But his anger was directed toward his colleagues. He needed to "tell the truth" and to castigate them. His wartime relationship with Alpha was based on loyalty and on public service, but, in the Aristotelian tradition, the highest kind of friendship is based on truth. Such critical truth telling allows friends to follow the rightful path, to "keep us worthy of ourselves."[30] And truth turned out to be more fruitful than loyalty, or rather, truth became a form of loyalty and the highest form of friendship. The anger that governed Miłosz's truth telling was accompanied by feelings of love. "In fact I love those people against whom I directed my anger much more than I show,"

Miłosz wrote in that letter to Merton. And, in another letter also to Merton: "For Alpha my chapter about him was a blow." Yet six years later they were friends again. Soon Andrzejewski became a dissident, declaring single-handedly his opposition to the 1968 invasion of Czechoslovakia. For Miłosz only death could fix a person's biography, and even then, the fixing was not set in stone.

I was very anxious when, during the International Czesław Miłosz Festival, I spoke in Miłosz's presence about *The Captive Mind* as a book born out of friendship. I was talking not so much about Miłosz's personal life as about his solidarity with his fellow writers, about friendship as a social institution. After my talk, Miłosz said to me: "You know, it is right, these friendships were very important for me." Elżbieta Sawicka, then a journalist at the daily *Rzeczpospolita*, asked him what he thought about such a characterization of his book; she quotes his reply: "I partially agree with it, although as far as friendship goes we can talk about it only in the case of Jerzy Andrzejewski. But certainly my student youth in Wilno consisted of constant association with friends. It is deeply present in me. . . . Dr. Wikta Winnicka . . . used to say: 'Czesio [diminutive of Czesław] is always nostalgic and suffers in exile, because he would like to play in mud with his little friends.'" Sawicka asked him also about my opinion about *The Captive Mind* as a book of friendship. "Of course, we discussed in the Polish group that interpretation of *The Captive Mind*," she wrote. "I tended to agree with Irena Grudzińska-Gross, but Adam Michnik objected, especially because of the chapter on Jerzy Putrament: What kind of friendship with Putrament?"[31] The letters from and to Putrament, published by Miłosz a few years later, show indeed that there was no friendship between the poet and the *apparatchik,* and yet one can find there a kind of fascination, especially on Putrament's side. He tried very hard "to direct this geyser [of Miłosz's talent] into a socialist tube," and repeatedly sent the poet abroad, attacking him in print only after his "choosing of freedom." Miłosz always remembered Putrament's interested support, and wrote about this unsuccessful writer very generously, without irony or bitterness.

Generosity is one of the characteristics of friendship, and Miłosz is generous in his constant remembering of dead acquaintances and friends. It is not always easy, as many memories are difficult and not welcome. "My dearest shadows—he writes about Andrzejewski and his wife Janka—I cannot invite you for a conversation with me, for behind us, as only we three know, lies our tragic life. Our conversation would develop into a lament in three voices" (*ABC,* 54–55). About Bujnicki, he declares: "While ending this writing, I almost physically sensed his presence, the non-importance of years that passed. He was in front of me and seemed to have a request. 'Say it.' But what was I to say? 'Say that it is not all.' I understand. . . . How could one even for a moment suppose that words would be able to catch something from one human life, which is precious and gigantic? Injustice is born from the very ineptitude of words" (*TB,* 182). This imperfection of words does not render invalid the act of remembering. Especially important is that it is not a one-sided relation, but, as in the rite of Forefathers, described by Mickiewicz, it is the interdependence of the living with the dead. "Since people disappear one after the other," writes Miłosz, "and questions multiply as to whether and to what extent they exist, religious space borders upon historical space, understood as the continuity of civilization." The history of a language, for example, is a space in which we meet our predecessors, and Brodsky used to say that he writes for those who were before him, not those who are still to come. When Miłosz declares that he can make future generations remember his dead friends, it is not an act of pride. All that the dead can do is to "make use of me, of the rhythm of my blood, my hand holding the pen, in order to return for a brief moment among the living" (*ABC*, 313).

THREE

Friendship and the Estate of Poetry

While youthful friendships grow from the common project of learning how to live, friendly associations of adult years are more selective, deliberate. In the case of our poets, the shape of their later friendships was determined by emigration. In his *Nicomachean Ethics,* Aristotle considers friendship necessary—nobody would want to live without friends, he writes, even possessing every earthly good. The sufferings of emigration consist in great part in being cut off from places, language, family, and friends. Miłosz used to say that it was the fame in his little town that alone interested him. Only the weaving together of new threads of friendships allows for settling down in a new life. It forms conditions of a new normalcy.

The exile of Miłosz started in a very dramatic way. He decided to "escape" while on a short visit to Poland from Paris, where he had been stationed as a low-level diplomat. Feeling entrapped in the country that was sinking ever deeper into Stalinism, he barely managed to leave, enlisting the help of the wife of the minister of foreign affairs. He returned to France and left his post; he was sheltered just outside Paris, in Maisons-Laffitte, the seat of the Polish émigré publication *Kultura*. At the beginning, few people knew his whereabouts. They were Nelli Micińska, who contacted on his behalf Jerzy Giedroyć, the founder and editor in chief of *Kultura;* Giedroyć and the other members of the *Kultura* team—Henryk Giedroyć, and Zygmunt and Zofia Hertz—as he was living with them. There was no official welcome; rather, quite the opposite—several months of isolation due to fears of kidnapping by Soviet agents. The year was 1951: Stalinism, Cold War. Separated from Poland and from his pregnant wife and little son, who were residing temporarily in the United States, Miłosz felt lonely and abandoned. He turned to writing, first explanatory declarations, including the already quoted "No," then the political treatise *The Captive Mind,* a political novel *The Seizure of Power,* and a novel about his childhood, *The Issa Valley.* This last book described the riches of his childhood and served as a basis for many of his later prose writings. It was an archeology of his past, a retreat into memory.

The contacts of Miłosz with *Kultura* were not accidental, but were initiated by Jerzy Giedroyć himself a year before Miłosz's "escape." Giedroyć asked his collaborator, a fellow resident of Maisons-Laffitte and a great painter, Józef Czapski, who was traveling then to New York, to visit Miłosz and indicate to him that *Kultura* would offer him shelter in case of his rupture with the communist government. It is important in all of today's debates about Miłosz's access to the communist regime that such a supreme student of Polish politics as Giedroyć did not have any doubts about the poet's independent politics. When Miłosz decided to remain in the West, Giedroyć and Czapski on his behalf asked the French authorities for asylum. The person who, in this first, very bleak period, was of greatest emotional support for Miłosz, was Zygmunt Hertz. In a remembrance written after Hertz's death, Miłosz said: "He watched over me tenderly, took care of me, and whenever I went to the city he made sure that I had a couple of francs for lunch and cigarettes. When I accepted his offerings, I was too preoccupied with my own troubles to value those gifts at the time, but I did not forget about them, and for years afterward there was a good deal of ordinary gratitude in my affection for him." Hertz must have been very forbearing: Miłosz was difficult, angry, explosive, often drunk and depressed. The friendship with Hertz was almost automatic. "I didn't treat Zygmunt as a friend at that time, as someone whom one chooses and with whom one is supposed to have an intellectual understanding. He was more like a classmate, assigned to us without our participation" (*TB*, 173–74).

At *Kultura*, Hertz played a subaltern role; his duties included packing, mailing, food delivery. He was an immensely gifted and energetic man, frustrated by the narrow limits of his responsibilities; that frustration can be easily detected in his letters to Miłosz. He had a great gift for friendship, and all his unfulfilled ambitions were placed in the people he cherished. His emotions and talents found expression in the correspondence with Miłosz—the letters (only the Hertz side) were published after 1989. He wrote a lot, and easily, trying to keep Miłosz informed about Polish affairs and gossip. His letters, all 248 of them, were written between 1952 and 1979, and are a great chronicle of the life of *Kultura* and of this group's contacts with Poland. Hertz reviews important articles, political decisions, characters and actions of common acquaintances; he also tries to keep Miłosz happy and writing. This is why, in his *in memoriam*, Miłosz declares that he cries over him for egoistical reasons. "Is there anything one can have on this earth that is better than a few friends holding each other by the hand, who together create a circuit and feel the current running through it? For me, after my emigration from there to America in 1960, Paris was just such a little circle of friends, but it was Zygmunt above all who held us together, it was his current we felt most powerfully, and now, as in a dream, our hands reach toward each other's but cannot connect" (*TB*, 179).

Miłosz had a very straightforward and old-fashioned attitude toward friendship. He exposed all the faults of Andrzejewski because he wanted to change him, pull him out of his ideological cul-de-sac. But friendship was for him most of all the virtue of mutual well-wishing, support, and attention. The word *friend* is used by him often. It was enough for him that he was the one who was bestowing it, that it was given, even if not explicitly accepted. For him and Zygmunt Hertz, the "tending of the estate of poetry," concern for Poland, and the shared experience of emigration were elements in common. That external element was only a leaven, a germ of communion. Friendship needs more warmth than judgment; it blossoms when built on agreement and not on having the upper hand. Miłosz survived his friend, and this is why he could trace the final shape of his life, its final reckoning. He did not sum it up, he only recorded it. Generously.

In the first period of his life in exile, Jeanne Hersch was the person who helped him most, more—if such things can be judged at all—than Zygmunt Hertz and the team of *Kultura*. I will return to her while talking about our poets' women and muses. She helped him, not only by her clear and definite anticommunism and by her disgust of Parisian intellectual fashions, but she also convinced him to write his short novel *The Seizure of Power*. She then translated that novel into French and helped in its presentation for a literary award that allowed Miłosz to bring his family to France and live off his writings. He was always very grateful to her, as he was toward Albert Camus, who was then his "ally." "Good, helpful, [Camus] belonged to these writers, so rare in Paris, on whom one could always count when in real trouble. I am expressing here my gratitude for his attention, cordiality in these times that were difficult for me, for his gift of friendship."[1]

Miłosz remembers this initial period of his emigration as having been humiliating. In 1981, I witnessed his meeting with the Polish Diaspora in Paris soon after he received the Nobel Prize in literature. I was shocked then, as were other younger émigrés present in the large basement of the church in which the meeting took place, by the cold irony, almost a fury, with which Miłosz treated the overflowing public. Today you are proud of me, he was saying, but when I needed your help you accused me of communism and you informed on me to the U.S. embassy, preventing me from joining my family. The violence of these words seemed to me disproportionate to the triumph which we came to celebrate. I did not know the dimensions of his bitterness. In the moment of his greatest need, he was rejected by the Polish Diaspora—he was for them a man who worked for five years as a diplomat for the communist government; and was therefore suspect, perhaps even a Soviet agent, sent to penetrate Polish milieus in the West. In the Polish émigré publications, his "escape to freedom" caused violent discussions between *Wiadomości,* a London literary weekly hostile toward him, and *Kultura.* The case became a pretext for a showdown between various factions: the attitude toward "Bierut's diplomat"—as Miłosz was called (Bierut was the president of Poland and the head of the Communist Party at that time)—was a measure of the opinions toward the old country, communism, and emigration. Miłosz was attacked as well by the other side, by his colleagues who remained in Poland. In an orchestrated effort poems were written against him, by, among others, Konstanty Ildefons Gałczyński and Jarosław Marek Rymkiewicz, and critical articles by Jarosław Iwaszkiewicz and Antoni Słonimski. Miłosz recalled that when he bumped into Iwaszkiewicz in Paris in 1954 or 1955, Iwaszkiewicz had "turned [to Miłosz] and snapped: 'I cannot greet you, darling'" (*YH,* 149). Joanna Pyszny rightly calls her article about the beginnings of Miłosz's emigration "L'Affaire Miłosz; or, The Poet in Purgatory."[2] He was in-between, cut off from both sides of this Polish cold war. He felt innocent, and that caused him to explode with anger and despair. He often said that it was a horrible period in his life and that he was uncertain how he managed to survive it. "L'Affaire

Miłosz" caused him to write a book about Stanisław Brzozowski—like himself, innocent and persecuted by "the forces of conformism."[3]

The attacks of the Polish Diaspora and of his fellow writers were just some of the causes of his distress. "Perhaps I would not have felt so humiliated in the 1950s," he wrote in *Year of the Hunter*, "had I not craved recognition as a poet. A couple of people—Jean Cassou, Supervielle—had some understanding of who I was, but I could sense through my pores the general aura surrounding my person: he's some kind of crank, maybe a little crazy, working at anti-Communism." In France, he was known as a prose writer, the author of *The Captive Mind*; and when he moved to the United States, he was "only" a professor of literature and translator of Polish poetry into English. But all of it finally ended. He was now enjoying France, "in retaliation for the humiliations I once suffered there" (*YH*, 9). He thought of his life story as a moral fable, a fairy tale in which the third, youngest brother, the stupid one, turns out to have been right all along.

In comparison with Miłosz's "escape," Brodsky's emigration was almost too easy. And yet how traumatic and painful it was! The *casus* Brodsky—his trial, his internal exile—were well known in the West, and W. H. Auden himself wrote the introduction to the first English-language edition of his poems. The fact that Brodsky came from Russia guaranteed more interest in his person. Also, times had changed; in the twenty years that separated the two acts of emigration the USSR had lost a lot of its attractiveness: only a few Western communist parties continued to express confidence in the future of its political system. Carl Proffer, the American editor of Brodsky's works, awaited him at the airport in Vienna; a few days later he met Auden, who "during those weeks in Austria looked after [Brodsky's] affairs with the diligence of a good mother hen" (*LTO,* 377). Thanks to Auden, Brodsky soon traveled to London, where they stayed together at Stephen Spender's. The reason for that trip—an international poetry festival— became the Western "debut" of Brodsky, the first of many such festivals he (and Miłosz) frequented. In the Brodsky archive one can read a letter from Auden with detailed instructions about the Russian poet's trip. Although Brodsky's spoken English was still limited, they understood each other very well. During the festival Robert Lowell, who befriended Brodsky, read English-language versions of the Russian poet's poems. Brodsky also met Seamus Heaney and John Ashbery, and Heaney would become very close to him. Lowell died in 1977, and during his funeral Brodsky met Derek Walcott, his future close friend. Even in death, Lowell played a role of a go-between for poets.

And so, two weeks after arriving in the West, Joseph Brodsky found himself in the very center of the establishment of poets. "Greatness, you may say, like poverty, looks after its own," Brodsky later wrote.[4] In 1972 in London, a poet could have no better recommenders than Auden and Spender. The newcomer Brodsky was greeted as he deserved—solemnly and with respect. He did not have to prove anything; his exile had not taken away his dignity, his status of poet. In a letter to him W. H. Auden put the word *emigration* into quotation marks. "Hope you are finding 'emigration' not too awful," he wrote on August 3, 1972. Auden himself was for a part of his life an exile by choice. Brodsky did not forget this beginning of his emigration and was not shy in expressing his gratitude. He wrote about it several times, most directly in his essay on Auden, "To Please a Shadow," and, fifteen years later, in a text commemorating Stephen Spender. Among Brodsky's prose texts both of these essays belong to the genre of elegies with a strong autobiographical bent; he described Auden and Spender through the lens of his own life. Spender hosted him thanks to Auden, but the initial impulse for this hospitality came from Akhmatova, who during her 1965 stay in England had talked about Iosif to Natasha and Stephen Spender. When she was going back to Russia, they gave her two gifts for Brodsky: a record of *Dido and Aeneas,* by Purcell, and a scarf. He was then in exile in Norenskaya, where, as Natasha Spender later explained, they were afraid he was suffering from cold.

If I am not mistaken, "In Memory of Stephen Spender" was the last essay written by the Russian poet before his death. It is, as the title indicates, an elegy for Spender, full of telling details about the poet, his wife, his family, Auden, and meetings and contacts Brodsky had with them. Brodsky's talent as a prose writer and portraitist here comes to the fore. Since Auden and Spender were, as was also Carl Proffer, the first people to truly take care of Brodsky in exile, he shows an almost filial respect for them. Also, Spender was only six years younger than Brodsky's father. But one can read from "In Memory of Stephen Spender" still another kind of "filiation" between host and guest. Brought up with a romantic idea of the link between friendship and poetry, already in Russia Brodsky had idealized Auden's and Spender's Oxford past, their poetic friendship. Reading them in Russia, he wrote, "made me feel at home at once. . . . It was their poetics. It unshackled me; above all, metrically and stanzaically. . . . I found terribly attractive their common knack for taking a bewildered look at the familiar. Call this influence. I'll call it affinity. Roughly from the age of twenty-eight on, I regarded them as my relatives rather than as masters or 'imaginary friends.' They were my mental family— far more so than anybody among my own contemporaries, inside or outside of Russia" (*OGR*, 468–69). Their later meeting of minds, therefore, was not accidental. Toward the end of the essay, Brodsky associates Spender more and more with his father. He thinks about his parents, about Auden: they are his family. He says good-byes to Spender lying in the open coffin and he looks on as the poet's son screws the bolts into the coffin lid. "He fights tears," Brodsky writes, "but they are winning. One can't help him; nor do I think one should. This is a son's job" (*OGR*, 482).

There is little here about Spender's poems; the feeling of gratitude is directed more to the person than to the work. It is a gratitude of the newcomer toward a person who showed him hospitality. I have found a similar feeling of gratitude in another text, also an elegy for a dead friend, written by the Italian writer Nicola Chiaromonte—I have in mind his essay "Albert Camus." Chiaromonte is linked with Miłosz, whose *Captive Mind* he recommended to *Partisan Review* readers in 1953; Miłosz mentions Chiaromonte in one of his poems— his name appears among those who are unjustly forgotten. In his essay about Camus, Chiaromonte describes the way in which the French-Algerian writer and his wife, Francine, showed him hospitality in Oran, during World War II. Chiaromonte was then a "multiple" exile, an escapee first from fascist Italy, then from Franco's Spain and Nazi-occupied France. He was "alone and homeless," and therefore capable of feeling "the value of hospitality." Here again, as in the case of Miłosz, we encounter Camus as the person who understands estrangement and extends his hand to help a newcomer. After a few weeks' stay, trying to get to the United States, Chiaromonte parted from Camus and his wife. He knew "that we had exchanged the gift of friendship. At the core of this friendship was something very precious, something unspoken and impersonal that made itself felt in the way they received me and our way of being together. We had recognized in each other the mark of fate—which was, I believe, the ancient meaning of the encounter between stranger and host."[5] This Greek model of friendship, of hospitality as a reciprocal gift giving and being joined by a common cause, renders very well the content and mood of the essay on Spender. Brodsky was touchy and proud, in a totally new situation, a step away from humiliation, without the possibility of using his only "organ" that was special: his language. It was a great privilege and also a stroke of luck to be taken in on terms of equality. This is what he remembered and recorded in his elegy of Spender.

In the second part of his life—the time of his exile—the main criterion in his choice of friends seems to have been art and, especially, poetry. His friendships were often linked to work; they were expressed by his working with somebody or receiving help with his work. His main literary friends were poets Mark Strand, Seamus Heaney, and Derek Walcott. In print he used the term *friend* more rarely than Miłosz did. Perhaps the Soviet propaganda about "Pushkin's friends" undermined the value of that word and Brodsky had to reclaim it, just as he did with the word *nation*. He did not feel cowed by such barriers; he reused, privatized, and renewed large parts of seemingly exhausted vocabulary. He liked to quote Akhmatova's saying: I don't use great words such as *poet* or *billiards*. He applied a diminutive to describe his poems—*stishki*—translated by his friend Lev Loseff as "versicles." He shunned pathos and pomposity. It is possible that he would apply the word *friend* more often had he lived longer and less tensely. It was the lack of haste that allowed Miłosz to recollect and savor his friendships.

Even before coming to the United States Brodsky was open to his future friends. He encountered the poems of Mark Strand before his emigration. Strand remembered the first American reading by Brodsky—in New York's 92nd Street Y, in 1973. The large hall was full, and among the public was the young poet Rosanna Warren, later to become one of the friends of the newly arrived Russian. I remember that evening very well—it was the first poetry reading I went to after my own arrival in America. After the reading, people stood in a long line to talk to Brodsky, and when Mark Strand introduced himself, Brodsky recited from memory one of Strand's poems. This was a great beginning of a great friendship. Since they lived in distant cities, they spoke on the phone usually once a week.[6] Although they were very different as poets, they promoted each other's work, and read poetry together at universities or bookstores. In 1987, while introducing Strand's lecture at the Academy of American Poets, Brodsky caught the essence of his friend's poetry. "Mark Strand," he said, "is essentially a poet of infinities, not of affinities, of things' cores and essence, not so much of their applications. Nobody can evoke absences, silences, emptiness better than this poet."[7] Brodsky's archive is full of funny postcards and letters written to him by Strand, always proposing new plans on how to make money, with new poems attached. These letters and postcards show a striking contrast between a magnificent self-sufficiency of Strand's poems, and a continuous worry about tomorrow's paycheck, which is so present in the "prose" part of these missives. Friendship often has a utilitarian side, a kindly helpfulness, taking care of another's needs. Friendly associations, according to Aristotle, have a social dimension; friends unite to meet life's requirements. Money is clearly one of them.

As stated earlier, Brodsky met Derek Walcott during the memorial service for Robert Lowell. Their friendship truly started to blossom in the late 1970s. In Brodsky's archive one can find a typed copy of a poem, "Dedication," signed "Derek," and, below, "Mitt luff, One way to pay for the apartment." Survival, rent, payment rates were always Strand's, Brodsky's, and Walcott's pressing concerns. But the poem is about something else. Walcott wishes "Joseph" "more strength and grace to the work" and later: "I wish you the blessing of Ovid / on your Roman elegies." It is a concrete work that Walcott has in mind, and his poem is intended to support his friend in his difficult undertaking. The poem itself is an act of friendship, declared, as the poem ends, with the words:

> . . . *You whom*
> *I have grown to love as a brother,*
> *And of whom I boast: My friend.*[8]

The boasting comes, not only from the pleasures of this concrete affiliation, but also because it is the cult of friendship that unites the two poets.[9] And several other common beliefs. They treated the poetic vocation with the same seriousness; they professed similar respect for tradition and classics, and for literary joke, pastiche, and imitation. Walcott is an excellent painter, Brodsky a passionate photographer and author of many interesting drawings, including self-portraits similar to Pushkin's "doodles." Both Walcott and Brodsky needed many adjectives if they were to be precisely described, as their national and cultural affiliations were too complex to be captured in one word. Brodsky presented himself as a Russian poet, English-language essayist, and an ethnic Jew. Walcott, who comes from the West Indies, has mixed African-European roots; he was a Methodist growing up among Catholics, living on St. Lucia but earning his bread in the United States. His poetry is located on the borders of several languages: educated in the British colonial tradition, in his poems and plays (he is also a playwright) he uses English, as well as British and French Creole. French was his first language. This national marginality linked to the belief in the centrality of the poetic vocation was the basis of the friendship of these two poets, or, in any case, a similarity with which their friendship was cemented. Both of them—by birth and by choice—were interested in the borderlands of empires.

Walcott understood very well Brodsky's ambition to write in English, his efforts to domesticate that language, to settle in it. About himself he said that English was not his choice: "I am in an English situation."[10] In an early poem devoted to Brodsky and the similarities between them, Walcott wrote that "Joseph"—the "you" of the poem—is "a man living with English in one room," and that the other emigrants from the borders of Neva are "citizens of a language that is now yours." This poem, "The Forest of Europe," shows the two poets somewhere in Oklahoma, in a snow-covered house, united by the same fever for poetry as the one that tormented Mandelstam imagined in another "barren" space, that of the Gulag, "space / so desolate it mocked destinations." "The Forest of Europe" was dedicated to Brodsky and printed in the August 7, 1978, issue of the *New Yorker*; it shows a great sense of commonality Walcott felt with Brodsky right from the beginning of their acquaintance—a commonality as poets and radically displaced people. The fate of Osip Mandelstam symbolized for them, and also for their friend Seamus Heaney, the supremacy of poetry; Walcott writes in this poem that it is "the bread that lasts when systems have decayed." A very "Brodskyean" line.

Their love of poetry found one of its expressions in a joyous attitude toward language. In 1990, Brodsky wrote a long (unpublished) poem for Walcott's birthday, using his own, Russian-accented rhymes. The poem opens:

> *What is it, Walcott, that one hears*
> *You've been around for sixty years?*
> *Is that a rumor,*
> *A naked truth, a pension bluff?*
> *Am I again a victim of*
> *Your English grammar?*

A year later, in May 1991, he wrote an introduction to the Swedish edition of Walcott's poems, opening it by stating that the publication of that volume was like the arrival of Golfstrom to Sweden.[11] It would be another year before Walcott received the Nobel Prize in literature.

Seamus Heaney, also a Nobel laureate, was a close friend of both Brodsky and Walcott's. "I have two very dear friends," Walcott said in that period, "Seamus Heaney and Joseph Brodsky. I love them because they are poets naturally, first of all, but I love them because they are friends. There is no competition there."[12] And during a different interview he specified: "I just feel very lucky to have friends like Joseph and Seamus. The three of us are outside of the American experience. Seamus is Irish, Joseph is Russian, I'm West Indian. We don't get embroiled in the controversies about who's a soft poet, who's a hard poet, who's a free verse poet, who's not a poet, and all of that. It's good to be on the rim of that quarreling. We're on the perimeter of the American literary scene. We can float out here happily not really committed to any kind of particular school or body of enthusiasm or criticism."[13] Heaney, just like Walcott, grew up on the linguistic border: his domestic language, he said in his Nobel lecture, clashed everyday with BBC English. The three of them shared poetic models: Mandelstam, Akhmatova, and, of course, Auden. Also, Brodsky had published a book of essays by each of them about Robert Frost (*Homage to Robert Frost*). From among all English-language poets, Heaney came closest to the East-Central European poets with his belief that poetry needs to "witness."[14] Their friendship was very intimate, as attested by a moving letter written by Heaney from Harvard on June 20, 1983, to "Joseph," as he reacted to the news of the death of Brodsky's mother. "A pang of unexpected shock occurred," he wrote. "I had never taken into account that your parents were still behind you all that time. Stupidly I had assumed that your spiritual state—Yeats's 'finished man among his enemies' stage?—of solitude and beyond-ness was some sort of absolute condition."[15]

The friendship of the three of them comes from the before-Nobel times. They made their living in New England, in the universities around Boston. Walcott was teaching at Boston University, Heaney at Harvard, Brodsky at Mount Holyoke. They were not far from each other, and their evenings at "Derek's apartment in Brookline," Seamus Heaney wrote to Hilton Als, "turned into a kind of time machine. It was like being back in your first clique as a young poet with all your original greed for the goods and the gossip of poetry instantly refreshed. Poems being quoted and poets being praised or faulted, extravagantly; anecdotes exchanged; jokes told; but underneath all the banter and hilarity there was a prospector's appetite in each of us for the next poem we ourselves might write. We were high on each other's company and that kept the critical standard-setter alive and well in each of us."[16] Miłosz was right: poets recognize each other like ants with their feelers.

This unusual alliance did not pass unnoticed. "I am writing this just weeks after the death of Joseph Brodsky," wrote a younger New England writer, Askold Melnyczuk, "who together with Heaney and Walcott, formed the triumvirate of 'exiled' poets who presided over the relatively tame literary communities of New England for more than a decade—by the strength of their art and the, to most of us, enviable strangeness of their experience. Each of them had seen things not vouchsafed us in American suburbs, and they offered access to dimensions of consciousness we'd otherwise not known about. They were explorers more than exiles. The three occasionally appeared together publicly—something we took as our due for living in the Athens of the east. At some level, I'd bet we even begrudged these men their fame, their glamour, their art. Provincialism is the great enemy of promise, as well as of achievement."[17] They each came from a different place, but were united by the similarity of their existential and poetic situation. The American poetic establishment accepted them as its own, perhaps because of the imperial expansiveness of the English language appropriating everything in its way. They came from the margins, but they represented the centrality of the English language's high culture. Or its dominance.

Miłosz lived in California, but he belongs with these three poets. He was older and was the first to be honored by the Nobel. This award is decided upon in Sweden, but its reach is truly global. It has existed for more than a hundred years, and so far has been awarded most often to French authors. Since the 1990s, however, English-language writers have been quickly closing the gap. Heaney is counted as an Irish Nobel, but Brodsky and Miłosz's awards belong to the United States. Walcott's award, if I am not mistaken, is attributed to Great Britain. The four poets have a lot in common. Miłosz (Nobel, 1980), Brodsky (1987), Walcott (1992), and Heaney (1997) share an emphatic respect for poetry and for the role of the poet in society. Also, they come from the borderlands of empires. The poetry written by Heaney and Walcott is a continuation, critique, and transformation of the tradition of the British empire. The poetry of Miłosz became known thanks to translations into English; and the duality of Brodsky, the last one in this quartet, consisted in his charging into

English, the language of the empire to which he moved. Perhaps English was the necessary though not sufficient reason to translate the "marginality" of these four poets into a universal human condition. The common speech allows for the sharing of our particularities; the English language, today's lingua franca, makes them general.

Miłosz often said that had he remained in France there would have been no Nobel for him. France, he said, was a country "forsaken by the spirit of poetry." He understood the role the English language played in the internationalizing of his poetry. To my question whether other poets helped in his receiving the Nobel Prize he replied: "The fact that my poetry was by then accessible in English was of primary importance. Moreover, in 1978 I received the 'little' Nobel, that is the Neustadt Prize. This is the most secure way. And it was a prize awarded by poets. I don't remember who was there, but I remember Brodsky, perhaps Herbert. So yes, I was helped by poets."[18]

In fact, it is easy to check that Miłosz was proposed for the Neustadt Prize three times, in 1972 by Kenneth Rexroth, in 1976 by Zbigniew Herbert, and finally, and successfully, in 1978 by Joseph Brodsky himself. Brodsky's "Presentation and Encomium" to the jury of the award, later printed in *World Literature Today*, consists of four long, dense paragraphs. Written only six years after his arrival in the United States, the text witnesses to an incredibly quick acclimatization of the immigrant poet. I don't have in mind his language, as the encomium was written in Russian and translated into English, but his place and influence within the poetic establishment, if such a term can be used. The first sentences of his encomium were often quoted: "I have no hesitation whatsoever in stating that Czesław Miłosz is one of the greatest poets of our time, perhaps the greatest. Even if one strips his poems of the stylistic magnificence of his native Polish (which is what translation inevitably does) and reduces them to the naked subject matter, we still find ourselves confronting a severe and relentless mind of such intensity that the only parallel one is able to think of is that of the biblical characters—most likely Job. But the scope of the loss experienced by Miłosz was—not only from purely geographical considerations—somewhat larger."[19]

Two years later, when Miłosz received his Nobel Prize, Brodsky was asked to write about him for *The New York Times.* The editors must have worried about *both* poets' "recognizability," since they added what was for that paper an unusual explanation: "The writer of the following article, an exiled Russian poet, teaches at Columbia and New York Universities and is an authority on Eastern European literature." Brodsky's encomium contains several sentences lifted from his "Presentation to the Jury." I am not sure if it was Brodsky himself or the editors who lowered the tone of the text, having in mind, most probably, the newspaper's mass reader; and the comparison to Job—puzzling as it was in the original—was abandoned as well. Yet Miłosz is still called "perhaps the greatest poet of our time."[20] Two years later, in an interview with Sven Birkerts, Brodsky's tenor is a bit different. He was impressed by Miłosz's Nobel: "I think he is the only Nobel Prize winner I know personally. I met once Heinrich Böll, whom I like as a prose writer. But that was it. . . . I like Miłosz a great deal and I was championing his case here for quite some time while—from the very moment I came. Because I think he's an especially good poet, and a very wise man." To a question about whether he can include Miłosz in the constellation of his masters, Brodsky replies in the affirmative, but he adds: "As for Miłosz, I don't really read him so frequently. Basically it's not so important—you get the main vector of the man and that's enough." This fragment was cut out from the edited interview.[21]

Miłosz too was "championing" Brodsky's case, proposing him, for example, to the Nobel Prize committee. In the Beinecke archive there is a draft of a Miłosz letter directed to "Mr. Freund" [?], starting with, "I feel honored by your asking my assistance in selecting a candidate." Miłosz recommends Brodsky, though I am not sure it is for the Nobel Prize. "I have been following his progress for several years, beginning with the time he still lived in Russia," Miłosz writes. "He has always been dedicated to one thing: writing good poetry in his native tongue. Such a persistence pays: his poetry has been developing both in depth and scope."[22] After the Nobel was awarded to Brodsky, Miłosz sent him a telegram: "Now the Polish-Russian relations have been restored to normal."[23] It is a curious way of congratulating someone on his award, especially since, as I have already written, they received them as American citizens. He also presented the Russian—or rather Russian-American—poet for other awards, and invited him to Poland, after the collapse of communism, of course.

Brodsky came to Poland for the first time in 1990—too late, and not from the eastern side, he said, remembering his unsuccessful effort to cross "the red line" of the Polish-Soviet border in the 1960s. During his stay in Warsaw and Kraków, he met with his readers and, according to Miłosz, hypnotized them with his melo-recitations. I have seen the videotape of one such meeting in Kraków, and, perhaps because of the presence of Miłosz, Brodsky's delivery of his poems seems very restrained. Miłosz also recommended Brodsky for an honorary doctorate at the University of Katowice, and the 1993 ceremony awarding that doctorate was the reason for the second and last of Brodsky's visits to Poland. On both occasions, when the Russian poet first landed in Warsaw, he was surprised to find that city very ugly. His reaction was due not only to the real shortcomings of this totally rebuilt city, and its contrast with the beauty of St. Petersburg, but, most probably, also to the romantic vision of a heroic city that Brodsky absorbed in his youth. In an interview he shocked the Varsovians by saying that the look of the city was not worthy of the victims who, during World War II, fell in its defense.[24] On his second trip, in 1993, he visited two of his very sick poet-friends, Wiktor Woroszylski and Zbigniew Herbert. Death was closing in on all three of them, visitor and visited alike.

The visit with Woroszylski, his wife, and daughter was a source of great pleasure for him. But seeing the sick Herbert was both delightful and painful. He considered "Zbyszek," as he called him using the Polish diminutive of Zbigniew, one of the best contemporary poets, and he had proved his high opinion by his usual means: prefaces, translations. He wrote an introduction to a selection of Herbert's poems published later in Italian and in English; he regularly taught at least three of Herbert's poems in his poetry classes. One of the poems was the "Elegy of Fortinbras" (a poem dedicated to C.M., that is Czesław Miłosz, and translated into English by Miłosz and Peter Dale Scott); the second was "Rain" and the third, "Achilles. Penthesilea." The poem "Rain" Brodsky translated into Russian, and the last poem, "Achilles. Penthesilea" into English. In a letter to Zofia Rata-jczakowa, written in the summer of 1993, after his return from Poland, Brodsky mentioned translating that poem and described in detail his visit to Herbert, who was bedridden with severe asthma. This visit is of great interest for us, as it bears directly on the fellowship of poets. Brodsky went to see Herbert because he loved him; once there, he intervened in the dramatic conflict that was raging at that time between Herbert and Miłosz. Herbert wrote a poem called "Chodasiewicz," which was a frontal attack on Miłosz. The poem was printed in a periodical and reprinted in the volume of Herbert's poems "Rovigo"—Herbert must have given that volume to Brodsky during the visit.

"I have spent three hours with Herbert," Brodsky writes in the middle of the second page of this long, Russian-language letter to Zofia Kapuścińska Ratajczakowa.

Zbyszek—absolute charm and he looks like a child. From that—the feeling of tragedy is even stronger. He understands all of it, but nothing can be done anymore, and this he also understands. To talk with him is, for me, easier than with anyone in the world, and this considering that we are conversing in English. He was in good form, he said that unexpectedly he has a lot of money. . . . I think that he is tormented by all this story with "Chodasiewicz." Miłosz too. "What am I to do now," asked Zbyszek. "Write another poem," I said, but, after turning back to the hotel, I open *Rovigo* and see that he has already done it, and the impression from the proximity of this little poem with "Chodasiewicz" is terribly nauseating. . . . All the rest of my time in Warsaw I have spent in the hotel, translating (into English) one poem of Zbigniew from *Rovigo* ("Achilles. Penthesilea,") where, indirectly, the matter is, I think, about his—Z.H.'s—feeling of guilt towards—whom, I have no idea, and "End and the Beginning" of Szymborska. "Achilles" is already taken by *The New York Review of Books.*[25]

Brodsky's visit to Katowice brought a whole series of publications and public discussions, including a session on his work. It was Czesław Miłosz who opened this session, with a paper "Thinking about Brodsky—Some Remarks." The paper addresses the topics that Miłosz considered most important for understanding of the life, work, and attitude of Brodsky, points he repeated on many occasions when he spoke about the Russian poet. Before I summarize some of the thoughts expressed in that paper, I would like to start with another quotation that shows Miłosz's extreme perspicacity in his approach to Brodsky's poetry. In a text called "On Joseph Brodsky," Miłosz declares that Brodsky's "tone, always recognizable, is solemn yet at the same time mocking, with continuous jumps from elegy and ode to satire, with a steady quasi-presence of a compassionate irony." In the paper he states that Brodsky was a man of culture, and of hierarchy, who worked within and managed "the estate of Russian poetry," building bridges back to the times of Akhmatova, Mandelstam, and Tsvetaeva. He spoke of a different role of poetry in Poland and Russia: "Each poetry develops in time, and entire generations participate in it; the estate of each of them differs most of all according to the laws of the language in which it is written." He points to the difference between the iambic Russian verse and free Polish verse. "Nowhere," he writes, is "the status of a poet . . . as high as in Russia and the calamities that fall there on the poet are a price paid by them for the recognition of their importance—by tsars and by tyrants. Death in a duel difficult to tell apart from a murder, death in a gulag, exile. In England and America there is no such custom, and the status of a poet in relation to Russia is low, because"—and here Miłosz quotes from a nineteenth-century Polish comedy—"who would hunger after your miserable life, sir."[26]

In his many asides, as we have seen in the above quotation, Miłosz compares Brodsky's poetic situation to Pushkin's—after all, for many years Miłosz was a professor of Russian literature. He notes that Brodsky, like Pushkin, is grounded in European culture, and that makes it possible for both of them to create masterpieces. While Pushkin built on the French culture that in his era was the common ground of educated European elites, Brodsky attached Russian poetry to the Anglo-American poetic tradition. But what Miłosz praises most in Brodsky is his "classicism"—the continuation of the Latin side of Russian tradition, his reliance on Christianity, on antiquity, even though Ovid and Horace come to him only in Russian translations. "Brodsky does not question the foundations of the Christian civilization, which are the Bible and Dante, as well as the history of poetry and art of antiquity. The motifs from the Old Testament ("Isaac and Abraham"), from the Gospels ("Nunc Dimittis"), and from Homer ("Odysseus to Telemachus") are testimony to this loyalty. Ancient Rome is for him the source of many metaphors; he talks about the empire as a certain situation of human societies. . . . The classicism of Brodsky can also be interpreted in another way: growing up in Petersburg, he became a poet of cities and their architecture. It is architecture that is the real heroine of many of his descriptive poems and essays."[27]

Miłosz was reading this essay in Katowice in the presence of Brodsky, and this created an occasion for many jokes and much laughter. Playfulness was an important part of their friendship, although here too they differed: a great companion of Miłosz's life was his deep laughter, and in Brodsky's case it was irony. "After each conclusion," Jerzy Illg noted in his report on the occasion, "Miłosz would turn to his friend for acceptance. *'Pravilno?'* 'Right?' 'Is it right?' And Brodsky would nod good-naturedly, and at the end, with a comical fatherly and at the same time son-like devotion he kissed Miłosz's forehead."[28] It was an almost carnivalesque reversal of their usual relation respectful of the age difference between them. From a son, a younger brother, Brodsky transformed himself into a father, as if he wanted to say: I am not taking all of this too seriously, it is only a game. When on the same occasion Miłosz, then eighty-two years old, said about the fifty-three year old Brodsky, "I am looking at the poets of Brodsky's age as very young people," Brodsky replied in Russian: "Are you looking the same way at Jesus Christ?" (39).

I hope it is now clear why I have described in such detail several literary friendships of both Miłosz and Brodsky. They were mostly about work. The management of the estate of poetry included an alliance (as well as a rivalry) between poets. Their thirst for awards may be greater than that of other artisans of words, since they are always unsure of the durability of their work. They have, like most people, to earn their living—something they can rarely do by writing poetry alone. They work for publications and editorial houses, they translate, review books, and teach. Often they recite their poems at poetry festivals or public readings, where they try to sell their books. They know each other, not only as readers of poetry, but also, if one can say so, as the members of a guild, colleagues in the same métier, in the same "cantine." Miłosz and Brodsky understood perfectly these needs and constraints; they, too, lived by them. By promoting each other they were helping poetry.

In August 1980, just before receiving his Nobel Prize, Miłosz published in *The New York Review of Books* a long article on a volume of Brodsky's poems, *A Part of Speech.* Entitled "A Struggle against Suffocation" (these words were taken from a Brodsky's poem), the long and thorough essay presented to the American public the as yet little-known poet. "The strong presence of Joseph Brodsky"—starts Miłosz—"has needed less than a decade to establish itself in world poetry."[29] For the essay, Miłosz read Brodsky's poetry in English and Russian, compared various versions, judged translations. He did not forget to mention their friendship, and their third poet-friend, Tomas Venclova. Brodsky's poem dedicated to Venclova creates, according to Miłosz, a space which "becomes an empyrean realm where three poets of different nationalities and backgrounds can celebrate their meeting in the teeth of reality which in that region is especially ominous and oppressive." The topic of empire is approached in this review as well, as is Brodsky's affinity with the work of Lev Shestov. Miłosz had known Brodsky for eight years and understood his work very well indeed. Even before writing that review, Miłosz included some of Brodsky's poems in the syllabus of his course on contemporary European poetry.[30] After Mandelstam, Brodsky was represented by the highest number of poems: six. All the poems that Miłosz discusses in his review are represented on this list. They served to show off the qualities Miłosz valued the most in Brodsky's poetry: the respect for tradition and religion, spirituality, the effort to deal with the passing of time and with death.[31]

In his teaching at Mount Holyoke College, Brodsky analyzed the already mentioned poems of Herbert, but also the works of Miłosz and Szymborska. These three Polish poets can also be found on a list, prepared by Brodsky and famous among students, who called it "Uncle Joe's great books list." There were more than one hundred titles on it, starting with the Bhagavad Gita and ending with Miłosz. The list is, it seems to me, a strikingly autodidactic tool of learning. The poems of Herbert and Szymborska that Brodsky's students analyzed were copied from the anthology of postwar Polish poetry edited by Miłosz himself. Before reading Herbert and Miłosz, Brodsky always delivered a long speech about Polish history, because Poland was, in his mind, a country severely burdened by history. A student of his from 1995, Liam McCarthy, wrote to me in an e-mail that Brodsky "proceeded to draw stick figure houses on the board, citing events during the course of the century [wars and insurrections] that effectively destroyed the houses, only for them to be rebuilt and destroyed again. He would cite dates and then scribble over the house (a triangular roof atop a square box), only to draw the same figure over again."[32] This superabundance of history caused Brodsky to excuse contemporary Polish poets for writing without rhyming. Rigid poem structure reminded Polish poets of the social order introduced in their country by twentieth-century totalitarianisms, he wrote in the introduction to the issue of *The Wilson Quarterly* devoted to the poetry of Herbert. This commentary applied also to the two poems of Miłosz: the "Elegy for N.N.," a line of which he took as a motto for his first volume of essays, and the fragment of the cycle "Voices of Poor People" named "Café." These two poems were not included by Miłosz in his anthology of postwar Polish poetry. Brodsky repeated to his students that they should learn Polish, because only in that language would they be able to read the best poetry of the world.

Polish poetry was but a small part of his self-imposed duties in the managing of the estate of poetry. The majority of his time and effort was devoted to Frost and Auden, Tsvetaeva, Cavafy, Rilke, and Walcott. He spent a lot of time with his students on deep, line-by-line analyses of chosen poems. Some of these analyses were later published, so we have a clear view of his way of teaching. Academic teaching was part of his breadwinning activity, but his activism on behalf of poetry was often totally disinterested. Sick and tormented by the need to hurry, he was more and more involved in various forms of promotion of poetry, poets, and literature in general. By the end of his life he was the literary director of the Players Forum in the International Theatre Institute in New York, helping to popularize the literature of eastern and southern Europe. He was also working on the creation of the Russian Academy in Rome, so that Russian poets and painters could stay there and work in peace. In 1991, he was the first non-U.S.-born poet to become the poet laureate of the United States.

In his inaugural lecture he proposed a battle for poetry, starting with the printing of millions of copies of essential American poems and their placement in every hotel room, side by side with the Bible; the Bible would not have anything against it, he used to say, since it is already flanked by the telephone book. His efforts were not fruitless, though they were not as successful as he wished them to be. It is thanks to him that in the public transit system of several American cities, where advertisement usually goes poems sometimes appear. The first poem that was posted in New York subways was Miłosz's 1936 "Encounter." I will never forget the moment when, on my way to work in a crowded number 6 train, I raised my eyes and encountered that poem. It was Brodsky who inspired American publishers to print and distribute free volumes of poetry; thanks to this I found myself once in a train compartment where every passenger was bent over a copy of Eliot's "The Waste Land." His deepening heart disease did not interrupt his poetry readings. In January 1996, he was to introduce a New York evening of poetry of Wisława Szymborska, but a snowstorm caused its cancellation. A few days later came his fatal heart attack, making that cancellation final.

Already in his youth Miłosz had "worked on the estate of Polish poetry," and translation was one of the ways to make it part of the estate of world poetry. His interest in translating English-language poetry into Polish started before World War II; he was one of those, he liked to repeat, who contributed to the ending of the French influence on Polish poets. He continued to translate after leaving Poland, first in his diplomatic posts and then in exile. In his "empty" periods, translating was for him what exercises must be for a pianist or rather for a composer. His translations were a kind of passion, an activity dictated by "friendship, because one could not earn any money out of it."[33] In the 1960s his translations of Yeats, Wallace Stevens, and Auden appeared in an anthology of English-language poetry published by a Polish émigré house in London. At the same time he was working on an anthology in English of contemporary Polish poetry. That anthology appeared in 1965, but even today—more than forty years later—it can be found in any good bookstore in the United States. In the opening words of that anthology Miłosz wrote: "Poets of each country resemble an eighteenth-century freemasonic lodge, with its rites, rivalries, and friendships. Being a member of such a lodge myself, I am glad to act as its representative abroad." He wrote these words in 1965, long before "joining" the American or international poetic lodge.[34]

If the act of translating had its basis in friendship, so was the method Miłosz used to accomplish it. Translating into English was a group effort, done with people whom Miłosz called his cotranslators. His first collaborator was Peter Dale Scott, with whom he published a volume of Zbigniew Herbert's poems; then Miłosz worked with his students Lillian Vallee and Richard Lourie; then with two poets, Robert Pinsky and Robert Hass, supported by Renata Gorczyńska, herself a writer and translator. The poet Leonard Nathan cotranslated with Miłosz the poetry of Aleksander Wat and Anna Swir; and Robert Hass remained with him until the end and has continued to translate Miłosz's poems after his death. Miłosz knew how great and important were the fruits of that collaboration. In 1998 he said: "I witnessed the change in the place of poetry on the

American continent, and I was able to see it from very close, because my much-missed friend Joseph Brodsky, as well as Robert Hass and Robert Pinsky, became famous for their energetic promotion of poetry for everybody."[35] In an obituary in *Gazeta Wyborcza,* Anna Bikont called Czesław Miłosz "a relentless PR-man of Polish poetry."[36] A Miłosz scholar, Aleksander Fiut, wrote: "It is uniquely thanks to the efforts of Miłosz that the phenomenon of 'the Polish poetic school' appeared on the American literary map."[37] The same opinion was expressed many times by poets such as Pinsky and Hass. And Adam Zagajewski commented: "Americans find in Polish poetry philosophy that is, as they say themselves, intellectual but not hermetic. This intellectuality is not an escape from life, not even from the everyday. They think that Polish poets found a magic formula of reconciling intellectuality with accessibility. This does not exist in American poetry. There you either have Wallace Stevens, interested only in ideas, or the poets of experience."[38]

The joining of intelligence with the quotidian, of ecstasy with history, is one of the characteristics of the poetry of Miłosz. The anthology he prepared, as well as the changes in American poetry due to the very works of Miłosz, became the reason for two extremely important poetic events. The first was the International Czesław Miłosz Festival at Claremont McKenna College, which took place over four days in April 1998. The second was an evening of poetry that took place in New York on March 13, 2002, under the title of Adam Zagajewski's poem "Try to Praise the Mutilated World." Both of these events belong at the same time to the history of poetry and to the history of friendship, these histories being linked to each other.

The festival was the shared idea of Robert Faggen, professor of literature at Claremont McKenna College, and Adam Michnik, who had gone there to give a series of lectures. It took them more than a year of preparation—the festival was truly international and vast. Miłosz called it "the feast of friendship, the importance of which for the collaboration of American and European poets I fully appreciate." Besides Miłosz, many poets came, and panels and discussions were scattered among numerous readings. The poet Edward Hirsch, a close friend of Adam Zagajewski, spoke about Miłosz as an American poet. Twentieth-century American poetry did not flow, according to Hirsch, only from its English sources; it is a river into which streamed the works of émigré poets. Hirsch continued: as the example of Miłosz shows, the émigré poets don't even have to write in English, it is enough that they are translated, absorbed by other poets with whom they resonate spiritually. Hirsch's words were indirectly confirmed by the presence and speeches of the translators of Miłosz— Robert Hass, Robert Pinsky, and Leonard Nathan, who are excellent poets themselves; their own works are sometimes a reply to the poems they translated together with Miłosz. They spoke at the festival about the centrality of Miłosz for contemporary American poetry, which has been in search of a historical dimension. The openness of the poetry of Miłosz encountered the openness and receptivity of American culture.

Throughout the years of living, that is working—because life for him went along with constant work—Miłosz not only became an integral part of American poetry but he also shaped it. He was absorbed into its circulatory system (in contrast to Brodsky, who was too separate, too inassimilable). During the Claremont festival, many poets—including the Irish poet Seamus Heaney; the Lithuanian Tomas Venclova; the Polish poets Adam Zagajewski and Bronisław Maj; Americans Edward Hirsch, W. S. Merwin, Linda Gregg, Jane Hirshfield, as well as Pinsky, Nathan, and Hass—emphasized Miłosz's influence on them or on the poetry of others. They read their poems and talked about Miłosz, but his poetic side was not the only topic of discussion. His students recalled Professor Miłosz, prose writer Miłosz, the author of essays, autobiographical fragments, novels, and papers. Helen Vendler discussed the Catholicism of the cycle of poems entitled "The World." Andrzej Walicki, Adam Michnik, Edith Kurzweil, and I quarreled about *The Captive Mind.* Slavicists Madeline Levine, Bogdana Carpenter, Jan Błoński, and Aleksander Fiut spoke about his poems and prose in the context of Polish literary tradition. Many other people came from overseas: his publishers, friends, family, disciples. The editor of the Kraków publishing house Znak brought in an exhibit of the Polish underground editions of his works. A musical group from Kraków played Irish music. A festive mood prevailed throughout. Everybody declared that they had never before participated in anything similar. And the person about and for whom this festival was organized was there among us, listening and, from time to time, laughing with relish. Miłosz was seated with earphones on his head, because his hearing was weak; wearing eyeglasses, because he could not see very well; and leaning on a cane, because it was difficult for him to walk. And yet the good energy expressed in his laughter brought smiles to the faces of a couple of hundred people who had come there to listen to his poetry and pay him homage. A big part of his talent consisted of his ability to convey an unusual characteristic—how to be happy.

The Claremont festival was a manifestation of the gratitude for the gift of Polish poetry. The fraternity of American poets expressed their thanks for access to another way of making poetry. The second of the events that I mentioned, the reading in New York, was proof that that gift had been accepted by a community beyond the poets themselves. Polish poetry served as a reply to the events of September 11, 2001. *The New Yorker,* in the issue published right after the attack, printed the poem of Adam Zagajewski "Try to Praise the Mutilated World." Half a year later, on March 13, 2002, Alice Quinn, then the poetry editor of that magazine, organized an evening named after the Zagajewski poem. In the auditorium of New York's Cooper Union twelve hundred people (the event was sold out and many could not get in) listened to poems of Miłosz, Herbert, Szymborska, Tadeusz Różewicz, Stanisław Barańczak, and Zagajewski. The poems were chosen, recited, and commented on by Edward Hirsch (who gave a stirring rendition of Różewicz's "In the Middle of Life"), Robert Pinsky, and W. S. Merwin. Other poems were read by, among others, Susan Sontag, Rosanna Warren, and Lawrence Weschler, Polish actress Elżbieta Czyżewska, translator of Zagajewski and Barańczak Clare Cavanagh, and Renata Gorczyńska. Among those whose poems were read, Adam Zagajewski was the only author present; he was a bit shy, surrounded by large photographs of his masters. Polish poetry provided a language capable of expressing the feelings of "mutilated" America. "Falls of Towers and the Rise of Polish Poetry"—Sarah Boxer wrote about the evening in *The New York Times* (March 16, 2002). There was no need to explain the poems read and recited. They expressed the feeling and mood of the city that was coming to terms with the disaster.

FOUR

Women, Women Writers, and Muses

Working on the estate of poetry, Brodsky and Miłosz often performed together on panels or at readings. Otherwise they met but rarely. Although very cordial, their relationship was not intimate. In personal matters they were both rather restrained; their attitude toward family life and women seemed quite different. This difference was expressed "obliquely" during a panel discussion in New York, on September 22, 1981. The mood of the occasion was festive. Miłosz laughed and joked, happy to have received the Nobel Prize in literature just a year earlier, seemingly liberated from some heavy burdens and doubts. It was a period of great creativity, perhaps also of a new romantic union. The Solidarity movement was still flourishing in Poland and the hopes linked to it were riding high. Well along in the conversation Brodsky asked Miłosz, laughing: "How would you define beauty?"

"When you see a girl do you ask yourself what is beauty?" Miłosz replied, also with laughter.

"No, the definition of beauty, my definition is—well—it's something that you don't possess," Brodsky said.

Miłosz: "Sometimes beauty may be felt in something you do possess."

Brodsky: "That's a Polish attitude, I think [laughter]."[1]

In this last sentence, the Russian poet caught the essence of the difference separating him from Miłosz, the difference in their relation to beauty, love, and women, and I am speaking here of literary tropes and traditions. The Polish poet had, if one may say so, a Catholic vision of woman: for him she was Eve—a temptation but also fulfillment. For Brodsky, as for Pushkin, the woman is an unfaithful lover about whom one can write only in the past tense. Miłosz describes her sinful, fragile, but marvelous body. Brodsky, "having embraced these shoulders," is searching the room for a ghost that used to live there.[2] It is time that takes women away from Miłosz. Brodsky is the Abandoned One.

Many of Miłosz's poems and prose fragments are devoted to women. Some of these texts praise life, some are elegies. In the biographical entry "Lena," in *Another Alphabet,* Miłosz describes his first erotic fascination—when he was six years old. This reminiscence, written down over eighty years later, is immersed in history. "Always the same: a woman and destructive time. Desired probably because she is so fragile and mortal."[3] This short fragment contains the main motif of his poetic vision of women: his rival is the transitoriness of human life. In two elegies he records the deaths of his wives—Janina, who died in 1986, and Carol Thigpen, who died in 2002. These two poems pose his most important questions.

"I loved her, without knowing who she really was," he confesses in the poem "On Parting with My Wife, Janina." They lived together for fifty years, during the last ten of which he took care of her as she was incapacitated by a devastating illness. The poem opens with an image of the fire consuming her body, and the tone here is one of grief, guilt, sorrow.

> *I inflicted pain on her, chasing my illusion.*
> *I betrayed her with women, though faithful to her only.*
> *We lived through much happiness and unhappiness,*
> *Separations, miraculous rescues. And now, this ash.*

The fire that engulfs her is not only literal; it refers to the theological doctrine of apokatastasis, the theory of the general salvation of all beings and of their final return to their primordial condition. The road to that return leads through the cleansing, "wise" fire. But the carnal salvation is not certain and death seems incomprehensible: "How to resist nothingness?"—he asks. The world turns upside down:

> *An apple does not fall,*
> *A mountain moves from its place. Beyond the fire-curtain,*
> *A lamb stands in the meadow of indestructible forms.*
>
> . . .
>
> *Do I believe in the Resurrection of the Flesh? Not of this ash.*

The poem ends with an incantation, a prayer for return, for hope.

> *I call, I beseech: elements, dissolve yourselves!*
> *Rise into the other, let it come, kingdom!*
> *Beyond the earthly fire compose yourselves anew!*
> (NCP, *471–72*)

The poem "Orpheus and Eurydice" celebrates his second wife and is a lesser deviation from the orthodoxy of Catholicism than the theory of apokatastasis was. His wife's death is final and accepted. The poem sums up his thought about creativity and dying; Miłosz himself was old then, his own death only two years away. This poem adheres to Miłosz's precepts about realism, as did the previous elegy— both of them located, however sketchily, in the geographic details of his married life. California forms the background landscape of both of these poems. In "On Parting with My Wife, Janina" we walk for a moment along the sea, most probably in California, where Janina Miłosz died. "Standing on flagstones of the sidewalk at the entrance to Hades," Orpheus struggles with gusty wind, surrounded by the headlights of cars piercing through fog. He then walks through long, cold corridors: we seem to be in the entrance to the San Francisco hospital, where Miłosz went to say farewell to his dying wife. Both geographic moments seem to underline Miłosz's belief in mimesis; even before the descent to Nowhere, the poet is holding to the earth with its measurable, material detail. He is Orpheus, who "felt strongly his life with its guilt," the guilt of his smaller or larger infractions, and also of the insufficiencies of his memory, which if it were better could have contained the dead ones, therefore keeping them among the living. He is an instrument, governed by music, so when he finds himself in front of Persephone to ask for the return of Eurydice, he re-creates the main themes of his poems but only those which have praised life. He sings

> *the brightness of mornings and green rivers,*
>
> . . .
>
> *Of the delight of swimming in the sea under marble cliffs,*
> *Of feasting on a terrace above the tumult of a fishing port.*

He is proud most of all of "having composed his words always against death / And of having made no rhyme in praise of nothingness." Persephone agrees to return to him his wife, under condition that on the journey back he does not speak to her or turn his head to look at her. Unlike the original myth of Orpheus, the poet keeps his part of the bargain—it is, in this case, the sign of his fidelity. He does not turn to Eurydice, but is overwhelmed by doubt and this doubt seems to be a breach that makes Eurydice unattainable. This may be a Catholic interpretation of the myth.

> *Unable to weep, he wept at the loss*
> *Of the human hope for the resurrection of the dead,*
> *Because he was, now, like every other mortal.*
> *His lyre was silent, yet he dreamed, defenseless.*
> *He knew he must have faith and he could not have faith.*

At the end of the road, when he was coming to the sun, the path behind him turned out to be empty. "Only now everything cried in him: Eurydice! / How will I live without you, my consoling one!" But his despair quiets down, because "there was a fragrant scent of herbs, the low humming of bees, / and he fell asleep with his cheek on the sun-warmed earth" (*SS*, 99–102).

Almost twenty years separate "On Parting with My Wife" and "Orpheus and Eurydice," but the question asked in the first one is also, of course, the very essence of the second one. The reply, however, is different. Eurydice, when the poet looks at her before starting his return to earth, has a gray face and absent eyes. She is lost. The image of Janina is more corporeal, the burning of her body is palpable. Fire is the element of the first poem, cold and darkness are parts of the second. This is why coming out into the sunlight is so important: it is the return to the world of life. The sun, the warm earth, and sleep are the signs of consolation. Life is here, in *esse*, and, as long as it lasts, it has to be lauded with trust and gratitude.

In his "Treatise on Theology," his final word on religion, Miłosz, following the young Mickiewicz, declares that Eve has a double nature; she is "the delegate of Nature and drew Adam down into a monotonous wheel of births and deaths. / . . . Thence perhaps man's fear before the promise of love, which is no different from the promise of death." But she embodies also the spiritual dimension of life, because she "received and assented to an appeal to become the Mother of God" (*SS*, 56). These two aspects of Eve are intertwined, each passing into the other. In Miłosz's poems about women, especially those that speak of love, the theme of corporality, or attachment to "the sun-warmed earth," dominates. "The woman is forever linked to the earth," he said in a conversation with Renata Gorczyńska (*PŚ*, 22). In the poem "A Confession," written a year before the death of Janina, Miłosz writes: "My Lord, I loved straw-berry jam / And the dark sweetness of a woman's body" (*NCP,* 461). He had used similar words twenty years earlier, in the poem "Annalena":

> *I liked your velvet yoni, Annalena, long voyages in the delta of*
>   *your legs.*
> *A striving upstream toward your beating heart through more*
>   *and more*
> *Savage currents saturated with the light of hops and bindweed.*
>   (NCP, *414)*

Love, that "sweet dance," serves

> *so that for a short moment there is no death*
> *And time does not unreel like a skein of yarn*
> *Thrown into an abyss.* (NCP, *406)*

The woman with her corporality is a sign of death, but she also al-lows for the reconciliation of soul and body, as in the poem "Father Ch., Many Years Later":

> *O my accomplice in sin,*
> *Eve under the apple tree, in the delightful garden.*
> *I loved your breasts and your belly and your lips.*
> *How to comprehend your otherness and sameness?*
> *Convex and concave, how do they complement each other?*
>   (NCP, *437)*

The biblical Eve is the sum total of all the female forms:

Who is she, and who will she be, the beloved
From the Song of Songs? This Wisdom-Sophia,
Seducer, the Mother and Ecclesia?

. . .

. . . the mysterious one,
Whom Adam contemplates, not comprehending?
I am these two, twofold. I ate from the Tree
Of Knowledge. I was expelled by the archangel's sword.
At night I sensed her pulse. Her mortality.
And we have searched for the real place ever since.

 (NCP, *403–4*)

"Eve under the apple tree" contains in herself femininity and masculinity, wisdom, sin, and holiness, maternity and consolation. She is everything, and the narrator of Miłosz's poems finds himself in her. His striving for unity, for the joining of Adam and Eve, is part of Miłosz's greatness. "How perfect / All things are," he writes in the poem "After Paradise."

Now, for the two of you
Waking up in a royal bed by a garret window.
For a man and a woman. For one plant divided
Into masculine and feminine which longed for each other.

 (NCP, *407*)

Most of the poems quoted here, the ones in which Miłosz's celebration of the physical appeal of women is the most explicit, were written when he was in his sixties. It seems to have been for him a period of rediscovery of physical love. But the enchantment of these poems has an undertone; it is—just as in Villon's ballads—the sense of *les neiges d'antan*. It is the Christian Eve, the one dragging Adam into death. The fear of the fragility and decay of the body, the horror of death is transferred onto woman: she is the one who helps to escape that horror and, at the same time, she is this horror's living reminder. Miłosz moves within the Catholic tradition, and even after years of living in proximity to Californian versions of Eastern and other religions, he never comes out of that tradition.

I have mentioned already that Miłosz was breaking the rules, the barriers, that he was talking openly about topics that Polish literature treated in an oblique, veiled way: questions about what it meant to be Polish, about Jews, religion, and women. Polish literature, Miłosz often said, does not know how to talk about Jews, how to address God, how to write about love, the body, femininity. There are very few cases of female friendships described or created in Polish literature. Sławomir Mrożek, a great contemporary playwright, explained the lack of female characters in his plays by being "the inheritor and product of a culture and language which badly express themselves in this matter, and when they try, it sounds so false, so helpless, adolescent, that it is better to say nothing about it. And even the sentence—there are no women in my plays—sounds helpless. . . . No, it is not 'there are no women,' it is we who are not there, people are not there, reality is not there. A cursed upbringing, cursed incapacity one has to drag oneself out of all one's life."[4]

Miłosz forcefully expressed that Polish attitude toward women, that ambivalence of attraction and repulsion. It is easily seen in his writings devoted to the poet Anna Świrszczyńska, known, though not enough, in the United States as Anna Swir. He wrote often about poets and writers, but rarely with similar emotion. In Polish, he edited a volume of her poems, wrote some essays about her, and published a book-length study of her work. He also translated into English, together with Leonard Nathan, a short volume of her poems, *Talking to My Body*. Besides Anna Swir's poems, the volume contains Miłosz's introduction, a conversation between him and the other translator about Swir's work and life, as well as a postscript by Miłosz. He also addressed her in the poem "Translating Anna Swir on an Island of the Caribbean":

> *By banana plants, on a deck chair, by the pool*
> *Where Carol, naked, swims her laps*
> *Of the crawl and the classical style, I interrupt her*
> *Asking for a synonym. And again I am submerged*
> *In the murmuring Polish, in meditation.*
> *Because of the impermanence of the mind and the body,*
> *Because of your tender embracing of our fate,*
> *I call you in and you will be among people,*
> *Though you have written in a poem: "There is no me."*
> (NCP, *598)*

The swimming of Carol, the poet's wife, harmonizes with his immersion in the murmur of Polish, her nakedness evokes Anna Swir's "philosophy of the big toe, / Of the female split, of the pulse, of the large intestine." Miłosz is enchanted by her delight in her body. "With that white mane of yours," he writes in that poem, "You could ride a broom, have a devil for a lover" (*NCP*, 598).

In none of his other literary biographies does he insist so much on the unity of life and oeuvre, on authenticity, on the veracity of poetic work that expresses in a radical way Anna Swir's physicality and femininity. That femininity, as was said already, both attracts and repulses him, and this is why he describes her as a broom-riding witch. She is dangerous to his manly self, which also makes her attractive. "Opening myself to her verses, I have been more and more conquered by her extraordinary, powerful, exuberant, and joyous personality," he writes in the postscript. "Reading her," he continues, "was like discovering in someone who is close to us an unsuspected, strange and admirable being. Perhaps I was even falling in love with her."[5] In the Polish book devoted to her, he addresses Anna Swir with the literary name of Telimena, the main female character of Adam Mickiewicz's *Pan Tadeusz*. "My poor, courageous, magnificent Telimena!" he writes, asking at the same time her pardon for applying to her a name of a comical character (*JT*, 105). His portrait oscillates between reality and literature, seriousness and caricature, a tone of respect and a patronizing attitude of the one who is leading the dance for both of them. He is especially dismissive of her feminism, explaining it away as an expression of solidarity rather than any ideology. At the same time, he is surprised and delighted at finding in her a great poet.

It is important here to return to the sentence from his poem, "I call you in and you will be among people." Miłosz was obsessed with pushing away oblivion, with saving people from an obscurity that is tantamount to nonexistence. In his books, on page after page, he recalls friends, acquaintances, family, even the newts he played with as a child and that "vanished so long ago." He gives them existence, "even a name and a title in the princedom of grammar / To protect you by inflection from nothingness" (*CNP,* 458). He repeats often that in his youth he was already sensitive to the passing away of people and things. In the case of Anna Swir, that saving "in the princedom of grammar" has an additional aspect. Thanks to his efforts, he writes in the postscript to the English-language volume of her poetry, she "is now regarded as a truly eminent poet of metaphysical orientation."[6] He placed her high in the estate of Polish and (hopefully) world poetry.

Anna Swir was, like all of the Polish population, deeply marked by the experience of World War II and especially by the Warsaw Uprising of 1944. During the uprising, she served as a nurse in a makeshift hospital, trying to keep, most often unsuccessfully, death away from the wounded and from herself. It took her many years to find language capable of expressing the tragedy of her city. Miłosz is rightly impressed with her volume *Budowałam barykadę* (*Building the Barricade,* 1974), a collection of poems that consist mostly of snapshots from the dying city, poems that are almost too piercing to read. Each of them feels like a close-up of a specific tragedy, and the fragmentation of time in them is particularly affecting: there is no continuity, in the war there is only the present. Their clear language and fierce commitment to reality make them the best Polish poetic testimony to the disaster of that insurrection. They are also quite unusual in their avoidance of any of the romantic embellishments so common in Polish war literature. History and religion are the basic categories of Polishness, and they have a long literary tradition behind them as well as an almost automatic vocabulary. Anna Swir does express in her poetry the sacrum of motherland, but in a particularly nontraditional and nonreligious way. In the matter of religion, Miłosz writes, "she was a typical member of the Polish progressive intelligentsia, that is agnostic, and you cannot find in her work any mention of church going" (*JT*, 28). This does not prevent him from declaring that her poems attain the proximity of the absolute. "Her poetry confirms the rule that should not be true in a Catholic Poland. . . . In the twentieth century the best poetry reaching for the Other Dimension, whatever we would call that dimension, is written by the poets not too confessional or extraconfessional, as if the very dictionary full of capital letters paralyzed the authors faithful to the catechism" (*JT*, 28).

Another woman writer Miłosz commemorated in a poem was Jeanne Hersch. "What I Learned from Jeanne Hersch" is composed of twelve moral and philosophical sentences, and is both discursive and didactic. I would like to quote, as examples, the first, fourth, and the last:

> 1. That reason is a gift of God and that we should believe in its ability to comprehend the world.
> 4. That truth is a proof of freedom and that the sign of slavery is the lie.
> 12. That in our lives we should not succumb to despair because of our errors and our sins, for the past is never closed down and receives the meaning we give it by our subsequent acts. (*NCP*, 711–12)

Miłosz does not write about the intimate aspect of his relation with Jeanne Hersch, and this reticence shows the limits which his reminiscences do not cross. He rarely mentions those women who played an important role in his emotional life. In a private letter, for example, he wrote to Renata Gorczyńska that the volume *Unattainable Earth* was in reality "hers,"[7] but no such information can be found in his published work. Jeanne Hersch helped him, as I already mentioned, in the initial period of his exile and cut short some of his ideological hesitations. Feminist writings often quote a passage from Joseph Conrad in which he writes about a hand that was placing a cup of tea in front of him when he was depressed, fruitlessly sitting at his desk. Miłosz behaved differently: of Jeanne Hersch he left us her head not her hand. Of all the kinds of amputation, this one seems to me the best.

A large part of Joseph Brodsky's literary criticism is devoted to two women-poets, Anna Akhmatova and Marina Tsvetaeva. Together with Osip Mandelstam and Boris Pasternak, they constitute for him the canon of Russian literature of the twentieth century. Not only the work of these two women but also their lives inspired his highest esteem. Still another person whose life awed him was Nadezhda Mandelstam, the widow of the poet and the author of two volumes of memoirs. Brodsky devoted two essays to her, one of them written after her death. The style of his writing about women is very different from that of Miłosz. The Polish poet has a very personal and easy tone, talking to us in a sorrowful but relaxed way. He reviews scenes, scents, colors of the past and tries to encapsulate them in words. Brodsky concentrates on the particular texts of the women he recalls. He writes with high tension, with something akin to an impatient hunt for the always escaping essence of life or work. His associations are poetic, his narration surprising.

The difference between the styles of Miłosz and Brodsky could be caused by their different ways of accessing to the past. Miłosz had a perfect memory and recall of the past, as can be judged by many of his reminiscences and by his novel *The Issa Valley*. It was poems that Brodsky remembered best. Miłosz's memory was narrative, Brodsky's lyrical. The dissimilarity of their memory corresponds to the inequality of their rootedness in life. Their attitude toward time was most different. Miłosz enjoyed the everyday, was an enthusiast and glorifier of the moments of perfect harmony, of *esse*. Brodsky was less easy, cut off as he was from the past of his family, left only with dramatic memories of his childhood. And he was sick. The heart problems he had are usually accompanied by a special kind of sensitivity. In 1994, when he was forced to visit a cardiologist during his stay in Sweden, he told him that he felt like a wounded animal who simply tried to survive. He expected to die any time; when leaving his hotel room, he would put his papers in order. "Hurry sickness" was the diagnosis of the psychologist who interviewed him on that occasion.[8]

Nervous tension is not a drawback of Brodsky's style, it is simply one of its characteristics. In his admiration for Miłosz there seems to be an appreciation of his embracing of life. Miłosz was very busy, yet he sounded like a person who was not pressed for time. Brodsky ran against time. In that fight he was not supported by religion or by history—national or private. His sick heart reminded him continually of the Fates' scissors. So, when writing about a poet or a writer—and such are the subjects of the majority of his essays—he did not follow their lives; rather, he analyzed their works, in that way defying death, "for language is the highest form of existence" (*LTO*, 186).

Miłosz is interested in the femininity of Anna Swir or Denise Lever-tov, while Brodsky does not write about that at all. Tsvetaeva—"a Job in a skirt"—is, according to him, the most eminent poet of the twentieth century, better even than Auden. Her poems entrance him by their temperature and accelerations—he paid homage to both of these characteristics in his translations of a few of her poems into English. These translations wonderfully express the tension of the originals and their continual escape forward. In his conversation with Solomon Volkov, from which the "Job in a skirt" characterization comes, he does not permit the classification of Tsvetaeva's poetry into a subcategory of "women's poetry." "Does a woman's voice in poetry really not differ in any way from a man's?" asks Volkov. "Only in the verb endings," Brodsky replies, having in mind Russian grammar. The only dimension in which Brodsky recognized the femininity of Tsvetaeva and Akhmatova is that "women have been much harsher in their moral demands [than men]," and "are more sensitive to ethical transgressions, to psychological and intellectual immorality." But the tragic tone of Tsvetaeva's and Akhmatova's poems is, so to say, genderless. "Is Job a man or a woman?"—Brodsky asks (*CJB*, 39, 43).

Tsvetaeva committed suicide during World War II, but luckily Akhmatova survived the war. Brodsky was twenty-one years old when he met her. It was a major discovery for him: "Such a good contact established itself between us because I understood with whom I was dealing. And she too to a certain extent found in me something that was a part of herself. And the other way around."[9] He was almost half a century younger than she, and liked to repeat that it was she who formed him. According to Tomas Venclova, Brodsky internalized Akhmatova; "his moral choices, his sense of self-worth, were as if subconsciously dictated by Akhmatova." In an analysis of Brodsky's poem "Sreten'e" ("Nunc Dimittis" in its English-language version), which recounts the story of St. Anna, Venclova finds Akhmatova's religiosity, even though it is not that of the author himself.[10] A great illustration of this influence is offered by a poem Brodsky wrote to celebrate the centenary of Akhmatova's birth, with the phrase: "Boh sohraniaiet vsio" (God will save everything). When his daughter was born, Brodsky named her Anna Aleksandra Maria, linking the names of his parents to that of the poet.

Brodsky's short poem "Didona i Eney" (Dido and Aeneas) was written most probably with Akhmatova's poem "The Last Rose" in mind. She had written that poem in 1963, opening it with an epigraph from a poem dedicated to her by the twenty-three-year-old Brodsky: "You will write about us on a slant." It was as if she were fulfilling that prediction. The poem is remarkable in showing Akhmatova's vision of herself as one of the women on whose shoulders rests the responsibility for their country. With the epigraph signed "J.B.," the poem appeared that year in the January issue of the periodical *Novyi Mir*.[11]

"It was the first appearance of the name of Brodsky in print," writes Tomas Venclova; "he was a well-known 'underground' poet at that time, and it became almost the main topic of discussion in unofficial circles."[12] But after Brodsky's trial the poem was reprinted without the epigraph, not only in Russia but also in Poland; the translation of "The Last Rose" appeared as early as 1964 and the epigraph had been censored. Brodsky liked to quote and recite this poem, and he often referred to Akhmatova as Dido, the Abandoned One. "Dido and Aeneas" pays her homage also by its form: its narration is elliptical in a manner that reminds the reader of her style and its meter is very restrained. It is possible that these were the reasons why Miłosz translated this poem—the only Brodsky poem he translated—into Polish. Brodsky translated six poems of Miłosz's into Russian, but none of them came from the list proposed in "the consolatory letter," discussed at the beginning of this book. Miłosz indicated at the end of that letter twenty-three poems he wished to be translated. Brodsky made his own choice. In that, too, he had a mind of his own.

For Brodsky and his friends Akhmatova was an embodiment of memory, opening for them the prerevolutionary Russian literary tradition that by then had few remaining witnesses. The landscape in which they grew was emptied by revolution, terror, and war, and paralyzed by censorship; it is therefore not too difficult to follow the influences on them, as they were few and enthusiastically proclaimed. They had to recover for themselves, not only ideas, but also customs, various kinds of poetry, and spirituality. Akhmatova was only one of the guides on that road of recovery, but she was the one with whom Brodsky listened to Henry Purcell's *Dido & Aeneas;* it was from her that he learned about Christianity as a basis of culture; she directed him not only to the Bible, to the classical tradition, but also to the "English orientation." She loved Shakespeare ("The Last Rose" must come also from him) and Byron, and English romantic poetry in general.

It is in this context—in the context of the English tradition and of Aeneas and Dido—that I would like to place the piercing scene of the visit paid by Isaiah Berlin to Akhmatova in November 1945. The city of Leningrad was then raising itself from the terrible experience of wartime blockade, unaware of the forthcoming attack of Stalinism. The encounter of Berlin and Akhmatova, unexpected and extraordinary, was described several times by Isaiah Berlin. The conversation was in Russian—Berlin was born in Riga when it was part of the Russian empire and knew the language perfectly. After many hours of waiting for the exit of a neighbor who sat with Akhmatova, the Russian poet proposed the recitation of her poems, but she wanted to start with two cantos from Byron's *Don Juan,* because "they were important for what was to follow. . . . Even if I had known the poem well," Berlin reports, "I could not have told which cantos she had chosen, for although she read in English, her pronunciation of it made it impossible to understand more than a word or two. She closed her eyes and spoke the lines from memory, with intense emotion; I rose and looked out of the window to conceal my embarrassment. Perhaps, I thought afterwards, that is how we now read classical Greek and Latin; yet we, too, are moved by the words, which, as we pronounce them, might be wholly unintelligible to their authors and audiences. Then she spoke her own poems."[13]

Anna Andreyevna attached great importance to that visit since she paid a heavy price for it. She was attacked by Stalinist propaganda, prevented from publishing, tormented, and persecuted. This had been the reason why she felt abandoned, Dido-like, by Berlin-Aeneas: he left and did not come back. What is important in this fragment is the seriousness with which she treated poetry. Her close friend Nadezhda Mandelstam wrote: "The first time I talked with Akhmatova, still in Tsarskoe Selo, I suddenly noticed, that she spoke about poets of the past as if they were alive and had only yesterday dropped in on her to read their freshly composed poetry and drink a glass of tea. . . . The resurrecting of dead [poetic] ancestors became for Akhmatova a natural act of friendship, a living and active relationship of a poet to his forefathers—friends and brothers in the house of a single mother, world poetry." According to Nadezhda Mandelstam, Akhmatova dreamed about the moment when she would meet her dead predecessors, including Osip Mandelstam, and would "feast" with them, preferably while their wives were absent. She was faithful to her literary forefathers, trying to reconstruct a tradition that was being threatened by wars, revolution, coercion of a totalitarian state, death of the poets themselves, and the ignorance and indifference of her contemporaries. What mattered was that "the torch inherited from our ancestors continue to be alight."[14]

Brodsky also took upon himself the responsibility for carrying on the torch of poetry. He called Akhmatova the Keening Muse, not only because of the tragic tenor of her poetry, including her *Requiem,* but also, perhaps, because she (and he) did like to use this "old word"—Muse.[15] Her early poem "The Muse" (1924) describes a visit of "this dear guest with her shepherd's flute."

> *And here she was. She gazed at me and waited*
> *Attentively, her veil tossed overhead.*
> *I asked her "Was it you then who dictated*
> *The script of Hell to Dante?" "I," she said.*[16]

Thanks to her, in the austere, prudish Soviet Russia the Muses were not only marble monuments on the banks of the Neva River but also characters peopling the landscapes of poetry. Brodsky called an entire volume of poems by the name of Urania, the muse of astronomy; and he wrote essays about Clio, the muse of history, Euterpe, the muse of lyrical poetry, and Mnemosyne, the muse of memory and mother of all the Muses. They were not literary trinkets or signs of erudition arrived at late in the life of the self-taught poet. They were the sign of the rejection of novelty and the choice of classicism. And, obviously, they were symbols of poetry.

Among many of Brodsky's drawings—and he had a talent for drawing—there is an affecting early self-portrait, showing him standing rather pensive, with his hands in his pockets, while a muse hovers in the air, one hand on his shoulder and the other offering him a lyre. The muse resembles a very cute young woman with curly blond hair, wearing a light toga, earrings, and sandals. Her immateriality is shown through the lighter lines with which she is drawn, though her eyelashes seem to be strongly touched with mascara. In many drawings from the 1960s Brodsky presented himself with a lyre or a laurel wreath. He is an unshaven man with disheveled hair surrounded by the symbols of poetry. In his poems, too, although he treats tradition very seriously, muses are called in with a bit of irony, almost always when he writes about inspiration and poetic creativity. He treats the vocation of the poet seriously but never falls into pomposity. For him, just as for Akhmatova, the Muse is a synonym for work.

In the period of his visits to Akhmatova—his apprenticeship—Brodsky wrote one of his first long poems, entitled "Sofiya" to honor Zofia Kapuścińska Ratajczakowa, a Polish woman then studying in Leningrad. The poem was written in 1962, when Brodsky was twenty-two years old, and, what is important, is also one of the first poems he wrote with a Christmas theme. The "Sofiya" of the title is not, as in the case of Miłosz, the bearer of wisdom, but a cross between a concrete woman, the author's soul, and a muse. Zofia was his Eurydice, lost now; he remains, Orpheus-like, with only a memory of her, and her photo. He will return to the character of Orpheus many times, including in a late essay (1994) devoted to Rilke's poem "Orpheus. Eurydice. Hermes." In the 1990 essay "Altra Ego," Brodsky comments on an exhibit in which the photos of famous creators were accompanied by those of the women who inspired them. Brodsky ridicules this idea; for him the Muse is identical with language: "it is presumably the language's own gender in Greek (*glossa*) that accounts for the Muse's femininity" (*OGR,* 83). In this essay Brodsky not only returns to Orpheus; he also mentions Akhmatova and repeats the motifs from her short poem "The Muse" that I quoted above. The Muse is not a poet's lover, she is the voice of poetry. "The ultimate distinction between the beloved and the Muse [is that] the latter doesn't die. The same goes for the Muse and the poet: when he's gone, she finds herself another mouthpiece in the next generation" (*OGR,* 95). Twenty-eight years separates the writing of "Sofiya" from the essay "Altra Ego," and thirty-two from the essay on Rilke. There is an amazing stability of motifs, references to masters, allusions, even though they accompany the author's moving from one language to another—definitely a radical change for a poet. Perhaps that stability, that clarity about what poetry *says,* was what allowed Brodsky's leap into a new language. It was a superficial change, while the essence remained the same.

In his poem Brodsky calls his attitude to Zofia "a strange love," but love is not his main topic. "Sofiya" is a successful literary exercise, running through various ideas and motives, with references to many poets, especially to Pushkin and Pasternak. Love is just one of the threads in it, although already in a form that will constitute the deep structure of all the love poetry of Brodsky, which speaks about feelings in the past, from a distance and with a distance, temporal or spatial. Such is the structure of the three-part poem "Polonaise" written nineteen years after "Sofiya" and also dedicated to Kapuścińska. "Does it really matter who's run away from whom?" he writes there. Miłosz also had some doubts about love poetry: the Polish poet Julia Hartwig remembers that when she showed him her first poems he said: "Oh, about love. . . . Love is not a topic for poems."[17] Both Miłosz and Brodsky approached the writing of love poems as artisans, looking at the texts of other poets more than at the object of their own attentions. "Love as content is in the habit of limiting formal patterns," wrote Brodsky in the essay "The Keening Muse" (*LTO,* 45). And in "Altra Ego" he categorically rejected any biographical interpretation of his love lyrics: "Even the most misogynistic, or misanthropic poet produces a spate of love lyrics, if only as a token of allegiance to the guild, or as an exercise. . . . 'To a man, a girl's visage is of course a visage of his soul,' wrote a Russian poet. . . . A maiden, in short, is one's soul's stand-in. . . . These are quests for the soul, in the form of lyric poetry. Hence the singularity of the addressee and the stability of the manner, or style. . . . A love lyric is one's soul set in motion" (*OGR,* 86–89).

The "singularity of the addressee," the literary "monogamy" of love lyrics, refers to "M.B."—Marina (Marianna Pavlovna) Basmanova—a great love of Brodsky's in the 1960s and mother of his son. I have already mentioned that the vicissitudes of their union absorbed the poet more than his prison, trial, and banishment to Norenskaya. Their union and separation was a topic of poems written over many years: "I was but what you'd brush / with your palm," he wrote in "Seven Strophes" (1981).

> *I was but what your gaze*
> *in the dark could distinguish:*
> *a dim shape to begin with,*
> *later—features, a face.*
>
> . . .
>
> *I was practically blind.*
> *You, appearing, then hiding,*
> *gave me my sight and heightened*
> *it. Thus some leave behind*
>
> *a trace. Thus they make worlds.*
> *Thus, having done so, at random*
> *wastefully they abandon*
> *their work to its whirls.*
>
> *Thus, prey to speeds*
> *of light, heat, cold, or darkness,*
> *a sphere in space without markers*
> *spins and spins. (*CPE, *286–87)*

Brodsky collected the poems for M.B. in one volume that he called *Novoye Stanci k Avguste* (*New Stanzas for Augusta*). He considered this the most important part of his work, and his friend and critic Lev Loseff agrees.[18] The title is an allusion to Byron and serves to underline the literary stylization of the volume at the expense of its biographical side. Analyzing one of the poems from the volume, "The Song without Music," Gerry Smith writes that it "articulates the most canonical attitude to male-female relationships by male Russian poets. The poem is elegiac; that is, the relationship is celebrated after it is over. Pushkin's "Ia vas liubil" [I loved you] is the quintessential statement of the theme of lost love, after which any other treatment of it seems indecorous. To this day it seems to be unthinkable for a male Russian to write love poetry about an enduring, requited relationship—especially if it is legally registered."[19] Brodsky would agree with this description; one of the "Twenty Sonnets to Mary Queen of Scots"—the sixth one—is a variation on Pushkin's poem: "I loved you. And my love of you (it seems, / it's only pain) still stabs me through the brain" (*CPE,* 228). The poems to M.B. speak more about his literary affinities than about the events of his life. They are some of the most beautiful love poems in the literature of the twentieth century—grateful, bitter, and desperate.

There are of course other works about love and women in the poetic oeuvre of Brodsky. They do speak about body and beauty, although in a predominantly ironic way. One of the "Roman Elegies," dedicated to Benedetta Craveri, enumerates "Lesbia, Julia, Cynthia, Livia, Michelina . . . Short-term goddesses," and hails "the smooth abdomen, thighs as their hamstrings tighten" (*CPE,* 278). But one can also find disgust at carnal experience, as in the poem "Debut," which describes a sad sexual initiation of two completely lonely people.[20] When he speaks about himself, he seems a protagonist of an old American movie: a man with a bitter past, alone, ironic, unkempt, drinking something strong, and looking through the window. His strangled feelings barely transpire through a restrained exterior, and he does not expect anything of life. In the poem "I Sit by the Window," he also performs, like Conrad, a kind of amputation—of his woman he leaves a knee:

> *I sit by the window. Outside, an aspen.*
> *When I loved, I loved deeply. It wasn't often.*
>
> *I said the forest's only part of a tree.*
> *Who needs the whole girl if you've got her knee?*
>
> . . .
>
> *I sit by the window. The dishes are done.*
> *I was happy here. But I won't be again. (*CPE, *46–47)*

Happiness, here invoked, would probably refer to the times passed with M.B., and "the dishes are done" undermines the tragic tone and "manly" suffering of the poet. The bitter tone in the love lyrics does not end in 1982, when the last poems of the *New Stanzas for Augusta* were written. The poem "Brise Marine" (1989) is another final good-bye:

> *Dear, I ventured out of the house late this evening . . .*
>
> . . .

Your body, your warble, your middle name
Now stir practically nothing. (CPE, 364)

Toward the end of his life, Brodsky softened. His last years seemed much happier. He married and had a daughter, and his professional life did not give him a lot of anxiety. For his wife, he wrote at least one love poem, a very joyous and funny one, called "Love Song." Its last stanza says:

If you loved volcanoes, I'd be lava,
*   relentlessly erupting from my hidden source.*
And if you were my wife, I'd be your lover,
*   because the Church is firmly against divorce. (CPE, 451)*

The poem was written in English, so it probably does not disprove the thesis of Gerry Smith that in Russian a love song cannot be written for a wife. That also shows how the English language enlarged Brodsky's literary (and emotional?) possibilities.

PART TWO

Fatherlands / Otherlands

FIVE

In the Shadow of Empire: Russia

Attitudes toward Russia form a difficult, hidden background of the friendship between Brodsky and Miłosz: they never discussed it openly. Miłosz often said that the two of them overcame the long-standing differences between Poland and Russia. Brodsky never declared as much.

The difference in their attitudes toward Russia can be deduced from a controversy over the entity called Central Europe. In the 1970s and 1980s the old concept of "Mittel Europe" became a new, anti-Soviet idea, produced or verbalized, mostly in the West, by exiles and refugees from the Soviet bloc. The concept was useful in the fight for the sovereignty of their countries. The existence of Central Europe—as opposed to "Eastern Europe"—was proclaimed by, among others, the Czech writer and editor of *Lettre Internationale* Antonin Liehm; by Ladislav Matejka, professor at Michigan and founder of the periodical *Cross Currents;* by Barbara Toruńczyk, the founder and editor of *Zeszyty Literackie,* the émigré Polish literary quarterly; and by writers Milan Kundera, Danilo Kiš, György Konrad, and Czesław Miłosz. It was a spiritual if not a territorial community, made up of the countries politically dominated by the Soviet Union but aspiring to sovereignty, democracy, and participation in Western culture. "Central Europe" was a multipolar, multiethnic, multilinguistic entity, kept within the "totalitarian East" by an imperial tyranny.

The most important, tone-setting essays about Central Europe were written by Czesław Miłosz and Milan Kundera.[1] As citizens of the territory, Kundera enumerated writers of Jewish origin and German language—this choice determined, perhaps, by their complex national identity. But as the project caught on, other names were added, together with new lands and even new history. Rooted in the past, Central Europe was leaning toward the future. To Kundera's "Bohemia," Miłosz added Poland and the Great Duchy of Lithuania, Konrad Hungary, Kiš the Balkans. This collaboration of writers from different regions of Europe corresponded to the regional solidarity of the dissidents from Poland, Czechoslovakia, and Hungary. The objective of this activity was to evoke sympathy for a "captive" (Central) Europe, so as to prepare her "return" to the West.

Russians—even those who were critical of their country—did not like the concept. The reasons were many, but the most important was that the term Central Europe was directed not only against the politics of Russia but also against its culture and traditions. And Russians were especially loyal to their culture, believing in its universal value and greatness. This may have been part of the imperial aura in which Brodsky's generation grew up. "None of us would have felt Jewish," wrote Ludmilla Shtern, Brodsky's friend and contemporary from Leningrad, "except that our motherland constantly, in one way or another, reminded us of it. We grew up with the Russian language, Russian culture, Russian literature, and Russian traditions. . . . We adored Russian nature, Russian forests and fields, Russian winter and Russian autumn, Russian vodka, Russian borsht, pickled herring with potatoes, and Russian 'bread which goes in the oven for us' (Gumilyov). . . . First and foremost we loved all that concerned Russia, Russian language and Russian culture."[2]

It is in this context, as a defense of Russian culture, that we should see Brodsky's article "Why Kundera is Wrong about Dostoyevsky."[3] It was a response to an essay by Kundera in which he described European culture as a domain of reason and Russian culture as one of feeling. There was nothing new in that juxtaposition, which was commonly aired in European writings about Russia. Kundera understood that opposition in 1968, when Russian tanks appeared on the streets of Prague. Brodsky ridiculed the idea of European culture in which there would be no place for Dostoyevsky. He did not accept, he declared, the division into West and East, the political approach to culture, with history explaining culture. Tanks are no argument in the domain of culture; language, literature, human thought are not limited by geography or political system, he wrote scathingly. The attack must have hurt Kundera, who still (as of 2009) does not give permission to reprint his text.

In his criticism of Kundera, Brodsky does not speak about Central Europe, but he touched on the issue directly in May 1988, during an international literary conference in Lisbon. The conference was organized by the Wheatland Foundation and was meant to bring together Soviet and East European émigré writers with their nonémigré counterparts. The Russian-Russian, East-European–East-European encounter, soon turned into a tangle between Russians and "Central Europeans." Among the participants there were Russian writers Lev Anninsky, Sergey Dovlatov, Tatyana Tolstaya, and Joseph Brodsky; to Central Europe belonged writers Danilo Kiš, György Konrad, Czesław Miłosz, Josef Škvorecky, and Adam Zagajewski. There were other invitees as well, the most outspoken of whom were Susan Sontag, Derek Walcott, and Salman Rushdie. They stood squarely on the side of Central Europeans, defending them against the Russians, who refused to accept the very existence of "Central Europe."

For the Central European writers, the attitude of their Russian colleagues was shocking. "The astonishing collision between the Russians and 'Central Europe'—a term they were hearing for the first time," Miłosz jotted down about this exchange in his diary-like *A Year of the Hunter.*

> Their unconcealed horror at the hostility of the Central Europeans, which they had trouble accepting, because Russians, of course, are raised from childhood to believe that they are admired and loved by everyone. . . . They don't comprehend the degree to which their thinking is imperialistic or, as Salman Rushdie remarks from the audience, colo-

nialist. Joseph Brodsky attempts to defend them, attacking the concept of Central Europe . . . which isn't news, of course; it has been public knowledge ever since his polemic against Milan Kundera. His friend and fellow Nobel laureate, Miłosz [the author writes here about himself in third person], in complete solidarity with his Hungarian, Yugoslav, Czech, and Polish colleagues, retorted that it is high time to break with Russian literature's taboo against any mention of the borders of the Imperium, and noted that it was Joseph Brodsky himself who first used the word 'Imperium' in his poetry to refer to the Soviet Union. (*YH*, 237–38)

Miłosz's recollection is very precise, and summarizes the main point of this late Cold War debate very economically. At the beginning of the conference, the East-Central European writers sounded tired of their oppositional role, their ardor extinguished; the reason was that, although nobody knew it yet, their battle was at that point already won. But the Russians immediately provoked them and woke up their fighting spirit. Tatyana Tolstaya, and after her other Russian writers, rejected the concept of Central Europe and declared that only individual countries exist. A writer has to write, she kept repeating; there is no link between Russian writers and the occupation of the countries of Eastern Europe. Konrad, Škvorecky, and Rushdie immediately reacted: the writer who uses the language of the empire should recognize its imperial position. Tolstaya, exasperated, replied that a writer has nothing to do with tanks. When Susan Sontag expressed her criticism of the Russian position, Joseph

Brodsky, till then a translator and mediator between the groups, entered the debate. The transcript of the conference reads:

BRODSKY (irritated, replies to Sontag): Of course, it's [the rejection of the concept of Central Europe] not an imperial position. Well, it is simply the only realistic attitude that we Russians can adopt towards the situation. And to call it "imperialistic," to charge us with a sort of colonialist attitude—colonialist disregard of the cultural and political realities . . . well, I think it's terribly myopic. I would add one more thing. As an anti-Soviet concept, the concept of Central Europe is not effective. That is, if I were a Soviet citizen and now I would just simply try to conjure it, well, I wouldn't be moved. I wouldn't be impressed. It simply doesn't work. What's more, we here—those who are sitting here—we are writers and we are defined not by our political system, although we presumably can't shed it. . . . A Russian writer is not a representative of the Soviet state. I beg you to distinguish between those things. That is, if you ask any one of us, "Would you like to have that tank removed from Eastern Europe?"—I take the liberty to speak for all of us—we would say yes, immediately. We feel terribly ashamed.

SONTAG: Nobody thinks you want the tanks. But what you call "realism" I call "imperial arrogance." . . .

BRODSKY: What would be republican humility then? If this is an imperial arrogance, if this is the only possibility. . . .

SONTAG: It's not to say "I'm not interested." . . . How can you not be interested?

BRODSKY: It's not that we're not interested. We simply think that, precisely because these countries are under our domination, under Soviet domination, the only way to liberate them is to liberate ourselves. . . .

SONTAG: But now you're talking power. I'm not asking you to liberate these countries. I'm asking you to speak in the name of literature. No one will think . . .

BRODSKY: In the name of literature, there is no such thing as a "Central Europe," either. Well, we've been over this ground. There is Polish literature, Czech literature, Slovak literature, Serbo-Croatian literature, Hungarian literature, and so forth. Well, it's impossible to speak about this concept even in the name of literature. It's an oxymoron, if you will. [Brodsky is repeating here the arguments of Tolstaya and grows more and more irritated, but when Miłosz joins the discussion, his tone changes immediately. The transcript continues:]

MIŁOSZ (interrupting Brodsky): *Divide et impera.* This is a colonial principle and you are for that.

BRODSKY: *Divide et impera.* In what way, Czesław? I don't understand you. Could you specify?

MIŁOSZ: The concept of Central Europe is not an invention of Kundera. You have an obsession that it is an invention of Kundera. Not at all. Central Europe, as Susan Sontag said, is an anti-Soviet concept provoked by the occupation of those countries. It's an obviously anti-Soviet concept and how can you, as Soviet writers, accept that concept? It's a very hostile concept to the Soviet Union!

BRODSKY: No, no, I accept it fully, but . . .

MIŁOSZ: And I should add that the conscience of a writer, for instance of a Russian writer, should cope with such facts, as for instance the pact between Hitler and Stalin and the occupation of the Baltic countries of which I am a native. And I am afraid that there is a certain taboo in Russian literature and this taboo is empire.

BRODSKY: All I'm trying to say is that I would be all for this anti-Soviet concept were that concept effective. It's simply not terribly effective. That's one thing. The second thing: the taboo of the Russian empire. Indeed, in the Soviet press, until this day, you don't encounter this concept. Well, it's never stated that the Soviet Union is an empire.

MIŁOSZ (turning to the audience): I would like to add that my friend, Joseph Brodsky, was one of the first, if not the first, to introduce the term "empire" in his poetry.

BRODSKY: Yeah, I know that.[4]

I will return to this exchange, but first I would like to underline Brodsky's very paternalistic (and imperialistic?) pronouncement that Russians need to liberate themselves before they liberate the countries of the bloc. Such an attitude—nothing will change till the Soviet Union changes—was a political cliché particularly disliked by the "East Europeans" as it was meant to keep them quiet. It was already more than outdated: these countries were to liberate themselves a year hence. This pronouncement was also one of the few in which Brodsky publicly spoke as a representative of a group—"we the

Russians." His irritation at Susan Sontag should be contrasted with his stopping at the edge of disagreement with Miłosz—where he immediately steps aside. Miłosz, too, reaches out to him: Russian poetry has a long tradition of using the term *empire* and Brodsky did not introduce it. The Polish poet seems to say: I am criticizing Russians but not Brodsky, Brodsky is a special case. And, uncharacteristically, Brodsky's reply turns incoherent.

They never changed their opinions about Central Europe. Miłosz not only participated in the creation of the concept, he continued to defend it even later, after the collapse of the Soviet Union, when it had already fulfilled its immediate political role. At a conference at Rutgers, in 1992, he expressed his sorrow at the lack of solidarity among the newly liberated countries that used to belong to that imaginary Central Europe. "I am a great admirer of the idea of Central Europe," he said. "My friend Joseph Brodsky doesn't agree with me. When I speak of Central Europe, he would say Western Asia—which is a point of view." It was still another instance in which Miłosz, but never Brodsky, publicly pointed out a difference of opinion between them. "Western Asia" must have been said with a smile. And when he used the term *friend*—was his intention to soften the disagreement? "But there is something," he continued, "that I believe unites those countries of a certain zone between Germany and Russia. They share a very turbulent past but also a common heritage, as for instance in their architecture. Going from Lithuania to Dubrovnik, one perceives a certain connectedness. The idea of Central Europe was in a way an experiment in harmonious existence among those countries, at least among Poland, Czechoslovakia, and Hungary; it was a nucleus. But today we are completely lost in particular problems."[5]

I was present during this session, to which Miłosz was unexpectedly invited—he was to replace Brodsky, who had been scheduled to be part of it but had lost his way on the New Jersey turnpike and come in late. I remember a kind of impatience with which the topic of Central Europe was received by the public; it already belonged to the past. Brodsky did not debate Miłosz's points, but continued to use the term "Eastern Europe," and said that the time had come when each of the countries would be judged by their individual worth, that is their economic success. And he predicted the dominance of the united Germany. It was the beginning of a new era.

The concept of Central Europe did not fit into the mental and political geography of Brodsky. A year after that conference, during his stay in Poland, a Polish theater director, Bogdan Tosza, asked him where he thought the center of Europe was located. "In Vilnius," Brodsky replied. "I have studied the map and the center of Europe is exactly there." Tomas Venclova, who, as we remember, is a Lithuanian, was standing at that moment behind Brodsky, and specified : "Concretely fifty kilometers north of Vilnius, in the place where the famous editor Jerzy Giedroyć was born" (*StS*, 49).[6] As we can see from these replies, "the middle of Europe" is not a purely geographic concept. When Chekhov left Kamchatka and found himself in Irkutsk, he wrote in a letter to his brother that he had finally returned to the "heart of Europe." Brodsky's and Venclova's words show the shape that Europe had in their mind: Russia constituted one half of their Europe, and therefore Vilnius was at her center. But although Miłosz, like Venclova, was born in Lithuania, he uses a different mental globe. His Central Europe stretches from Lithuania to Dubrovnik, and his beloved Vilnius is located on her border. Besides, for Miłosz, the very meaning of the concept of Central Europe consisted in not having a center, in multipolarity, in local centers, and even "transferable centers," because Kraków replaced for him the Vilnius of his youth. In the 1990s, new countries emerged out of the Soviet empire, yet both Brodsky and Miłosz maintained their geographic convictions. Brodsky was fighting for recognition of the Europeanness of Russia, Miłosz for solidarity with the small, freshly liberated nations previously occupied by Russia. Hence his fidelity to the concept of Central Europe, the concept by then fading and almost quaint.[7]

Miłosz's faithfulness to the idea of Central Europe does not mean, however, that he did not consider Russia as belonging to Europe—quite the opposite. As pointed out by Per-Årne Bodin, while Kundera's vision of Central Europe was anti-Russian, "Miłosz integrates the culture of Eastern Christianity into Europe through the myth of the Great Lithuanian Duchy."[8] His concept of that country—a utopia in the past—was of a multinational, multicultural entity that included Russia, or at least its western part. Thanks to a long career of teaching Russian literature to American students, Miłosz, according to Bodin, abandoned the characteristically traumatized Polish attitude to Russia. He was interested in Russian spirituality and studied Russian philosophers of religion. He thus accomplished two things: first, he incorporated Russians into his own worldview; second, he integrated them into European philosophical discourse as a positive pole. Miłosz confronts Lev Shestov not only with Albert

Camus but also with Simone Weil; Sergey Bulhakov with Stanisław Vincenz; in this way Dostoyevsky and Swedenborg are placed side by side. It is through the concept of the Great Lithuanian Duchy, writes Bodin, that "Russian language, Russian culture, Russian philosophy, Russian religious reflection are integrated into a European whole in a very decided and sometimes even—from the Polish point of view—provocative way" (19). The role of the émigré philosopher Lev Shestov is particularly important: Miłosz writes about him often, emphasizing that it was Shestov who formed a common intellectual plane between him and Brodsky. According to Bodin, Miłosz's sense of sacrum found its expression in the language of Russian mystical epiphanies; Polish culture avoids such forms of spirituality. "Miłosz finds in Dostoyevsky," Bodin writes, "what Shestov found in him, the closeness to life and its complexity, which cannot be expressed in abstract schemas or general rules" (21). And he concludes: "It seems that Miłosz uses the image of Russia in the description of himself, of his religious quests, epiphanies, dualism, and his own anti-utopian convictions and notions. The Image of Russia becomes part of the biography of the poet himself" (23).

Miłosz reaches out to the Russian culture to express something that he calls "the 'Eastern part' in me" (*NR,* 143). He does not accept this part without resistance, as he writes in his *Native Realm,* in a chapter devoted to Russia. This book, as the second part of its title states, is "a search for self-definition," and Russia forms a large part of that definition: namely, its changeable border. Russia taught Miłosz how to express ecstasy, how to move toward and accept mystical feelings. Yet, such feelings needed to be restrained. Russian mystical writers, Miłosz declared, express a philosophy in which the tie between intention and deed is severed. The basis of Russian culture—Miłosz rephrases here that reason-versus-emotion critique of Russia—consists of a duality joining a great love toward everything that is alive to a submission to the decrees of God, fate, or the state, because the world is evil and there is no justice in this life. This duality means that without any inconsistency a man could kill another human being whom he sincerely likes—that with a stoic resignation, he can commit the most atrocious evil while feeling compassion for his victim. In elucidating this "essence" of Russian culture, Miłosz quotes from Adam Mickiewicz's *Forefathers' Eve,* the canonical Polish patriotic nineteenth-century text, expressing Polish and Catholic rejection of the Russian empire. He concludes this section of his book with an annex (left out of the English-language edition) with numerous quotations from the most vociferous French critique of Russia, *La Russie en 1839,* by Marquis de Custine. A contemporary of Adam Mickiewicz and a devout Catholic, Custine expressed opinions identical to those of the Polish Great Emigration that languished then in France, unable to return to their country, swallowed—it seemed for good—by the Russian Moloch.[9] Theirs was the traditional Polish anti-Russian attitude, stressing cultural or even civilizational differences between Poland and Russia. Miłosz is therefore integrating into Polish culture a certain mysticism and an openness to epiphany (his "Eastern part"), but at the same time keeping them at a distance as a socially dangerous severance of reason from emotion. One should add here that Brodsky "adored" Custine and was planning to write an introduction to a Russian edition of his book. His was an attitude found often among Russian "Westernizers" who combined severe criticism with a deep love of their country.

Miłosz returned time and again to this border within himself, the border that was marked by his devotion to Latin and to the Catholic Church. He was conscious of his own double attitude toward Russia, his attraction to some of its aspects, and his rejection, much more frequent, of the others. He generalized this hesitation, this duality, and projected it onto all Slavic cultures. All Slavs, he maintained, felt an ambivalence toward their countries, attachment combined with repulsion, pride with shame, love with hate. These feelings are always joined, and they constitute a contradiction never to be resolved. In his writings about Russia he continuously remembers Poland, "that area between the Germans and Russia" (*NR,* 137). Russia permits him to illuminate and condemn Polish shortcomings, to undermine Polish certitudes, to distance himself from Polish phobias, Polish nationalism, "Polish obsessions" (*NR,* 142). Remembering Russia allows him to build what Wojciech Karpiński called "his strategy toward the Polish past: a play of rebellion and fascination."[10] For him, Poland and Russia are grown into one another, perhaps because he comes from a land marked by both of them. Thinking about Russia, he cannot not think about Poland—and about the reality of empire.

The expression "grown into one another" does not perfectly reflect the relation between Poland and Russia: using the terms of Mickiewicz, Miłosz sees Russia as an abyss, boundless and chaotic. The fear of being engulfed, swallowed, is one of the "Polish obsessions," as is the shame of being a conquered subject of the empire.

Miłosz wrote about this anxiety in the late 1970s, with bitterness and irony:

> *In the shadow of the Empire, in Old Slavonic long-johns,*
> *You better learn to like your shame because it will stay with you.*
> *It won't go away even if you change your country and your*
> * name.*
> *The dolorous shame of failure. Shame of the muttony heart.*
> *Of fawning eagerness. Of clever pretending.*
> *Of dusty roads on the plain and trees lopped off for fuel.*
> *You sit in a shabby house, putting things off until spring.*
> *No flowers in the garden—they would be trampled anyway.*
> *You eat lazy pancakes, the soupy dessert called "Nothing-served-*
> * cold."*
>
> *And, always humiliated, you hate foreigners.* (NCP, 376)

This remarkable fragment of *Separate Notebooks* ("Page 29") explains Miłosz's "ear" for the imperialistic tone of the Lisbon speeches of the Russian writers, and his immediate siding with the anticolonial stance of Salman Rushdie, Derek Walcott, and Susan Sontag, all three of them belonging to minorities, although different ones. He recognized the well-meaning blindness of the Russians, their certitude that they see the world as it is. Although he grew up in an independent Poland, when he was born Poland was part of the Russian empire; his birth certificate was written in Russian. He witnessed the consequences of national humiliation in the generation of his parents and always remembered the past submission of the people he belonged to. It has been said that one feels guilty about what one does and ashamed of who one is. Miłosz often wrote about his guilt—he was a deeply Catholic poet. He also wrote about shame stemming from humiliation: personal, when he was an exiled, unappreciated poet in France, or national—the historical humiliation of subjugated Poles. He knew what it was to live in the shadow of the empire, to be powerless, to be dictated to by people—even well-meaning ones—with their tanks. And he did not like to use the heroic tropes to embellish that experience.

It is in this context that we can examine again the puzzling fact that Miłosz always adds the attribute "my friend" when talking about Brodsky, while Brodsky never does so. Brodsky, we said, respected the age difference between them, and Miłosz was encouraging his younger colleague. But Miłosz was always deliberate and precise in his use of language, and the insistence on repeating "my friend" while talking about Brodsky, alive and dead, in his presence and in print, begs for deeper explanation. In our archeology of their relationship we can find a layer which has to do with the issue of empire. This repetition, this insistence seems to be addressed at some presupposed, implicit objection, rebuking something that is forcefully present in Miłosz's mind. As we have seen in the quoted poem, he feels or at least recognizes in himself the traces of the shame of a subject of the Russian empire. And Brodsky represents Russia. Is Miłosz saying: he IS my friend, although he is Russian and I am Polish? When Miłosz repeats that the two of them overcame the conflicts between their countries, Brodsky keeps silent. When Miłosz talks about their friendship, Brodsky keeps silent. This silence reminds me of a fragment from the diary of another Polish writer, Witold Gombrowicz, a specialist in detecting shame and ambivalence. "With Geneviève Serreau and Maurice Nadeau," he writes in an entry from 1963. "Little supper. Truffles à la Soubise and Crème Languedoc Monsieur le Duc. I am talking, they are listening. Hmm. I don't like it . . . when from Buenos Aires I went to provinces, to Santiago del Estero, I was silent and the local writers were talking. . . . The one who talks always wants to prove something, the one from the provinces."[11] Perhaps Miłosz wanted to prove something. He was from the provinces.

But—and here is another of Miłosz's ambivalences—being from the provinces certainly did not cause him to feel inferior toward Brodsky. His phrase "my friend" was to overcome a different cleavage—a deep historical and class separation between the two of them. In another remarkable poem—"1913" (translated by him with Robert Hass)—Miłosz describes two travels, one undertaken by his presumed ancestor in 1913, when the world was about to collapse, the second by himself in the present. The ancestor is going abroad, and his "factotum Yosel" is traveling in the same train, though in third class; on his contemporary visit to Venice, he takes coffee in Piazza San Marco with "Yosel's grandson . . . / Talking of our poet friends" (*NCP,* 424). In the Polish original of the poem, Yosel—the Yiddish version of the name Iosif-Joseph—is not identified by the word *factotum,* but by a probably untranslatable noun denoting a Jewish tenant who is renting and managing the property of his landed lord, be it an inn or an orchard. That word—*pachciarz*—is negative, encompassing an abysmal class, religious, and racial difference between the owner and his factotum. They were from the same part of Europe, as Miłosz wrote in his first letter to Brodsky, and the poem is the clearest indication that the

Polish poet remembered the "geological" dimension of their relationship, which, in his insistence on calling Brodsky "my friend," he tried to show did not matter. Brodsky, too, remembered it when he called him "Pan Czesław."

The motif of the humiliation "in the shadow of the empire" is recurrent throughout Miłosz's work. "My country will remain what it is, the backyard of empires, / Nursing its humiliation with provincial daydreams"—he writes in the poem "Return to Kraków in 1880" (*NCP*, 427). Russia, too, appears in his poems with great regularity, though not always named as such. In the poem "On the Other Side" (1964), Miłosz describes a landscape through which his soul would walk after his death, a landscape that is both inferno and Russia:

> *Then I trod in wheel-ruts*
> *On an ill-paved road. Wooden shacks,*
> *A lame tenement house in a field of weeds.*
> *Potato patches fenced in with barbed wire.*
> *They played as-if-cards, I smelled as-if-cabbage,*
> *There was as-if-vodka, as-if-dirt, as-if-time.* (NCP, *200*)

No splendor or proud monuments; the empire, for him, is violence, poverty, and degradation.

Miłosz rebels against the imperial strength, history, and culture, as is clearly visible in his attitude toward the great Russian poet Osip Mandelstam. Beloved poet of Brodsky, Mandelstam was born in 1891 in Warsaw, which was then a provincial city of the Russian empire. In 1914, a year after having published his first volume of poetry, Mandelstam reacted to the creation of Polish patriotic (read: anti-Russian) battalions of Józef Piłsudski, by writing a scornful poem directed to the Poles and reprimanding "the Polish, Slavic comet" for reflecting the Habsburg, that is alien, light. For Mandelstam the Poles belonged to the great family of Slavic nations whose natural homeland was in the Russian empire. That poem, written in the spirit of Pushkin's anti-Polish poems of 1831, could not endear Mandelstam to Miłosz.

In 1937, shortly before Mandelstam's arrest and death in transit to a camp, the Russian poet wrote an untitled work that is known as his ode to Stalin. The poem is an object of many controversies; it seems that Mandelstam's widow and Anna Akhmatova tried to suppress its publication, though the author himself was proud of it. Clare Cavanagh has written that its existence darkens and "complicates our portrait of the artist's final days in multiple ways."[12] The ode is, in fact, a very surprising and confusing work of art. In its construction, it follows Pindar's model of rigidly structured praise. It has seven twelve-line rhymed stanzas, with a regularly patterned changing number of syllables and accents; unfortunately, the English-language versions reflect only the content of the work, not its form. There are definitely two persons, two characters present here, the artist who describes, and the "warrior," whom the artist has to "praise, guard, and cherish." Sometimes the artist seems to be more important than the object of adulation. Here are the initial lines:

> *Were I to take up the charcoal for the sake of supreme praise—*
> *For the sake of the eternal joy of drawing—*
> *I would divide the air into clever angles*

> *Both carefully and anxiously.*
> *To make the present echo in his features*
> *(My art bordering on audacity),*
> *I would speak about him who has shifted the world's*
> *Axis.*

The word *axis—os'—*is a play on the poet's first name, Osip, and on the first name of Stalin, Joseph, hence the "audacity" of a line above. A series of almost perversely complex praises follow, with the poet always reflecting on his act of praising and predicting his own death. Toward the end of the ode, he says: "I shall be resurrected . . ."[13]

Miłosz criticized this poem harshly, declaring at the same time his adoration of other works of the poet. His essay "A Commentary on the 'Ode to Stalin' by Osip Mandelstam" appeared in a modest Kraków periodical, *NaGłos*,[14] and would probably have passed unnoticed had it not been reprinted in the weekend edition of the daily *Gazeta Wyborcza,* at the initiative of its editor-in-chief, Adam Michnik—challenged to do it, as he said to me, by Miłosz himself, who thought he had written something "politically incorrect." An editor at *Gazeta,* Joanna Szczęsna, reworked the essay for the newspaper reader: she cut out, for example, a few sentences about Brodsky, which constituted an aside. This is very interesting for us, because it is typical of Miłosz's recalling on any occasion his by then dead friend. The most important change, and the most conspicuous, consisted in the replacement of the descriptive title from *NaGłos* by Miłosz's words "without shame or measure," taken from his sentence: "Calling the things by their name, the 'Ode' is a hideous Byzantinism, which in its adulation does not know shame or measure." When the essay was later reprinted in a volume, Miłosz removed this sentence at the suggestion of the volume's editor, Marek Zaleski: it was, I assume, an indirect acceptance of certain arguments of his critics. In the version edited and printed by *Gazeta,* the meaning of the essay was not changed, but its tone became more harsh. A series of sharp criticisms followed. Mandelstam was defended by, among others, Russian-language writer Fazil Iskander, by Anatoly Nayman, and Polish critic Adam Pomorski. Miłosz felt offended by the editorial cuts of the newspaper editor. In a telephone conversation ("Here is Miłosz!"), he said to me, using, as usual, rather antiquated language: "It looks like an attack on Mandelstam, Michnik already explained himself."[15] Miłosz wrote a reply to his critics but did not give it to *Gazeta.* It appeared in another daily, *Rzeczpospolita,* under the title "The Poet and the State" (December 7–8, 1996).

This controversy clarified Miłosz's views on Mandelstam and on the place of a poet in society. He protested the cuts and the change of title, but there was no difference in content between the second essay and the first one, which opened with the statement: "The Polish—but not only Polish—legend of Mandelstam as a martyr for freedom of thought does not correspond to the facts. It is a bit as if one were to find, among the martyrs for faith in the Rome of antiquity, a pagan accused by malicious rivals of lacking loyalty toward Caesar." (It is interesting to note the use of the context of the Roman empire, which is so often invoked by both Mandelstam and Brodsky; it is Russia that makes Miłosz think of Rome.) In the second essay, he acknowledges Mandelstam's "mastery of craft" in the ode to Stalin, so often mentioned by his defenders, but goes on to say that all mastery pales when one considers the object of the apology, "the criminal, whose name should be covered with infamy for centuries." He also rejects the argument, advanced by the Russians, regarding the centrality of the relation between the poet and the czar; it goes so far as to claim a certain equality between them. Miłosz describes the fate of Mandelstam—his support for the revolution of 1917, his "Bolshevization," his need to belong to the people—without accusatory zeal, but also without his customary compassion. Although he finds the love of Russians for their state admirable since it is "the exact opposite of the Polish fondness for anarchy," the ode to Stalin arouses his disgust. Miłosz also wrote odes—one to Wałęsa and one to John Paul II—but he never praised a tyrant. In the Polish romantic literary tradition, the poet may raise his voice to challenge God, but he never lowers himself to the level of a tyrant.[16] In this response to the critics in *Rzeczpospolita*, Miłosz declares: the Polish poet defends the existence of his stateless nation, while the Russian poet "is thinking about the force needed by the state."

In an aside edited out from the first text about Mandelstam, Miłosz declared that he had no occasion to talk about this issue with Brodsky, but that the "ode was [for Brodsky] a not-so-small problem." Miłosz was mistaken. Brodsky appreciated the ode to Stalin very much, as attested by at least two testimonies. One of them comes from a conversation with Solomon Volkov, printed posthumously and not authorized by Brodsky. "To my taste," Brodsky said, "the best thing written about Stalin is Mandelstam's 'Ode' of 1937. In my view, this may be the grandest poem Mandelstam ever wrote. Even more. This poem may be one of the most significant events in all of twentieth-century Russian literature. That's my belief. Because this poem of Mandelstam's is simultaneously both an ode and a satire, and out of the combination of these two opposite aspirations arises an utterly new quality. This is a fantastic work of art." He then goes on to analyze the literary technique Mandelstam used in the text and to explain that Mandelstam "was taking a remarkable theme that runs all through Russian literature, 'the poet and the tsar.' In the final analysis, this theme is resolved to a certain degree in the poem inasmuch as it points to how close the tsar and the poet are. To do this Mandelstam makes use of the fact that he and Stalin share the same first name [Osip=Iosif=Joseph]. So his rhymes become existential" (*CJB*, 31–32).

The relationship between the czar and the artist—the poet, but also prose writer, film maker, composer—is a topos present throughout the history of the Russian state; it was especially alive during the height of Stalinism. Stalin's famous interventions, for example, into the work of Boris Pasternak and Dmitry Shostakovich became the source of legends. Brodsky continues that Russian literary tradition: there is no separation of literature and state. A poem is an ultimate reality, it "resolves" things, its power is stronger than physical force. By writing his poem, Mandelstam "invades" the intimate sphere of Stalin: "If I were Stalin," Brodsky says to Volkov with striking violence, "I would have slit Mandelstam's throat immediately. I would have realized that he'd violated me, he'd moved in, and there's nothing more frightening or shocking than that" (*CJB*, 31). He expressed a similar opinion, only slightly less violently, in a letter written in 1993 to Professor James Rice. The poem is part satire, part ode, and expresses no fear or ambivalence—it is a magnificent attack à la Sherman.[17] This is obviously a sincere expression of admiration for the poem, and for the extremely skillful inclusion of hints of criticism in extravagant praise. Brodsky is awed by the challenge the poem constitutes for the "czar" and by the audacity of the poet who places himself at the czar's level.

What are we to make of the conviction of the privileged relationship between the czar and poet? Both Anna Akhmatova and Marina Tsvetaeva wrote that Pushkin's name obliterated that of the czar who tormented him—the period in which they both lived is called "Pushkin's epoch." The South African writer and Nobel laureate J. M. Coetzee is also fascinated by this relationship between the word and power. Conscious of politics, he wrote that "only at the price of retreating into a rigid formalism can the issue of Mandelstam's sincerity, with its political as well as its moral implications, be evaded." But then he arrives at a conclusion somewhat similar to Brodsky's. Stalin seemed to have been especially sensitive to the way his image was to be transmitted to posterity by great Russian poets. No poets recognized as great were killed in his purges, at least intentionally; this is why Stalin called Boris Pasternak and asked about the value of Mandelstam's work. The relationship was reciprocal: the poets understood the importance of their words. A great poem was a threat to Stalin, and that explains, in Coetzee's words, "the lengths to which [Mandelstam] is prepared to go—self-abasing obsequiousness, cloying concern for Stalin's happiness—to mask the threat." These were Mandelstam's "usurpatory urges" he tried to mask. From that confrontation, Coetzee writes, Mandelstam came out "outgunned, but not disgraced."[18]

The tone of the ode to Stalin, so disgusting to Miłosz, is not foreign to Brodsky's own work. Although he never wrote an ode to the czar, he did place himself face to face with the czar of his times, the general secretary of the Communist Party of the Soviet Union, Leonid Brezhnev. When going into exile he wrote an open letter with a romantic, Pushkin-like pathos, undermined, however, in typically Brodskean (and Pushkinean) fashion, by irony and insolence:

> I want to ask you to give me the opportunity to preserve my presence, my existence in the Russian literary world, at least as a translator, which is what I have been [known as] until now. . . . I belong to Russian culture, I feel part of it, its component, and no change of place can influence the final consequence of this. A language is a much more ancient and inevitable thing than a state. I belong to the Russian language. As for the state, from my point of view, the measure of a writer's patriotism is not oaths from a high platform, but how he writes in the language of the people among whom he lives.
>
> I owe everything I have in the world to Russia.
>
> I believe I will return, poets always return, in flesh or on paper.
>
> I ask you to give me an opportunity to exist further in Russian literature and on Russian land. I do not think I am guilty before my homeland.

At the end: If my people do not need my body, my soul will be still useful.

Respectfully, JB[19]

Among his own poems there is a work called "On the Death of Zhukov" (1974), which, like Mandelstam's ode, links the elegiac encomium (for the death of the national hero) with satire (the hero dies calmly in his bed, without weeping for his dead men). The pitch of the praise is, of course, much lower—the protagonist is, after all, a general and not Stalin, and the overall tone of the work is much more satirical. Besides, the poet lives in exile and does not depend on the object of the poem, so it is some kind of poetic exercise. But ten years earlier, in 1964, while in internal exile, Brodsky wrote a poem with a surprising title "Narod"—"The Nation" or "The People." In Brodsky's milieu that word was often used ironically—it was one of the main staples of the propagandistic vocabulary of the Soviet state. The poem expressed solidarity with the people, as do some of Akhmatova's writings. But by Brodsky's literary entourage the poem was considered to be a *parovozik*—"a little locomotive"—that is, an ideological concession that poets would write in order to get into print their other, more important poems. Writing about it in the article entitled "About Akhmatova's Love of 'Narod,'" Lev Loseff disproves this opinion, quoting not only Akhmatova's admiration for the poem but also some lines from her *Requiem* in which the term *nation* or *people* is similarly used. The tone of "Narod" is exalted; it is a combination of the bitter and the sublime.[20] The poem was printed only once in an early samizdat publication, but later Brodsky rejected it together with many early poems he considered immature.

Miłosz, too, wrote a poem called "A Nation," which was at the same time critical and pathetic; one of his most often-quoted works, it is cited both by his admirers and, more often, by his critics. It opens with these striking words: "The purest of nations on earth when it's judged by a flash of lightning. / But thoughtless and sly in everyday toil"; and it closes with: "A man of that nation, standing by his son's cradle, / Repeats words of hope, always, till now, in vain" (*NCP,* 91–92). The poem was written right after World War II, and it expressed all the bitterness and shame of a witness to five years of death, demoralization, and defeat.

The patriotism of Brodsky's poem "Narod" or of his letter to Brezhnev does not seem to be directed toward the Russian state. Valentina Polukhina called him a stepson of Russia because, while still in his country, he never wrote a "civic" poem.[21] In exile, in his interviews, he often expressed his feelings of ambivalence about Russia. In 1987, attending the ceremonies surrounding his Nobel Prize, he said in Stockholm to his Polish editor, Jerzy Illg: "Poland is a country toward which—perhaps it is silly to talk like this—my feelings are stronger than toward Russia. . . . It is clearly subconscious; after all my ancestors, they are all from there, from Brody, hence the last name."[22] This is a declaration made to Poles; in interviews granted to Lithuanians he says that his ancestors lived in Lithuania and spoke Lithuanian.[23] Both of these declarations are true and serve to introduce a distance, to keep Russia at arm's length. But he also said that there was nothing more important for him than Russia. "I am part of Russia, but an opposite statement is equally true. I don't think about Russia, there is not in me a process of thinking about Russia, because it would be thinking about myself" (*StS*, 126).

Brodsky's relation to Russia cannot be defined simply as love, and his ambivalence can be clearly seen in the conversation with the editor-in-chief of *Gazeta Wyborcza*, Adam Michnik. I should say, before proceeding, that it is difficult for a person who has grown up in Polish culture to understand and talk about the issues of empire from a perspective other than that of victimhood or resistance. For Poland, empire means oppression. Even the proudly remembered Polish empire—Rzeczpospolita Obojga Narodów, or the Commonwealth of Two Nations—is remembered and valued as an anarchic one-class democracy, with an elected king, independent and numerous nobility, and raucous miniparliaments. What every Polish child is taught is that Poland was then a unique place of tolerance and diversity. The benign vision of Polish conquests and occupations as civilizing missions is another version of the same outlook, ahistorical and usually unchecked on the level of popular culture. That culture is the culture of a nation-state, and today's Poland—the country of one nationality, one religion, one ethnicity—is understood as a final standard toward which the entire Polish history has been striving. This is a vision that makes understanding the attitude of Iosif-Joseph Brodsky toward the Russian empire very difficult.

The *Gazeta Wyborcza* conversation took place on November 10, 1994, a year and a half before Brodsky's death, in a small New School apartment Michnik occupied while lecturing in New York. One has to add that Michnik is a Russophile who avidly follows Russian politics and knows Russian language and literature. He is also a former dissident and political prisoner, and this conversation's disagreements between him and Brodsky were not a result of Michnik's ignorance. I was present at the encounter and I remember its tension, only partially reflected in the transcript that appeared later in *Gazeta Wyborcza*.[24] Michnik identified with the rebellious tradition of Russia, symbolized for him by Chaadayev and the Decembrists, and he ascribed to Brodsky the same tastes and tradition. Michnik's assumptions as to Brodsky's opinions were shared by Polish admirers of the Russian poet: he was anti-Soviet, and therefore had to be a liberal, prodemocratic dissident. Yet Brodsky always repeated that he was not a dissident, and in the conversation with Michnik he rejected this assumption; he was interested only in the individual or in the cultural dimensions of Russia. "If I do represent any tendency," he said, "it is an understanding of culture that does not need political history." He was irritated by all generalizations used by Michnik. "I don't consider myself a member of the Russian intelligentsia," he said. "It would be good to reject these mental categories—Russia, East, West. . . . Who has a right to discourse about two hundred million people?" But then he himself starts to generalize, blaming his interlocutor for it ("It is your fault, Adam"), and the vision of Russia evoked by his words is very pessimistic. "Russia of today is a totally new anthropological zoo. . . . In Russia a history happened that no one understands. It is not only that numberless people were murdered, but also that the lives of millions and several generations run differently from the way they were supposed to. As Akhmatova said—human life, like a deflected river, flew in a different river bed. People were dying having lived lives that were not their own" (6, 8).

As I already remarked, these words of Akhmatova were often recalled by Brodsky in relation to himself and his family. They express a vision of Russia as a country that was devastated, unfulfilled, distorted. Freedom was possible only outside of politics and history, in the life of individuals, in their resistance against imposed categories and behaviors. What is important in Russia, Brodsky said in 1975, is a solidarity among individuals, "a civilization of friendship" between "people whom you can trust."[25] Instead of talking about Russia, he wanted to talk about concrete people, their lives and achievements. "We grew up in the spirit of absolute individualism," he said to Michnik about the people he "trusted." "It was probably a reaction to the collectivism of our Russian existence. . . . After coming to America many of us—I don't know why I feel like using the pronoun 'us' instead of 'me'—I understood one simple thing: in Russia we were more American, much more individualistic than the real Americans. America as an embodiment of individualism was a category of our consciousness." And he adds, ironically, about himself: "I am a dog. Of course I do possess intellect, but in my life I direct myself by smell, hearing and sight. . . . I gave up being governed by common opinions."[26]

Brodsky sidesteps here the issue of Russia in its relation to politics, claiming for himself an apolitical status. He did follow politics; he objected to the Soviet invasion of Afghanistan, and he wrote some political poems about Bosnia's war or Poland's martial law—these were "human rights" reactions of a Western-like liberal. But he never forgot Russia's imperial reach, and the terms of his political thinking did not follow a Western liberal path. His attitude toward Central Europe is a case in point. An entire part of the conversation with Michnik, unfortunately edited out and lost, pertained to Russian-German affinities and a great plain uniting Russian Euro-Asia with the German West. Brodsky gave a short speech which reminded me then of the common attitudes that Russia and Prussia held against Poland and other nations located between them. Brodsky spoke about his strong attachment to a mystical spirit of Russia, a spirit that was shared by Germany. It happened late in the evening, and it was somehow misunderstood or forgotten by the participants of the interview, and then edited out in the first transcription of the tape. The Poles present at the scene, and those who transcribed and edited the interview, did not have an "ear" for such a topic coming from a person they considered their friend. It was assumed that he was one of "us," that he thought like *we* did.

He did not, actually, and another case in point is Brodsky's attitude to the Ukraine. While it seems that the dissolution of the Soviet empire did not affect him, he was shocked by the Belorussian, and especially, Ukrainian decisions to secede from Russia and create separate states. Lev Loseff wrote in his biography of Brodsky that Brodsky's vision of Russia was "from the White to the Black Sea, from Volga to Bug River." He reacted to the creation of the Ukrainian nation-state by writing a poem, which Loseff described as a "long invective directed at Ukrainians" (*LL,* 262). In Pushkin's and Mandelstam's tradition of writing about and to the Poles, he addressed himself to the Ukrainians; the parts quoted by Loseff are brutal and full of offensive ethnic stereotypes. The violence of the poem could be ascribed to the fact that Brodsky's family came from the Ukraine, or, at least, their last name came from the city of Brody in what is now western Ukraine. Brodsky considered Ukraine part of greater Russia. Kievian Rus is the founding mother of Russia, just as for Serbs Kosovo is their cradle. The violence of his invective evokes that troubling Kosovar analogy.

Brodsky read that poem in public just once, at Queens College; somebody transcribed it from the tape of the reading and published it (to predictable outrage) in a Ukrainian newspaper. Tomas Venclova told me that, after having heard the poem, he advised Brodsky not to publish it. The advice was followed and the poem was not published; Loseff calls it the only case of Brodsky's political self-censorship (*LL*, 263). This self-limitation was certainly not due to his fear of being "politically incorrect"—like many émigrés from the Soviet sphere, sensitive to the state control of the language, he considered restraint about ethnicity, gender, race, and religion as a new form of oppression. He made several public pronouncements against Islam and "the East," written down in his essay "Flight from Byzantium."[27] These statements reflected his deep-seated conviction about the opposition between the West and the East, and the superiority of European culture (*LL*, 159–65). So, when he "rejected"—as he was saying—the West-East divide, it was a matter of keeping Russia in the West. He didn't accept the concept of Central Europe because it was pushing Russia further into the East. Miłosz, too, did not want to push Russia outside of Europe, but Brodsky's Europe was more tilted to the East.

A few years after coming to the United States, Brodsky started to write about Russia in an elegiac mode, as if Russia was for him only a memory.[28] For all his devotion to the Russian language, it is difficult to imagine him producing, like Miłosz, a history of the literature of his country—his love of literature did not have the geographic and national stability felt by Miłosz. His personal development had a form of an expansion to the outside, beyond Russia, not so much into the West as into its Latin culture. Even as a young man he was "enlarging his speech," reaching for non-Russian models. After leaving his country, for a period he functioned in Russian, promoting the poets closest to his heart—Mandelstam, Akhmatova, Tsvetaeva. But gradually he moved away from Russian topics. In the second volume of his essays few texts relate to Russian culture, and in the last volume of poetry Italy becomes more important than Russia. "The more one travels, the more complex one's sense of nostalgia becomes," he writes in the essay "A Place as Good as Any" (*OGR*, 35). As he was never truly settled in politics or history, he could not abandon himself to nostalgia. About Russia, as about his family, he was talking "obliquely," "on a slant"—most often when addressing the issues of language or empire.

He often repeated that for a poet the biggest danger comes from repetition and clichés. Akhmatova, Nayman has reported, liked to say: do not repeat, your soul is rich. The advice applied not only to writings, but also to living—Brodsky was always seeking to escape from banality. Once, in a conversation with me, objecting to some platitude, he said that the Russians blame everything on their government, Americans on their parents, and Poles on history. A free man, he wrote somewhere else, did not blame anyone. His radical dislike of the political uses of history formed only a part of his general rejection of the repetition that life imposes. He continued the tradition of Russian literature, but did not take upon himself the Pushkinian role of the national poet, or, Solzhenitsyn-like, of a True Russian. His Russia was the "portable Russia" of her poets. The poets were for him the true Russia, the one outside of political history. His attitude thus was totally anthropocentric, individual-oriented, and this led to his insubordination, his refusal to fulfill the most obvious social requirements. The best example is his dropping out of school when he was fifteen—a thing very rare at that time in his social class. His resistance was almost physical, as proven by the fact that in his seven years of education he went to five different schools. Here the contrast with Miłosz is glaring. The Polish poet graduated on time from every school he attended (he had to repeat one extremely difficult exam at Vilnius University Law School), yet he was very proud of his rebellious spirit—a priest had him thrown out of the classroom because of the insolent look in young Miłosz's eyes. Brodsky never claimed any merit for his rebelliousness. It was only due to my nerves, he would say, and my dislike of repetition.

Miłosz accepted the rules and protested within them, Brodsky was often a wild card. He rebelled, for example, against the role of the victim of communism, and was visibly unhappy whenever, in numerous well-meaning introductions, he was presented as such. The speakers would quote his daring reply to a judge's question during his trial of 1964: " From where do you know that you are a poet?" "I don't know . . . perhaps from God?" This quote was presented as an act of resistance, while in Brodsky's memory it was an honest reply of a person who was embarrassed by the ridiculousness of the whole "judicial" setup. In internal exile, he wrote, read, worked, and later described that period (perhaps only in order to act against cliché) as one of the best in his life. Expelled from his country, he did not fall into the role of a pining refugee; he challenged the very validity of such a role in the text "The Condition We Call Exile." He did not allow his critics to prevent him from writing poetry in English. Quite the opposite: he repeatedly presented himself as somebody who is not classifiable. "Who are you, the author asks himself in two languages," he writes in the essay "Collector's Item," and he replies: "Well, I don't know. A mongrel, then, ladies and gentlemen, this is a mongrel speaking. Or else a centaur" (*OGR*, 150).

The figure of the centaur appears often in Brodsky's poems, one of the shapes hiding the author. The cycle of four poems entitled "Centaurs" is about the encounter of elements that are incompatible. The cycle was written after Brodsky received his Nobel Prize in literature, but it still expressed a deep discomfort with life, not a temporary, passing malaise. The narrator seems to be staring death in the face. Saying good-bye to life is particularly visible in another poem, written after that cycle, "Epitaph for a Centaur." The poem's ironic opening lines state: "To say that he was unhappy is either to say too much / or too little: depending on who's the audience" (*CPE*, 369).

If we would take seriously Brodsky's dictum that the biography of the poet is only in his works, we could take these lines as a fragment of his autobiography. This was the interpretation given to the poem by Mark Strand, who read it during the funeral mass for Brodsky in the Catholic church on the Venetian Island of the Dead. The centaur of these poems best reflected Brodsky's maladaptation to life, portraying "Intransigence, Incompatibility—that sort of thing which proves / Not so much one's uniqueness or virtue, but probability"

(*CPE,* 369). Maladaptation is here presented, not as a result of free will, but as an inborn incompatibility of "his animal part" with his humanity. This is one of many instances in which he explains his insubordination as due to his impatience rather than to his courage. He must be proud of this characteristic since he values instinctive rebelliousness in individuals and in nations, as his pronouncements about Poland will show in the next part of this book.

The Polish philosopher Zygmunt Bauman wrote that a fatherland is a place where a person is like a plant drawing its saps from the soil, and not a free-moving animal. Brodsky's centaur is always in motion: "For years, resembling a cloud, he wandered in olive groves, / marveling at one-leggedness, the mother of immobility" (*CPE,* 369). Stability eluded the poet even in his fatherland, and became impossible in exile not only because of his geographic displacements. For Brodsky, it is hybridity that causes alienation, since it denotes the incompatibility of the spirit with matter. This, I believe, is his way of representing his living with his heart disease and the always present danger of sudden death. The coming of death is clearly foreshadowed in the "Epitaph for a Centaur," and not only in the title. The poem ends: "he died fairly young—because his animal part / turned out to be less durable than his humanity" (*CPE,* 369). Here, too, the pathos of the death is ironically undercut: the materiality of the centaur's body contradicts his spirituality. The body gives off an odious smell, gets sick, fails him, and is the seat of brutal, aggressive instincts. This joining of human and animal elements makes out of the centaur a walking ruin, a monument in motion, strong and brittle at the same time. It is one of many references in Brodsky's work to antiquity—

the centaur himself being a sign of the classical past—but this reference is highly personal, autobiographical. The all-important characteristic of a centaur is his double nature, which prevents him from belonging fully to any realm. Brodsky's heart was failing his indomitable spirit. Not only did he not belong to Russia or the United States, he was also suspended between life and death.

In Greek culture the centaur was in the category of monsters,[29] and the monstrosity of centaurs was preserved in European culture and poetry. Writing about the Polish poet Zuzanna Ginczanka, the scholar Agata Araszkiewicz points to a literary tradition—in the works of Maurice de Guérin, Leconte de Lisle, and José Maria d'Hérédia— of writing about centaurs as violent but wise monsters.[30] Ginczanka was also denied "one-leggedness"—she died in the Holocaust, unable to pass for a non-Jew because of her exotic looks. She is known mostly for her tragic, ironic, and nontitled "Non omnis moriar"–like poem, but she also left a poetic volume titled "O Centaurach" [On Centaurs]. Brodsky pinned to a wall in his New York study an old picture of a centaur and centauress. Such figures signified for him not only hybridity and ambivalence, but also the crossing of boundaries, doubleness, "androgyny" as Miłosz said, in the matters of language and culture, the attachment to both the Russian and English languages, the Russian and American empires. This attachment transpires often through imperial detail—a self-portrait in the form of a centaur or of a chipped statue, as in the poem "Torso." Brodsky was continuously returning to these images, as if finding a home in the signs of empire, an empire in ruins. Unlike a nation-state, empire would survive itself. Nation-state could pass away. Empire meant immortality.

One reason for the recurrence of imperial symbols was that his childhood was spent among the ruined pseudoclassical marbles of the Neva embankment. In the chapter of his book on Brodsky called "The City as a Means of Education," Lev Loseff writes that the young Iosif grew up in a Petersburg full of signs of empire, many of them incorporated into the most important buildings of the city and visible from the windows of his apartment. Even as a child, Brodsky had in front of him an image of an ideal fatherland—an empire based on classical symmetry, on the rhythmic repetition of the same motifs, on a harmony that was identical with force and immortality (*LL*, 23–24). These symbols of empire remained forever impressed on his retina. The high ceiling and walls of his "room and a half" were stuccoed with garlands; the nymphs and chipped torsos were reflected in the river's canals. When he was young, Brodsky wrote, the word *West* meant for him Venice in winter, that is "a perfect city by the winter sea, columns, arcades, narrow passages, cold marble staircases, peeling stucco exposing the red-brick flesh, putti, cherubs with their dust-covered eye-balls: civilization that braced itself for the cold times" (*OGR*, 15). Marble, stucco, monuments constantly reappear in Brodsky's poetry. Even the snow of the long winters of Leningrad functioned as a reminder of empire—as in "the snow, this poor man's marble," from the poem about his mother ("In Memoriam"). Rows of marble statues reflected in the river are for him a sign of empire, as in the poem "Torso":

> *If suddenly you walk on grass turned stone*
> *and think its marble handsomer than green,*

or see at play a nymph and faun that seem
happier in bronze than in any dream,
let your walking stick fall from your weary hand,
*you're in The Empire, friend. (*CPE, *78)*

The poem, dated January 1973, was written in the first months of Brodsky's stay in America. It seems to say: I arrived. A ruined imperial landscape promised to become a home.

Brodsky ironically described leaving Russia as switching one empire for another. But as the term *empire* appears in his poetry very early, we can treat it as a frame for all of his work. He wrote about empire at the very beginning of his poetry writing, in "Ex Oriente" (1963) and "Ex Ponto" (1965). These short poems were variations on the poetic "letters" addressed by Pushkin to Ovid and a prefiguration of Brodsky's own exile, a topic that any Russian poet reached for almost automatically. And vice-versa: the figure of the exiled poet invoked empire. In January 1968, the twenty-eight-year-old Brodsky wrote a poem called "Anno Domini" (*CPE,* 5–7), in which he further developed the theme of empire, clothed in Roman garb. It is the moment of the invasion of Czechoslovakia by the "friendly" armies of the Soviet bloc, an event Brodsky felt ashamed of as a citizen of the USSR. The town of Palanga, located in then Soviet Lithuania, is given as a place of inception of the poem. The narrator, a lonely man separated from everything that is dear to him, writes from a sad province of the empire. This sad, province-in-empire tone characterized all of Brodsky's Lithuanian poems.[31]

Not only Lithuania triggered the topic of empire: his repetition of this term caused Valentina Polukhina to call a chapter of her book about Brodsky "Poet versus Empire." The United States, ancient Rome, Greece, Byzantium, Venice, or Mexico—all these geographic terms were associated with imperial images. Venice especially attracted Brodsky as a former empire, today in ruin. The narrator of such "imperial" poems is always an alienated, ironic, or cynical observer—a character Brodsky may owe to the poems of Pushkin. And the empire itself, or rather its borderland (because the narrator is never in the empire's center) is in a state of decomposition. In the 1960s, when Brodsky wrote "Anno Domini," the Soviet Union was already in decline, but only the imagination and sensitivity of a poet was able to catch it and describe it. Brodsky was an extremely intelligent person, but his poetic intelligence was even greater than his purely rational power. It was not a matter of politics but of poetics.

Brodsky never abandoned the topic of empire, either in poetry or in his essays. The action of his two (and only) dramas, written toward the end of his life, takes place in generic imperial scenery. While mentioning Brodsky's uses of the term *empire*, Miłosz, as usual, assigned the best of intentions to his friend: Brodsky wanted, he said, to purify the Russian language from pollution, to return to "the tested and clear words: empire, tyrant, slave."[32] In the first English-language review that Miłosz wrote about Brodsky's poetry, he says: " 'Empire' is one of Brodsky's prankish words. . . . That their country is also an empire may, for the Russians, be a source of pride, and for Americans, with their strange habit of breast-beating, a source of shame, but the reality is inescapable. For Brodsky, 'empire' also means the very dimensions of a continent, the monumentality itself of which he is fond."[33] Miłosz understands Brodsky's love of empire, especially of its *prostor*—the openness of its space; but as for him, he could never pronounce this word without clenching his teeth. His poem "Epitaph" (1986) sounds like a reply to Brodsky. In this poem, not translated into English, Miłosz writes that when empires fall, as they do and should, they perish together with their rich statues, and we hear in the air the crying of captive peoples, of those who did not live long enough to witness the "agony of the beast." Brodsky felt shame at the thought of the invasion of Czechoslovakia—as though he shared in the responsibility for it; Miłosz identified with the suffering of the conquered. He wrote "Epitaph" three years before the fall of Berlin Wall, not knowing these were the last years of the empire that oppressed him nearly his entire life—the empire condemned "by time, with its contemptuous though tardy judgment."[34]

For Brodsky's generation, as I already mentioned, the term *empire* was a nickname for the Soviet Union.[35] The emotional and intellectual connotations of that term were very complex. There was pride in the power of a country controlling eleven time zones; its sheer dimensions inspired wanderlust and gratitude. There was a love for its culture and language. And there was rejection of the oppression it imposed, of the ridicule of its political system, of the cruelty, mindlessness, and pomposity of its rulers. The irony of the term *empire* undermined the Soviet propagandistic claim of world-wide working-class solidarity. The contemporaries of Brodsky—the unpublished poets, the geologists who were also musicians, electrical engineers who wrote novels—were at home not so much in the Soviet empire as in

Russian culture. They were attached to the empire, to its geographic and historical grandeur, but full possession of the language, full knowledge of the culture was their way to feel a part of a community, perhaps the only way in which many of them could "belong." What they had to offer to their country was respect for tradition, and that meant the continuation of imperial themes: empire was an integral part of that culture, its pride and shame.

According to Miłosz, the classical architecture of Petersburg was at the basis of Brodsky's art, yet the language used by Brodsky is not "symmetrical." He was reacting against the pseudoclassicism of the Soviet newspeak and that made his language anticlassical, fragmentary, resembling a ruin. It reflects the late empire. Unlike Miłosz's calm, ringing speech, his language followed Pushkin's "insane eclecticism." This is how Lev Loseff defined the characteristics of Brodsky's style: changes in tone, in themes, in cultural background.[36] It is a language, writes Sylvia Molloy, "always thirsty, always wanting, never satisfied."[37] The empire is decomposing, the narrator sick and lonely; in this way the theme of empire is linked to the image of ruins and death. It is the decomposition of the empire that explains, according to Mikhail Lotman, the eclectic character of the language and style of Brodsky. "A ruined totality [of empire] engenders a ruined discourse, a melting pot of themes, quotations, languages and styles held together by elementary particles, hints, allusions."[38] The linguistic mobility of Brodsky is the adaptive mechanism of an escapee from a crumbling empire.

Miłosz is right when he declares that the role of a poet is different in the empire from what it is in a country like Poland that is painfully focused on history. Brodsky rejects history and politics because he is entrusted with responsibility for the greatest treasure of the empire—its language. This is where immortality of empire resides. "Because civilizations are finite," he wrote in an essay on Derek Walcott, "in the life of each of them comes a moment when centers cease to hold. What keeps them at such times from disintegration is not legions but languages. Such was the case with Rome, and before that, with Hellenic Greece. The job of holding at such times is done by the men from the provinces, from the outskirts. Contrary to popular belief, the outskirts are not where the world ends—they are precisely where it unravels. That affects a language no less than an eye" (*LTO,* 164). The outskirts are thus the same as in Pushkin's "letters" to Ovid. There too we can find borderlands of the empire that exists outside of time, the stretched-out space, geography plus power. The function of the poet is to write because language, like music, is everywhere the same; it is always composed of vowels and consonants, though it may have a new set of words, even a different alphabet. As he wrote in his "Lullaby of Cape Cod":

> *The change of Empires is intimately tied*
> *to the hum of words, the soft, fricative spray*
> *of spittle in the act of speech. (*CPE, *119)*

The surprising stability of this "linguistic" self-identification—the only one he has, though proposed with irony—explains also the trajectory of Brodsky from Russian to English, another language of empire. What interests him in empire is the material reach of its language.

A proof of such an attachment can be found in a documentary made two years before his death by two young Russian filmmakers who invited him to Venice, where they filmed him, walking, talking, and laughing with his friend Yevgeny Rein. In one scene, Brodsky, standing on a bridge over a canal and dressed in a raincoat and tweeds, looking like an Englishman, says to the camera that even though the Soviet Union collapsed, the Russian language maintains its imperial character, just as English is still an imperial language, though the British empire is no more. And I am using both of these languages, he says, English and Russian, or rather Russian and English, and therefore my worldview is two-imperial. He then adds, after a short pause, and with an impish smile: "You could call me a double-headed eagle."[39]

This statement is a great example of Brodsky's ability to use irony to express poetically (and visually) an idea that would take pages to explain. The double-headed eagle is, of course, the symbol of Russian empire, but also so much much more! And Brodsky had more than two heads: he was a citizen of at least three empires, if not four of them. He was born in the Soviet Union fifty years before it collapsed. He died as an American citizen and resided within the borders of that empire. After his death, he was buried in Venice, a former empire, and, more broadly, in the soil of what used to be the Roman empire. In the last years of his life it was that last empire that continuously attracted his attention. It is there that he resides today, the citizen of protoempire, and, therefore, a custodian of all imperial languages, whatever their alphabet.

SIX

Iosif Brodskij and Poland

It is difficult to recall now the isolation from the outside world that characterized the Soviet Union of Brodsky's childhood and youth. After he dropped out of school at age fifteen, he traveled a lot, working with geological expeditions in Siberia and Central Asia. Later, he often visited his friends in Moscow and Lithuania, and went for vacations to the Caucasus. Today, these territories belong to separate nations, but at that time they constituted provinces of the Soviet empire. Travel within the borders of the empire was not easy. Trucks had the beginning and the end of their journeys written on them in large letters, and kolkhoz dwellers were pinned to their homes exactly as Peter the Great's peasant serfs were. But Brodsky did not complain about that; the crossing of internal borders was not difficult for him.

The real border, the one that truly bothered him, was with Poland, on the Bug river, because behind it the "West" began.

Brodsky was not a typical representative of Russia; in fact, there was nothing typical about him at all. As he somewhat ironically wrote in "I Sit by the Window": "My song was out of tune, my voice was cracked, / but at least no chorus can ever sing it back" (*CPE,* 46). Nevertheless, his relationship to Poland was part of a longer political and cultural history of mutual Polish-Russian influences. Other great Russian poets of the twentieth century also felt a need to reach into different cultures: Boris Pasternak was fascinated by Georgia, Osip Mandelstam by Armenia. Brodsky's generation in the 1950s and 1960s reached out to Poland. That generation came of age in a period of invisible, slow bleeding away of communist ideology. In 1956, the Polish "October" and Hungarian revolt shook the "Socialist bloc." Although a separate state and not a Soviet republic, Poland was then located firmly within the Soviet empire; there was even a rhyme saying "the chicken is not a bird, and Poland is not a foreign country": *Kuritsa nye ptitsa, Polsha nye zagranitsa.* Compared to the Soviet Union, Poland was culturally, artistically, and intellectually open to the West—more so than any other country of the "bloc." And the Russian intelligentsia and their Polish friends did use that opening as much as they were able to.

This situation was captured, like everything else that was important, in a contemporary Russian anecdote. It started with a question: What is different in the ways a Swede, a Pole, and a Russian engage in group sex? In Sweden, group sex is when a Swede has sex simultaneously with several people. In Poland, group sex is when a Pole tells a group of his friends how he witnessed group sex in Sweden. And in Russia, group sex is when a Russian tells how he was in a group of people listening to a Pole who described witnessing group sex in Sweden.

The joke, of course, speaks about the indirect route Russians had to take to reach what Osip Mandelstam (and Brodsky after him) called "world culture." And not only Russians: the same is true of a whole generation of the intelligentsia, born around the time of World War II, from many of the Soviet republics. In the 1960s, Tomas Venclova read, as did many of his friends, "almost all of Western literature in Polish: Proust, Kafka, Musil, and even Thomas Mann, because these books were not accessible in [Soviet] Lithuania in any other language. We bought them sometimes on the black market, sometimes in stores; on the black market we were able to get even Gombrowicz or Miłosz. . . . Friends of mine, some of them beginning writers, some simply intelligent people, learned Polish very early on to know what is happening in the world. I know that it sounds strange, but even *Trybuna Ludu* was useful . . . not to mention *Życie Warszawy*, *Przekrój*, and especially *Twórczość*. . . . For me and my friends it all started in October, after 1956."[1] That was when some bookstores in the Soviet Union opened to the publications of the just de-Stalinized Poland.

Although Venclova and Brodsky lived in different parts of the Soviet Union and did not know each other till the late 1960s, their search for "world culture" led, by geopolitical necessity, along the same path—through Poland. Lev Loseff, the biographer of Brodsky, declares that the poet learned Polish in order to read Camus and Kafka (*LL*, 45). "In those days," says Brodsky in an interview, "the bulk of Western literature, and of news about cultural events in the West, was not available in the Soviet Union, whereas Poland was even at that point the happiest and the most cheerful barrack in the entire camp. People there were much better informed and they were publishing all sorts of magazines and everything was translated into Polish; the publishing house Czytelnik was printing God knows what. I remember I was reading Malcolm Lowry, some of Proust, some of Faulkner, and also Joyce I first read in Polish. So that was the practical consideration: we needed a window onto Europe, and the Polish language provided it."[2] In another interview he says: "There was very little that was translated and we were learning about what was going on from Polish periodicals such as *Polska, Przekrój,* or *Szpilki.* We read them very attentively."[3]

In contrast to Soviet periodicals, which were solemn in tone and circumspect, some Polish periodicals, especially *Przekrój,* were light, satirical, witty, full of fashion photographs and articles about Western art, literature, and philosophy. *Przekrój* was known for translations of Western short stories, *Twórczość* presented Western literature, *Dialog* printed new foreign plays. In an atmosphere of an "emphatic and self-asserting diet of Russian verse" (*LTO,* 360), young members of the Soviet intelligentsia found these periodicals intellectually and artistically inspiring, and attractive in their lightness. For example, Gałczyński's poetry and short theater pieces, with their detachment and "absurdist" gaiety, were profoundly liberating. For the Russian intelligentsia, Poland became an object of "cultural snobbism" (Piotr Fast), or even "Polonomania" (Irina Adelgeim).[4] Venclova and his group of friends, to quote one example, loved things Polish and played at speaking a bit in Polish among themselves; whenever Brodsky came to Vilnius, he would fall into that playful way of speaking and enjoy it very much. The Polish writer Andrzej Drawicz said that when he first met him in Leningrad—at the beginning of the 1960s—Brodsky was "ecstatic about Poland," and that "he maintained that Poland was the poetics of his generation."[5] His attachment to Russia and, later, to the United States was full of ambivalence, and Tomas Venclova maintains that Brodsky truly loved only three countries: Italy, Poland, and Lithuania.[6]

Their generation grew up admiring the Polish anti-Nazi resistance and romantic insurrections, Venclova told me, and certain early Brodsky poems attest to that. In the 1960 poem "Song," for example, he mentions two Polish musical motifs: the anthem and the song about the Battle of Monte Cassino. The Nazi invasion of Poland is also the background of the poem "September the First" (1967).

> *At Poland's border, Germans raised striped bars.*
> *Their roaring tanks, like fingernails that smooth*
> *the tinfoil on a piece of chocolate,*
> *flattened the uhlan lancers.*[7]

These poems contain images of World War II that are unlike the ones continuously celebrated in Soviet film, books, and painting. Perhaps these images offered Brodsky his own, noncliché manner of commemorating war's ravages, which marked his childhood and even his youth.

Part of the interest that Poland held for this generation stemmed simply from its geopolitical location. Brodsky liked to say that Lithuania was a step in the right direction—toward the West. And Poland was a step further. Many Western books mentioned by Venclova or

Brodsky were accessible in Russia only in Polish. The degree to which the language was in fact learned by the poets and how much demanding literature was actually understood (Joyce! Proust!) must have varied (Venclova was probably among the most accomplished readers of Polish translations of Western literature), but it was in Polish nevertheless that the Russian intelligentsia, among them young Leningrad friends of Brodsky, glimpsed Western novels, short stories, and learned about existentialism and other Western "isms."

In Polish-Russian relations it was nothing new for Poland to be Russia's medium for Western culture. Poland was always, so to speak, Russia's Western horizon. Through that "border" came ideas and words. "Polish (both spoken and written) became [in the seventeenth century] the natural linguistic mediator between West European languages (including Latin) and Russian," writes A. V. Issatschenko in his chapter of the history of Slavic literary languages. "The majority of early Russian borrowings from German and the Romance languages bear distinct marks of the Polish pronunciation. . . . Polish remained the mediating language between Russia and the West until the nineteenth century. . . . For a long time, Poland was also a prestigious model in literary matters. Polish metrics was mechanically imitated in Muscovy where a few *poetae docti* (most of them born in Poland) used Polish versification rules in Church Slavonic compositions."[8] This imitation was soon abandoned, as the metrical principles of Polish and Russian are very different—there is much greater metrical similarity between Russian and German or English. This could explain to a certain degree the attraction that English-language poetry held for Brodsky. And also why he called Polish poetry "a French poetry with a Slavic soul."[9]

The importance of Poland as a transmitter of Western culture oscillated with the changes in the political situation in Russia. In the 1950s and 1960s, that role again became vital. The isolation of the USSR magnified Poland's "Western" appeal. Travel to and from Poland was very difficult, yet some direct, human contacts did occur. There were, for example, Poles who studied in the Soviet Union; the road to "world culture" was facilitated for some, including Brodsky, by friendship with them. Before emigrating in 1972, he had never crossed that western border to Poland. He felt frustrated and confined. But he did have direct contact with Poland in the person of a young Polish woman: Zofia Kapuścińska. Several of his early poems, written in the years 1960 to 1965, are dedicated to her and contain Polish motifs.[10]

Kapuścińska, later a professor at Katowice University under her married name, Ratajczakowa, thinks she first met Brodsky in 1960.[11] In the interview with Husarska, Brodsky said of her: "I knew a girl who was from Poland, Zośka was her name; she was studying in Leningrad then. She was married to a physicist, an athletic fellow, so it was a dangerous acquaintance. She knew I was writing poetry, so she gave me, or rather I heard in her apartment, a record with [Konstanty I.] Gałczyński reading some of his poems and I liked them very much. . . . Since I was interested in poetry, I started translating it." It does not seem, however—to judge from the letters Brodsky wrote to Kapuścińska—that an athletic husband existed at all. The main danger to their relationship came from that rigid, irremovable border that, after the young woman returned to Poland, prevented their seeing each other for many years.

In one of his letters to Kapuścińska, Brodsky calls that western border "a red line" (March 15, 1963). "Nobody was so distant from me [as you are in Warsaw], even when I was roaming through Yacutia," he writes in a letter of January 16, 1962 (Yacutia is a part of eastern Siberia). On October 10, 1962, he wrote a poem, dedicated to "Z.K.," about a "borderland," and in another letter from that period (undated), he declares: "If you knew how often I think about Poland. I have a strange feeling that on a clear day she could be seen from here. It is so close."[12] This was a source of incredible frustration: so close, yet continually out of reach. As I mentioned earlier, when finally Brodsky did come to Poland from the United States in 1990, it was, he said, "too late, and not from the right direction" (*LL,* 47).

He did not doubt that Poland belonged to the West. He wrote on March 15, 1963, in the already quoted letter: "I believe that among you, in the West, there is more justice, more naturalness in life. That you do not need heroic efforts to feel calm. That among you it is internal and comes to life earlier than among us. . . . I have to tell you," he continued, "that I love Poland without restraint, that I wrote poems [about Poland] for which in the good old times I would have been shot, but I love her with one-tenth of my soul, and my feeling which I am confessing right now has one-tenth strength. It is a pity, and it is not a pity, because the remaining nine-tenths is my love of freedom, which is everything."

He could not accept the rigidity of the border, though his love of freedom did not have a strictly political character. "The red line" separated countries with the same political system, and Poland did not in fact belong to the West. Poles, as he said later, were not, after all, real foreigners. Discussing with Volkov the relation of Anna Akhmatova to the painter Józef Czapski, Brodsky exclaimed: "Czapski was a Pole, a Slav. What kind of foreigner was he to a Russian poet!" (*CJB*, 230). But when Kapuścińska wrote a letter to him which proved that she perfectly understood his poems, he was moved by being understood by a "foreign woman." And, finally, didn't he himself feel like a foreigner in his own country? "I am sitting at dawn, I write a poem, and then I go onto the street, and see people, my potential readers and understand that I am a total foreigner," he wrote to her (on March 15, 1963). His exile did not change the picture of his life in Russia. "It doesn't matter if I was writing a poem about John Donne or about a cabbage head in the garden; [in Russia] I always felt this terrible divergence between writing and life. And when I've found myself here [in the United States], all of this became more natural and simple. Here I am truly a foreigner."[13]

The letters to Zofia Kapuścińska express Brodsky's double awareness of foreignness and common Slavic identity, and define how he understood the Western character of Poland. Polish everyday life was governed by a different culture, one that was based, according to him, on continuous conversation. In a letter from "Sankt-Petersburg," as he sometimes called Leningrad, dated October 11, 1963, Brodsky described a visit of Joanna Pollakówna, a young poet herself, and daughter of the Polish poet and translator Seweryn Pollak. "My God, how you all know how to converse, each of your words so touching. One is defenseless against that, there is always a feeling as if somebody placed their hand on your breast and looked directly into your eyes: this is how you [Poles] speak, such is the strength of your words." Joanna Pollakówna had been telling Brodsky, Era Korobova, and Anatoly Nayman, in whose apartment the conversation took place, about her reading of Proust. And she was speaking in Polish, a language that "is of tenderness and precision, and that's a terrific combination."[14]

With the language came its culture. Young Soviet intelligentsia read the Polish poets Norwid, Gałczyński, Szymborska, Grochowiak, and Harasymowicz; and developed interest in Polish prose writers, Polish film—especially Wajda's movies—and Polish actresses. They also listened to Polish jazz. Whenever he mentioned Zofia Kapuścińska, Brodsky would emphasize that she introduced him to the works of Gałczyński and other Polish poets. "I began with Gałczyński," he continued in the interview in which he mentioned the dangerous husband of the Polish student, "and went on to do translations of [Julian] Tuwim, [Jerzy] Harasymowicz, [Stanisław] Grochowiak, [Zbigniew] Herbert, and [Cyprian K.] Norwid. I even wanted to translate Mikołaj Rej [a Renaissance poet]. I was a great admirer of Polish poetry." According to Lev Loseff, Brodsky's reading of Polish baroque poets prepared him for his later absorption of John Donne and the English metaphysical poets. And he loved Norwid, whose similarity to Tsvetaeva he enjoyed (*LL*, 46). Asar Eppel, a writer and a good translator of Polish poetry into Russian, says that the kind of poetry written by poets like Norwid, Gałczyński, or Szymborska did not exist in the Russian "treasury of poetry."[15] Brodsky translated all three of these poets, and several others, stretching the vocabulary and styles accessible to his fellow poets and himself.

Many Russian poets in that period earned their living by translating, and Brodsky was one of them. He translated from Greek, Spanish, Czech, Italian—whatever poems were there to work on, proposed by editors and journals. But his Polish translations were more numerous than from any other language (English later won over) and seemed to be of better quality than others (according to Victor Kulle).[16] He continued to translate from Polish after he left Russia, including the six poems by Miłosz. In his last years in New York, he translated Aleksander Wat ("Mice"), Herbert, and Szymborska, the last two into English. During his 1964 trial, he said not only that he was a poet but also that he was a translator of *Polish* poetry. It was while translating that he learned the language well, and, as if in anticipation of what happened later in his relationship with English, he wrote some doggerel in Polish, mostly as dedications or jokes. As an example, I would like to quote from his charming dedication in Polish to "Zośka" on her personal copy of the poem "Prorochestvo" (Prophecy, 1965):

> *Pani o wielkiej urodzie*
> *mieszkającej w pagodzie*
> *chińskiej—*
> *mlle Kapuścińskiej.*

The quoted part rhymes and says, literally,

> *To a lady*
> *of great beauty*
> *who lives in a Chinese pagoda*
> *Mlle Kapuścińska.*

Stanisław Barańczak has translated these light verses for this book as follows:

> *To the great beauty,*
> *Who is so snooty,*
> *She lives in a pagoda,*
> *Strictly on Scotch and Soda*
> *(Both Chinese—*
> *Jeez! . . .),*
> *Is cuter than most Sophies,*
> *And I'm one of her trophies.*

Another little Polish poem written by Brodsky consists of Christmas greetings, accompanied by a drawing of an archangel, sent to Andrzej Drawicz and his wife, Viera. The greetings say:

> *Looking with sad eyes*
> *here and there, Joseph Brodsky [sic!] sends you*
> *Drawiczes, New Year wishes.*[17]

I feel that, for Brodsky, using a language was always linked with rhyming: rhymes were the heartbeat of a language. A language was a living thing, with a rhythm and a voice.

Brodsky's Polish was still alive thirty years after his letters to "Zośka," in 1993, when he received his honorary degree in Poland. This is still another proof of his exceptional talent for languages, and of his extraordinary capacity for absorbing cultures. "I am a sponge," he said about it in the conversation with Husarska. And, as with everything else, he did it his own way. His study of Polish does not remind one of the usual language lessons: it was active, all-encompassing. In the years 1964–65, while in exile in the Archangelsk region, he read the weekly *Przekrój* (Natalia Gorbanevskaya was sending him her subscription issues). In a June 14, 1988, letter from New York to Andrzej Drawicz, Brodsky remembers that "sometime in 64–65 Gorbanevskaya mailed to me in the country [he means where he was in exile] an issue of *Przekrój* with a face on its cover as beautiful as any I have seen since: it was a woman designer, it seems, from Kraków or perhaps from Gdynia, Teresa Wierzbiańska. I hope," he continued, "that in the matter of looks the country did not change that much" (*StS*, 16). It is as if Poland, like France with her Marianne, had for him the face of a woman.

Poland clearly was a source of many kinds of cultural goods and standards: to immerse themselves in Western culture, the Soviet intelligentsia needed more than words. That culture, after all, consisted of objects, music, smells, and images. Going back over his letters, "Zośka" saw that in almost every one of them Brodsky had asked her to send him candles. This shows, I believe, the need he had to make his life aesthetically complete with words, sounds, images, and light. And it was not only Poles who supplied him with candles. Anna Akhmatova brought two beautiful candles for him from her stay in Syracuse, and asked Anatoly Nayman to deliver them to his exile in Norenskaya.[18]

Brodsky kept in touch with Zośka for years, and, at his request, she sent him records of classical music and books, Polish and foreign, which then were easily accessible in Poland and rather cheap. In a conversation with me, she said that she was the one who had mailed to exiled Brodsky the volume of English-language poetry with photographs of the poets, the same volume he mentions in his essay about W. H. Auden, where he says that the anthology was sent to him "by a friend from Moscow" (*LTO*, 361). In the interview with Husarska he said: "I started to read English [when] I was living up North, in my place of confinement or banishment, and somebody sent me an anthology of 20th-century English poetry as well as the collection of John Donne's poems and sermons. I simply started to make those things out." In a letter to me, Zofia Ratajczakowa explains that she had mailed this anthology to friends in Leningrad, for them to deliver it to Brodsky in Norenskaya. That book marked a turning point: Brodsky abandoned Polish and started to concentrate on English. Paradoxically, this is one very important instance of Poland's influence on his life.

The anthology was studied by Brodsky with serious dedication, and was a source of great poetic discovery. His English was not very strong then; he needed the help of a "veritable boulder" of a dictionary. He described these discoveries in his essay on Auden. Later, in exile, Brodsky dined with Auden at the Spenders' in London. Having to seat Auden on a chair that was too low, Mrs. Spender placed the *Oxford English Dictionary* on it. He was "the only man," Brodsky wrote, "who had the right to use the OED volumes as his seat" (*LTO*, 383).

While candles and books were being sent to Brodsky in Russia, Brodsky's poems traveled to Poland. Andrzej Drawicz was the first to translate them into Polish. In fact, Poland was the first foreign country where Brodsky's poems were published. Loseff writes in his biography that during Brodsky's life, fifteen of his books of poems and essays were published in Poland, "more than in any other language, including his native one" (*LL,* 46). In the Soviet Union, he appeared in 1960 in the samizdat publication *Syntaksis.* His poem for children "The Ballad of a Little Tugboat" was published in *Kostior* in 1962—his first official publication in his homeland. He was then already twenty-two, and had been writing poetry for almost six years. Two years later, his poems started to appear in the Russian émigré press: his trial made it impossible to print his poems in his own country.[19] In the United States, his poems first appeared in *The New Leader* in 1964, after he had been sentenced to exile.[20] Of course, he was well known even before having been published, mostly because of samizdat, whose reach was very wide and included Poland. Stanisław Barańczak first read his poems in 1963 in Poznań; in Warsaw around that time, I saw a samizdat notebook containing three handwritten poems of Brodsky. In Russia, his poems were recited from memory by many of his contemporaries, and were even, to his irritation, set to music and sung in private apartments. In this "pre-Gutenberg" era (Nadezhda Mandelstam's phrase), people learned his work by heart and, though he was an "unpublished" poet, he was better known than many of his voluminously printed contemporaries.

His poems in Drawicz's translations appeared in 1963 in the weekly *Współczesność* (Contemporaneity), and his early friendships with Poles, especially with Andrzej Drawicz, and with the poets Wiktor Woroszylski and Witold Dąbrowski, lasted all their lives. The 1993 ceremony at Katowice University was an occasion marked by warm conversations between Drawicz and Brodsky; several times

the Russian poet was moved to tears.[21] "This [what happened in Ka-
towice]," Brodsky said,

> is one of the strongest feelings in my life. And I have had sim-
> ilarly strong experiences twice in my life. Once—it was prob-
> ably in 1970 or 1971—when I learned that a poet whom I
> respect very much, the English poet W. H. Auden, was writ-
> ing an introduction to a volume of my poems; and a second
> time was around the time I received the Nobel Prize in 1987.
> It was in London. I went to the BBC radio station, to say a
> few words to my readers in Russia. And somebody called the
> station, speaking Polish. I was summoned to the phone. The
> call was from Witek Woroszylski, who was then staying with
> Leszek Kołakowski [in Oxford]. Witek says: "I congratulate
> you. I would also like to thank you for the poem you wrote for
> me and Drawicz." "What poem?" I ask. And he: "A Martial
> Law Carol." "Aha," I say, "that one. Not at all." And then he
> says: "You simply don't know, don't understand how it was."
> It turns out that somebody cut this poem written in English
> out of a newspaper and slipped it under the door of their cells
> while they were incarcerated. Without exaggeration I can say
> that this made a bigger impression on me than the Nobel
> Prize and all that was linked to it. And since I am reminiscing,
> the third event that shook me so much was indeed yesterday's
> experience [here in Katowice] in the Wyspiański Theater.[22]

Never before, it seems, had Brodsky been exposed to so much gen-
uine admiration as in Katowice, and he lost his usual composure. He

knew how to react to hostility, he explained afterward, but was totally disarmed by affection. Hence his tears.

On the occasion of receiving the honorary doctorate from Katowice University, Brodsky said, "Poland is dear to me." He spoke in English—he decided not to give his speech in Russian, fearing he might offend Polish national sensibility. Thanks to the Poles, he said, he understood what independence is. The compliment was significant, coming as it did from one of the most independent people of the second part of the twentieth century. What he must have had in mind was political independence: he was part of a generation that possibly learned some of its ideological detachment toward communism from Poland. It is worth noticing that the image of an independent, rebellious Poland forms a part of long-standing Russian cultural baggage. Brodsky liked to repeat approvingly what is to me a rather derogatory saying of Akhmatova, who, quoting Mandelstam, would say that Poles do not know how to fight but know how to rebel. This saying has a long and unpleasant history, having been used by Catherine the Great as well as other occupiers of Poland to ridicule Polish efforts at resistance. (Bismarck is rumored to have said that Poles are poets in politics and politicians in poetry.) But for Brodsky, and perhaps for Akhmatova, it meant that, unlike Russians, Poles would always resist, never break down, no matter what the outcome of their rebellion. Brodsky found proof of it even in Polish vocabulary: the word *niepodległość,* meaning political and social independence, represented for him a special concept, translatable into its etymological origin (as he believed) of "never lying down under something." He rendered it in English as "un-prone-ness," "un-submissive-ness." As he saw it—and this was the main topic of his speech at Katowice University—Polish rebelliousness was determined by linguistic inevitability.

In expressing his gratitude to Poles for that rebelliousness, Brodsky emphasized the innate, involuntary, predetermined nature of their dissent. Poles cannot help it: they have to rebel even if it is not reasonable. In the Katowice speech, he talks about this instinct approvingly: "It was neither the force of your arms nor a conscious choice to resist that brought that political system down, but one word [*niepodległość*], or just its prefix [*nie*] euphorically triggering your instinctive response to it."[23] If I feel a bit uneasy about this statement, it is because we all come from cultures that value Aristotle's "autonomy of will" in politics, conscious choice over instinctive response, however noble. Is stubborn instinct superior to free will? Would Poles' *deliberate* resistance, planned and successful, be less valuable? Was it truly so instinctual? Also, Brodsky's claim reminds me of his negative attitude to the Decembrists' insurrection, especially to the fact that they lost (he blamed it on their character). Paraphrasing Pushkin's disdain for the Pugachev Rebellion, he ridiculed the Decembrists' effort for its "mindlessness."[24] The Polish public took the Katowice speech as one long compliment.

Brodsky praises stubbornness and rebelliousness in individuals, but what about entire nations? What is interesting here is a certain ambivalence—felt, I imagine, by those who grew up in an imperial culture—toward brave people on the empire's margins, especially if these people have a history of serial, unsuccessful efforts at liberation. Brodsky was always acutely aware of the imperial character of Russia, and he radically subverted the empire's pull upon himself by feeling (and being) an outsider. But he saw Poles as a "small nation," and Poland as "a small country," or so he wrote in the introduction to the Italian edition of Zbigniew Herbert's poetry.[25] The smallness is of course relative (Poland has 40 million inhabitants), and stems for him, I believe, from Poland's political weakness in relation to Russia. His is, *nolens volens*, an imperial gaze passing over a small, rebellious province.

Brodsky's imperial perspective may have been a reason for some friendships manqués with Poles. Gustaw Herling-Grudziński, an exiled writer and author of one of the most important testimonies about the Soviet Gulag, met with Brodsky at a dinner in Rome in 1981, right after the imposition of martial law in Poland. They were brought together by another émigré, Chicago-born writer-translator Ronald Strom, who wanted them to become friends. "The dinner was a total fiasco," Herling wrote later, "and even ended with a quarrel. . . . It was the matter of martial law, Brodsky spoke about it with, to my taste, too much of sometimes overly Russian understanding. . . . But maybe I gave into a provocation? This suspicion does not let me in peace whenever I remember that evening in Trastevere."[26] This was, I believe, a rather typical encounter between suspicious Polish émigrés and Russians. The wound of empire was open.

There was a habit in Russia of sometimes assuming Polish cultural superiority (deriving from the Latin influences and other contacts with the West), while claiming Russian priority in matters of morality and religion. It is enough here to mention Dostoyevsky, who despised Poles as being devoid of true spirituality. That was definitely not Brodsky's attitude. Yet some remarks of Brodsky (he liked to say "those Poles" with a smile and a little shrug), led me to ask Anatoly Nayman, Brodsky's contemporary and a member of his poetic group, about their "sizing" of Poland. "Don't fool yourself," he said, "Poland is not important to Russia."[27] Indeed, in Nayman's *Remembering Anna Akhmatova*, a book that relates readings, intellectual and artistic influences, and literary culture of the late 1950s up to the mid-1960s in Leningrad and Moscow, the only indication of anything Polish is Akhmatova's quoting of Mandelstam about the Poles who only know how to rebel. Yet, Nayman too learned some Polish, read books in Polish, and translated Polish poetry into Russian, including Szymborska's work.[28] The same is true of another book describing the youth of Brodsky and his friends, Ludmilla Shtern's *Brodsky: A Personal Memoir.* Shtern writes about her friends who learned Polish: "Not that the Polish culture held any special attraction for these young Russians. It just happened that Polish magazines were allowed to circulate in Russia legally, and the Polish language was fairly close to ours. These magazines were our windows on the Western world."[29]

For Brodsky, as we have seen, Polish language, poetry, and contacts were much more important than they were for Shtern or Nayman. But all of his statements about his feelings about Poland come from his texts—speeches, letters, interviews—directed to Polish recipients. In the most important part of Brodsky's work, his poetry, the Polish theme ends with his emigration. And there is nothing about Poland or its culture in his essays; they express the intellectual and poetic interests of his life in the United States of America. I have already mentioned his early poems, many of them dedicated to "Z.K."

(Zofia Kapuścińska) and containing Polish motifs. "A Martial Law Carol" was a kind of a letter written to his friends. Another later poem, "Polonaise: Variation," also dedicated to Kapuścińska, contains Polish (and musical) motifs, but the polonaise itself was a common form in Russian music; it served as the first anthem of Russia. Thematic mentions should not, perhaps, be the only way in which the impact of a culture is detected. Ann Kjellberg, for example, considers Brodsky's poems about Lithuania similar to the "Polonaise" and related "in spirit" to Miłosz's "Elegy for N.N.," a poem Brodsky admired, translated into Russian, and taught in his college poetry classes every year.[30] A sentence from that poem, "And the heart does not die when one thinks it should," was taken as a motto for Brodsky's first volume of essays, *Less than One*. According to Brodsky, it was one of the greatest lines of poetry written in the twentieth century. But one cannot detect any definite direct literary influences of either poet on each other—in their poetry they made no literary concessions to the other's tastes. As admiring as they were of each other, as important as their friendship was, they each wrote in their own way. Their mutual admiration did not leave traces in their poetry.

Brodsky addressed the issue of literary influence in his essay about W. H. Auden. "Man is what he reads," he writes (*LTO*, 365). In a conversation with Miłosz in 1989, he said something similar: "Everything that you read influences you one way or another, imperceptibly or directly or whatever it is, most likely imperceptibly" (*CCM*, 106). And in another conversation he replied irritably to a question about John Donne's influence on him: "He did influence me. Naturally he influenced me, but then who am I that John Donne should have influenced me? You can't see it in my poems. At least I don't think you can see it. . . . Almost anything you read has some influence."[31] His impatience with the interviewer was a reaction, I assume, to what he considered an imposition of a poetic ancestor; he wanted to build his pedigree all by himself. The beginning of his Nobel lecture was devoted to the influences he did want to acknowledge: Mandelstam, Tsvetaeva, Frost, Akhmatova, "my beloved Auden." "In my better moments," he said, "I deem myself their sum total." He speaks not only in his own name, he adds, but as a representative of a generation that was "born precisely at the time the Auschwitz crematoria were working full blast, when Stalin was at the zenith of his godlike, absolute power." That generation strove for and was able to re-create the continuity of culture—a continuity that "was supposed to be interrupted in those crematoria and in the anonymous common graves of Stalin's archipelago" (*OGR,* 44, 55). To rebuild cultural continuity, they needed to reach back in time into that culture's past, and in space, to the outside. Poland, with her poetry and openness to the West, was part of that "outside."

Poland helped to reconnect Brodsky and his generation to the continuous flow of European culture. It brought in cultural models and languages, Polish and others, that enriched his idiom. It gave him respite from "the diet of self-assertive Russian verse," and provided him with absurd humor, with poetic "magical realism," with colorful objects. All of it helped him to "enlarge his diction."[32] Rather than talk about influence—as influence, like a waterfall, assumes a difference of levels, a flow from higher to lower—one should talk about "spongelike" absorption, appropriation, exchange, transformation, dialogue, continuity. Brodsky loved Polish culture and made good use of it. Polish culture absorbed him and made him her own.

"Poles are a happy nation," he said in 1993. "In half a century they have had as many as three great poets: Miłosz, Herbert, and Szymborska" (*StS*, 7). And in fact, the most stable part of his relationship to Poland came through poetry. "My Poland comes from books," he said in his Katowice speech; "Poland for me is a state of mind or a state of heart rather than a real—police or democratic—state." He felt a great affinity with Polish exiles, whose homelessness brought new friendships. In 1982, at the invitation of Barbara Toruńczyk, he became a member of the editorial board of the newly created, Paris-based literary quarterly, *Zeszyty Literackie* (Literary Notebooks). And his closest Polish friends were all editors, poets, and translators: Woroszylski, Dąbrowski, and Drawicz, as well as, when he found himself in the West, Toruńczyk, Barańczak, Zagajewski, and of course Miłosz. These later friendships form the second chapter of Brodsky's relationship to Poland. He did not read Polish any longer; he did not need it, so to speak. And the three poets—Barańczak, Zagajewski, and Miłosz—were exiles, representing an extraterritorial Poland, "the Poland that comes from books": a country for all poets.

His Polish friendships form an important part of the history of what Miłosz called the confraternity of poets. Brodsky, Barańczak, Zagajewski, and Miłosz collaborated, helped, and translated each other, promoting each other's poetry. Here a special mention is owed to Stanisław Barańczak, to whom, together with his wife, this book is dedicated. His translations of Brodsky's poems and essays into Polish placed Brodsky firmly within the Polish canon. Consequently, when

Brodsky came to Poland in 1993, he met an admiring public fully aware of and conversant with his work.

Brodsky was emphatic about the importance of the Polish instinct for "independence." For him, it was that striving for independence, though not this alone, that undermined the Soviet empire. "It wasn't Solzhenitsyn who finished off Soviet power," Brodsky said in the conversation with Adam Michnik, "but events in Poland [during the Solidarity era] when the Kremlin found itself in a highly unusual situation—in a state of ambivalence. The Kremlin realized that if it sent in the army, it would lose, and if it didn't send in the army, it would also lose. Ambivalence is the greatest catastrophe for an ideologue. The moment it appears, it devours everything: it destroys the will to act. The moment that 'and' appears, it's the end, the end of the system."[33]

Brodsky was right: the collapse of the Soviet empire began in its western territories. Already at the end of World War II, in May 1945, a young staff member of American embassy in Moscow, George F. Kennan, had predicted in an internal memorandum that the Soviet Union might prove unable to swallow the newly annexed western territories. "It should not be forgotten," he wrote, "that the absorption of areas in the west beyond the Great Russian, White Russian, and Ukrainian ethnological boundaries is something at which Russia has already once tried and failed. . . . These western districts [were] a hotbed out of which there grew the greater part of the Russian Social Democratic Party which bore Lenin to power. . . . [They] proved indigestible to tsardom." Kennan argued that absorption of western conquests undermined the Russian political tradition of "unlimited centralization of autocratic power, the Byzantine scholasticism of political thought, the exclusive self-segregation from the Western world, and even the mystic dreams of becoming the world's Third Rome." He predicted that from these territories the "clouds of civil disintegration" would come.[34] And come they did. This is also what Brodsky said—as usual, in his unusual way.

SEVEN

Loneliness as Always: America

In the traditional western-European geographic imagination, America was described as nature. Starting in the sixteenth century, Europe thought of herself as a culture in opposition to America—seen as a territory outside of history and tradition. This juxtaposition continues to form the basis of European descriptions of America, although the terms of this contrast are slightly changed. As an example one can take the well-known work of Jean Baudrillard, *America*. The new continent (still considered new after so many centuries), is seen as an "astral" desert, composed of highways, motels, and minerals, all contrasting with the dense culture of France and the rest of Europe. The contrast between Europe and America functions also within America itself, and is a basis of political conflict. It appears in the clash of urban and suburban cultures, of both coasts with the middle of the country, of the north with the south. In opinion polls Europe's preferences in matters of politics, religion, and customs are similar to those of New York, Boston, or San Francisco. Europe is a hard kernel within America's body.

When Miłosz arrived in California—at the beginning of the 1960s—the distance between Europe and the United States was much greater than it is today, and the intellectual standing of America in the eyes of Europeans was rather low. Although he was teaching at Berkeley, one of America's world-class universities, he felt that he was in the middle of nowhere. He went there out of necessity: "I did not choose California," he wrote in *The Separate Notebooks*, "it was given to me" (*NCP*, 364). He had come because of a job offer—as many economic migrants before and after him did. He needed to make a living: he had a family to support. He knew that twentieth-century America produced a culture, but believed it was only a mass culture. Even during his childhood "the movies meant that America was beginning its expansion," and today "artists and writers from all kinds of countries journey to America as to a land of opportunities" (*ABC*, 26, 27). He understood that he was one of those who would help in this expansion, because his was an important voice in the generation that abandoned the French language, with all its culture, for English. English would become the language by means of which he gained recognition and the highest literary laurels. America recognized in him her own poet.

California owes a lot to Miłosz, declared Leonard Nathan in his elegy for the Polish poet, his West Coast neighbor. He also asked whether Miłosz's poetry would have been different had he lived those forty years somewhere else. It is impossible to answer this question; Miłosz was a fully mature poet and writer when he started his Berkeley tenure. Some themes and preoccupations of his later work—actually of the second part of his opus—seem to be linked to the place in which they were written. Ewa Bieńkowska enumerates among them the wide-angle lens with which Miłosz looks at the world, his consciousness of the universality of human life.[1] His mind was open and receptive, continually examining his surroundings, and there is no doubt that he made the most of those forty years in California. Thanks to him California appeared in Polish poetry as the land of ecstasy—as in one of Miłosz's best-known poems, "The Gift": "A day so happy. / Fog lifted early, I worked in the garden" (*NCP*, 277). But, in keeping with the nature-culture opposition, California was most of all a "scorched emptiness," an unchosen land of untamed nature.

At first, Miłosz's life there was difficult. He found the separation from Poland and his readers very painful; his wife was afflicted by a long illness, not only of body but also of mind; and one of his sons also fell ill. Few of his acquaintances visited California, and he felt as if he lived on a different planet. "The view of the Bay, the islands, and the skyscraper city seen from the Berkeley hills is spectacular, but lunar" (*ABC*, 59). He nevertheless declared his need to grow roots in the place where he lived. And he lived in so many places, countries, houses. "I am here," is the first, terse sentence of his most Californian book, *Visions from San Francisco Bay*. He wrote the book to resist the disorientation that results from emigration; it was a clear-eyed decision to accept what is happening, an attempt to settle in. The phrase

"I am here" bestows a material dimension to his "visions," a solid footing in that "lunar place." "I am here. Those three words contain all that can be said—you begin with those words and you return to them. *Here* means on this earth, on this continent and no other, in this city and no other, and in this epoch I call mine, this century, this year. I was given no other place, no other time, and I touch my desk to defend myself against the feeling that my own body is transient. This is all very fundamental, but, after all, the science of life depends on the gradual discovery of fundamental truths" (*VF,* 3).

"The touching of the desk" is therefore a search for a fixed point, so that one can orient oneself rather than get lost. It is the desk, because through writing the poet builds up and gradually enlarges the space in which he can settle. For it is space that forms the central concept of *Visions from San Francisco Bay.* Miłosz is quoting his relative, the poet Oskar Miłosz: all our ideas have their origin in our concept of place. One of the chapters of the book takes up the problem of "facing too large an expanse." His imagination is always spatial. "There are many cities and countries in my mind," he writes, "but they all stand in relation to the one which surrounds me every day. The human imagination is spatial and it is constantly constructing an architectonic whole from landscapes remembered or imagined; it progresses from what is closest to what is farther away, winding layers or strands around the single axis, which begins where the feet touch the ground" (*VF,* 6–7). Time is also important, for the ground which was touched first, at birth, forms a primal map, kept in mind even during exile. In *From the Rising of the Sun,* Miłosz wrote about faithfulness: "Even if I were gathering images of the earth from many countries on two continents, my imagination could cope with them only by assigning them to positions to the south, north, east, or west of the trees and hills of one district" (*NCP*, 293). The possibility of happiness is also spatially determined, since "one of its conditions is that a certain modest human scale not be overstepped" (*VF*, 37). Even self-consciousness depends on space, because it consists of a movement toward one's own center, unfortunately futile, as "one can never be sure if that center truly exists or is identical with oneself" (*VF*, 39). Movement in space supports, conditions, and surrounds our life.

In Europe, space is pregnant with meaning, because numberless generations tamed and named it. That meaning is accessible for the poet and therefore the space belongs there less to nature than to culture. In California and in the rest of America the situation is different, as nature is omnipresent, it is "an endless void, populated here and there, and from time to time rising up into cities" (*VF*, 141). During the panel discussion with Brodsky at the Institute for the Humanities, one of the discussants, the editor of the *New York Review of Books*, Robert Silvers, asked Miłosz about his attitude toward America. "My clinging to one language, Polish, in a way is symbolic also of my clinging to certain attitudes which are un-American," said Miłosz. "Un-American. Because I have no tenderness for nature. . . . I am far from romanticizing nature, and if I have to choose I choose the world of history. Because history is human, encloses us in a certain cocoon built by the language, built by tradition, built by our civilization, and there is a profound opposition of the world created by humans and nature, which doesn't know good and evil." Silvers protested: "But you wrote that beauty of the earth is something that cured you," and went on to quote Miłosz's poem "Rivers," written around the time of the panel discussion. Miłosz responded, "But beauty is something else than nature."[2]

Miłosz feels that nature is hostile, that it continuously threatens man's physical fragility. The relentlessness of hunger and thirst, the sicknesses, the "humiliation of death," provoke rebellion in the poet, who writes that "the human being is worthy of admiration because he suffers so much and remains undaunted in spite of it" (*VF,* 150). America, this "illegitimate child of Europe," was founded by the poor, by the unhappy ones pushed by needs that were physical rather than spiritual. This is why the emigration to America, as opposed to the emigration to France, was for Miłosz a voyage outside of culture. Too few layers of human time were deposited in California. So even though he recognized that what was happening in California could be the sign of things to come—he was writing in the years of student protest and technological revolution—there was not enough culture to defend human beings, as far as it is possible, against nature. The human being is one in an endless multitude, facing a nature "impenetrable in its opposition to meaning" (*VF,* 68). It is only by one's continuous effort that meaning can be produced.

Miłosz generalizes his own condition of emigration onto all of humanity and calls America the country of the greatest and most extreme exile. It is a continent of chronic homelessness. "Human particles were torn from their ground earlier and on a larger scale in America than anywhere else, and this made America the unintentional precursor of modern life. . . . This land of the exile became almost a paradigm of all exile, and especially of the exile from a mental space made hierarchic by the Throne of God." Religion is also governed and built around space. "European civilization was founded on certain spatial equivalents of religious truths. These were vertical patterns—Heaven, Earth, Hell—as well as horizontal—the perilous travels of knights in search of the Grail, the legend of the Crusades" (*VF,* 207–8). Space without religion is senseless, useless—a nowhere.

The biblical echoes are not accidental—*Visions from San Francisco Bay* is a religious book. Miłosz asks himself who he is, where his loyalties lead him, who he wants to become and who he wants to remain. The world that surrounds him is not that of a small village of his childhood, centered on a church. California is full of religions, cults, desperate searches for various forms of spirituality. Miłosz makes what is for him a typical double movement: he is open and curious about other religions, while remaining totally faithful to his Catholicism. His curiosity, his recognition of human diversity do not bring acceptance of other religions, but accord other faiths an unquestionable right to exist. This is not a very common émigré attitude: the very situation of being an exile, as described apropos of Miłosz by the perspicacious Polish writer Jan Błoński, forces that person to define himself or herself *against* something, especially against the West, because this is the only way of maintaining one's originality.[3] Miłosz was against these new religions, against the West, against adapting himself to the new world; but he was curious, and this was one of the reasons for his intellectual and poetic productivity. The firm footing he found within himself created a foundation, thanks to which he did not fight fanatically against what was new, did not reject it vociferously as so many emigrants did. "I am here," he says, I know who I am. And then he looks around him.

Here, where he is, he establishes his "little homestead of hopes and intentions" (*VF,* 11), his little estate spun from his work, as from a spider's thread. Everything is an effort and a creation—culture, everyday routine, maintenance of life's order, always threatened by the hostile outside. Nothing is obvious, given once and forever, even if previously considered "natural." Migration, especially into the state of nonculture, undermines old automatisms. The truest and most intimate landscapes of childhood turn out to be as much a product of imagination as the most "extreme" landscapes of California, with the difference that they were absorbed much earlier. In the end, Miłosz writes in his *ABC,* the landscapes of California merge with those of his Lithuanian childhood, but the space is not orderly or hierarchic. We should envy Dante, the poet of exiles, that his world had a center— Jerusalem (or Florence)—over which the Heavens were bent. Our world is amorphous, and human plants, governed by chance, put their roots wherever they happen to find themselves.

"Everything depends on the man and his internal health," writes Miłosz in his first letter to Brodsky. That "everything" includes the meaning of his life. Here, in California, space is the greatest enemy: too much space imprisons as thoroughly as too little of it. This is why exiles belong to the same category as prisoners and hermits. The high hill over the San Francisco Bay, where Miłosz's home stands, is a good place to ask: Who am I? To this question, basic also to American literature and culture, the reply is: A disinherited man. A man who every morning has to domesticate anew the accidental place of his life, who has to impart a meaning on that place, because this is the only way in which it will have a meaning. The California that he knows is composed of

> *Grayish clay, dried-up creek beds,*
> *Hills the color of straw, and the rocks assembled*
> *Like Jurassic reptiles: for me this is*
> *The spirit of the place. (*NCP, *364)*

And it not only looks like a cross between the moon and the world of reptiles, it is dangerous:

> *In Death Valley salt gleams from a dried-up lake bed.*
> *Defend, defend yourself, says the tick-tock of the blood.*
> *From the futility of solid rock, no wisdom. (*NCP, *215)*

Nature, however, is only one part of Miłosz's vision of America, especially insistent when he is looking at San Francisco Bay. There is another dimension which he appreciates: the tradition of Anglo-Saxon democracy. He frequently praises the Constitution written by, as he says, highly educated and extremely well-read men. In the Constitution "human equality and everybody's right to happiness are not venerated relics." He does not forget his émigré status and always expresses solidarity toward his less fortunate brothers. What repels him in America is the "demonic character of the fight for survival that appears here in almost unveiled form."[4] It is a country of great extremes, of people who are enormously rich and terribly poor, with a gigantic system of prisons, full of wretches who had no luck. He remembers them, as he remembers those who were exterminated at the very beginning of the building of the American state. He looks at all of this through his own experience and his own physicality. Miłosz's speaking "I" feels compassion even toward a continent.

In *Visions from San Francisco Bay* Miłosz transforms the distance, his isolation, and depression into discipline and strength. America poses for him a challenge to adapt in such a way as to remain himself. He surrounds himself with the cocoon of tradition and overcomes the danger of dissolution in the new world. He writes about secluding himself in a small space, for only in that way, bending over his desk, is he able to continue the thread of his work. He is shielded by history—the opposite of nature, created by people, expressed in their lives and preserved in their memory. This is how he presents the matter in his poems and prose.

This, for example, is how he spoke about it on October 16, 1985, on a panel at Mount Holyoke College, in which he shared the podium with Peter Viereck and Joseph Brodsky.[5] The topic of the panel discussion, entitled "Does History Speak?" was the relation between history and poetry. "My poetry," Miłosz declared, "is permeated by reflection on the flow of time. The flow of time is for me the personal life, and the events and meaning of personal life . . . the reflection on history is an exercise of memory, with all the possible subterfuges, which we observe when we reflect on our personal life. There is a certain lack of clarity or even self-deception when we try to make sense of our personal life. For that reason the idea of the last judgment is very healthy." His is a personal, individualistic vision of history: it is contained in individual lives and its meaning (or even existence) depends on the divine presence. God does not act in history, but does guarantee it. "An enormous desire to endow history with meaning in my opinion is connected with the loss of religious faith, the loss of religious imagination . . . and a need to see a direction in history." He confesses that he does not possess any theory of history or conviction about its finality. He evokes, in support of his words, the "little conversation" between O'Brian and Winston, the characters in George Orwell's *1984:* "What is the past? The past is what is recorded." "What Orwell wanted to say," concludes Miłosz, is "that if the events of the past, both of our personal life and of our history, have no existence in the mind of God, they can be transformed and can serve the use of people who are in power."[6] Without God there is no history.

The great French linguist Emile Benveniste said that history can be written only in the third person of past tenses, without the expressed relation between the speaker and the listener, between "I" and "you." In his poems Miłosz often rebelled against that kind of impersonal history, that "elephant that tramples the nations" and whose "other name is Extinction."[7] His history is different, personal, always filtered through a concrete, individual life, noticed and retained in memory; only later does the generalization arrive. It is enough to mention his poem "Campo de' Fiori," where the extinction of Jews is shown through the solitude of the death of one person, Giordano Bruno, from the perspective of a narrator who sees this association and is talking to us. The separateness and particularity of a person is the basis of history, it is anthropo-history, thoroughly human. In that vision we see some of his most important convictions: profound religiosity, an antisystemic attitude toward social life, concentration on individual life as a measure of social justice. Living in the times of a triumphant Marxism, Miłosz rejects history as justification or even explanation of baseness, history as salvation or class warfare. History is the flow of time expressed in how separate human lives face external conditions. His is a classical attitude, perhaps even conservative, because he returns to the idea that history is governed by human characters and their moral choices performed in everyday life. The portraits of writers in *The Captive Mind,* or the history of the life and death of his Vilnius friend the poet Teodor Bujnicki, function like seventeenth-century "Characters": the external conditions form the background, unfortunately extremely cruel, against which unfolds the drama of decision making, of the rise and fall of people with their particular shortcomings or virtues. Miłosz and his contemporaries lived in dark times, and his judgments are merciful. One's character is important, but there is also the desperate need of luck. And some of the shortcomings can turn out to be a good thing. He often repeated that he did not fall into Marxist orthodoxy because of his sense of isolation, his stubbornness, and his egoism. They served him well.

Miłosz's thoughts on history were pronounced at Mount Holyoke in the presence of Brodsky, and it was an interesting nonexchange of opinions, one of the many occasions in which the poets avoided confrontation and emphasized what they had in common. Brodsky was the first to talk, followed by Viereck. Miłosz politely agreed with them on several secondary points. But his own view of history was very different, though expressed without polemical ardor. Brodsky too, when replying to Miłosz, continued his own train of thought without any polemics. They were soloists, each playing a different piece of music. The difference between their visions of history was enormous, perhaps too large for them to debate it publicly.[8] There were other occasions on which he spoke of history, for example in his essay on Cavafy, where the term "'history' is equally applicable to the endeavors of nations and to private lives. In both cases history consists of memory, record, and interpretation" (*LTO*, 57). Usually, however, he approaches the topic of history "obliquely," through poetic association, escaping didacticism. His talk during the evening at Mount Holyoke College, as well as his essay "Profile of Clio," start with a summary of Auden's poem "Homage to Clio" and with the juxtaposition of Clio, the muse of history, with Urania, the muse of astronomy, but considered by Brodsky the muse of geography because she governs space. The basic difference between life and art is that life consists of repetition, of a routine. Art on the other hand despises repetition, rejects routine, for repetition turns immediately into a cliché. It is a great advantage of art that it always has to be surprising, always revelatory. History is art, because "Clio is the Muse of Time, as the poet [Auden] said, and in time nothing happens twice" (*OGR*, 118). During the conference at Rutgers, he bitterly supplemented this judgment: "History never does repeat itself, for the very simple reason that one of the primary mediums of history is murder: each time a different man dies."[9]

In his writings, then, Brodsky rejects history. He points to its accidental character, its brutality: for him history is not produced by the intentional work of people. "By itself reality isn't worth a damn. It's perception that promotes reality to meaning" (*LTO*, 152). A historian, he writes in "Profile of Clio," can work only on what does not exist anymore, and therefore knows nothing for sure. He is also unable to predict what has not happened as yet. In history only surprises are certain: we are always surprised by history because, in our repetition-based life, we never accept history's uncertainty. We search history for rationality, thus always becoming its victims. Urania is a bit more friendly: "Any movement along a plane surface which is not dictated by physical necessity is a spatial form of self-assertion, be it empire-building or tourism" (*LTO*, 398). History constitutes for Brodsky the same kind of danger that nature constitutes for Miłosz—blind, mindless force, crushing human bones. His escape from history, like Miłosz's escape from nature, leads through culture, but he understands it differently. Our defense against history—against total destruction—is contained in language. Poetry, the highest form of language, domesticates, organizes time, discovers the past, bows before our ancestors' shadows. The poet has to ignore history, which, in its vulgarity, enslaves human beings and kills them in the end. "Basically, talent doesn't need history" (*LTO*, 153). The escape from history is the escape from the role of a victim, from any determinism. And from unforgiving time.

For Brodsky, Poles have a right to be preoccupied with history since they are its victims. As for himself, he does not need it because he looks at the world from the perspective of empire—and empire, even after its collapse, continues to exist in its art and language. He does not want to discuss crimes and punishment, he rejects political and state-oriented forms of argument, as if they had value only for the small, dependent nation-state. There is still another reason why he does not want to accept "historical thinking about causes and results." Within the empire he himself is "a little country," a victim, minority—in the Soviet Union a persecuted poet, in the United States an émigré. He does not want to accept this role, nor does he want to place a claim for damages. In "Profile of Clio" he writes that although he is ethnically a Jew, he does not identify with the Jews killed during World War II, but with the twenty million Russians killed, because there were more of them. His friend Derek Walcott, whose origin could easily fit into the horrendous pattern of the sufferings due to colonialism, takes a similar stand. History, according to him, consists of searching for the guilty, and inexorably ties people to their past. Instead of history, which is degrading and calls for revenge, Walcott proposes a narrative, or a myth, which, because of its continuous present, opens time, making the new world equal to the old one. His long poem *Omeros* shows that the world of the Caribbean islands is as epic as Greece, because it contains a journey, a return to the native island, the fear of ancestors, gods. He rejects linear thinking, the straight line linking today to the past.[10] Because the straight line, in the words of Peter Viereck, "is the longest distance between two points. And the bloodiest."[11]

Walcott's attitude to history and narration is often contested on aesthetic grounds. "Despite imperious passages of broken terza rima," the poet and critic William Logan writes in a vitriolic review of Walcott's poetry, "[*Omeros*] is spoiled by its clumsy narration."[12] I will return to this review while talking about the question of the native "ear" and the rejection of "nonnative" poetry. For now, it is enough to say that Walcott, like Brodsky, looks for his identity in culture and not, like Miłosz, in his genealogy, that is history. Or, to put it more correctly, Walcott and Brodsky placed their genealogy in culture. But they did not agree in everything. During the conference in which Miłosz debated Brodsky on the matter of Central Europe, Walcott also spoke. He had been hesitating, he began, before speaking: "I've a very great difficulty here between friendship and ideology. And I think that's a penalty of ideology." This conflict causes in him "flashes of rage and an alternation between that and nausea. . . . The imperial voice dominates this conference and its range increases with every representation by European tribe, by European nation. This is not merely a historical posture of ancestry and tradition which goes under the general name of 'civilization.' I am talking about tone . . . about a linear concept of progress and experiment in literature which I find no different from the presumptions of the priest and the conquistador. You writers of Europe continue that tone, that responsibility of carrying the banner and the cross or the book. I have found no breadth, no expanse of imagination and, even at the risk of sounding corny, no evangelical vision. What is the meaning of your empires? To hear all this from contemporary writers is only to deepen my conviction that for all its wars, its museums, its literatures, its revolutions, the provinciality of Europe and of Russia increases. Writers are not inheritors of history."[13]

As we remember, the debate between the Russian delegation and the writers of "Central Europe" introduced a divide between those representing an empire and those who represented the captive nations. Walcott, who spoke before the exchange between Miłosz and Brodsky, noticed that both sides were united by the sense of superiority of their culture, of the primacy of the priestly role of the writer, their missionary soulfulness always paid for by the victims among the converted. Salman Rushdie and Susan Sontag were equally critical.

"I offer this as a thought to the Russian writers," Rushdie said, "that if you're living and writing from inside one of the world's great empires, even if you occupy a weak position inside that empire, it seems to be very difficult to see beyond the frontiers" (118). And Susan Sontag continued this line of thought by stating: The power of the colonizer consists in the ability to describe the colonized: if you say that Central Europe does not exist and the writers from there declare its existence, don't you have to deal with it? It was at this point that Brodsky became irritated and said: "Of course, [the position of Russian writers] is not an imperial position." But his own words, spoken four years later at the Rutgers conference, had implied that Russia is condemned to be either imperial or nothing at all. "The trouble is that geography, at least European geography, doesn't leave history very many options. [Clio is governed here by Urania.] The bigger the country, the smaller the number of its options. The options are either to be strong or intimidating and wring the necks of its neighbors like dishrags, or to be insignificant, splintered, impoverished. For seventy years in this century, Russia has played the former role; now it is time for it to play the second role."[14] He did not debate democracy, civil society, social development, treating all these terms as propaganda. Like Pushkin, like Mandelstam, like his Russian colleagues at the Lisbon conference, Brodsky did not look at Russia as a society but as a state. And he measured the power of that state. He did not support it or its imperial ambitions. But isn't it comprehensible that a state does not want to be "insignificant, splintered, impoverished"?

It was not accidental that Brodsky looked at Russia through the prism of its statehood. He continued the Russian cultural tradition:

after all, the first written history of Russia consisted in following the development of the Russian state. At the instigation of the Russian czar Aleksander I, Nicolai Karamzin worked on the multivolume *History of the Russian State*, establishing (or expressing) the priority of the institution of the state over that of the nation. Again the contrast with Poland is useful here. Brodsky inherited the concept of history as a history of the state, and he escaped from it into individualism. Miłosz's history was that of a nation and of its resistance; such history served to defend the dignity of Poles, who lived "in the shadow of the Empire." This is why, in his discussion with Brodsky, he said *divide et impera.* He reached back—to Latin, to Roman history—for him the Soviet Union was an *imperium.* For Brodsky, too, it was an *imperium,* though he lived in its prosaic, rotting present. From which he escaped.

I return and circle around the theme of empire in part because I am interested in Brodsky's attitude toward the second empire, the one in which he finally settled for life. I have quoted Tomas Venclova's comment that Brodsky loved Poland, Lithuania, and Italy, but that toward Russia and the United States his attitude was quite complex. In his declarations, he always stressed that he and his generation idealized America as an embodiment of individualism. His essay "Spoils of War" was devoted to the signs of America's material greatness he remembered from his youth: the jazz program of Willis Conover in the Voice of America radio station, UNRRA (United Nations Relief and Rehabilitation Administration) food packages, American films. "The Tarzan series alone, I daresay, did more for de-Stalinization than all Khrushchev's speeches at the Twentieth Party Congress and after"

(*OGR,* 8). This definition—America as a continent of individualism—remained with him till the end, even though he was bothered by its conformism, mass culture, vulgarity. The very fact that he was free to leave, that he was an autonomous individual, placed this country above Russia. In 1990 he summed it all up: "What is empire? When I think about it, I have several things in mind, not only the terrain submitted to a political system or administered by a certain political authority. I think as well about a space, in which a certain concept of time is present, in which a primary idea dominates. For me America is an empire of individualism. This is the central idea of this reality: human autonomy. Or else: sovereignty which can reach total autonomy."[15]

As is clear from the above quotation, for Brodsky the word *empire* was not positive or negative, it had a factual value. And America was the best of existing political systems. Because a political system, as we can understand from his play *Marbles,* is best when it leaves us in peace. The space then is joined to freedom. Unlike Miłosz's vision of California, there is never too much space, and it surely does not imprison. Brodsky writes about the juncture of space and freedom in his poem "Lullaby of Cape Cod," which we can consider a functional equivalent of Miłosz's *Visions of San Francisco Bay.* The similarity between these two works is only situational: both marked the moment of acceptance of the place in which the poets found themselves. They differ, of course, in their genre and length, although the thematic complexity and diversity of the "Lullaby" is no less than that of the prose volume of Miłosz. Here, as in Miłosz, it is a matter of "the touch of the table corner" and "of the sharp nib of the pen" which signifies the encounter of the old self with the new place. But the table by which Brodsky is sitting also has a bottle of whiskey on it, an indication of the difference in how the two poets adapt to their new situations. (Only in writing, I should add, because in life Miłosz liked whiskey more than Brodsky did.) Emigration does not change them: they remain themselves. Miłosz finds strength in tradition and religion, Brodsky cannot find peace.

"Lullaby of Cape Cod" is one of the best known and best liked works of Brodsky (*CPE,* 116–29). In an interview, he described it as "a lyrical sequence. It was more like playing piano than singing an aria." It definitely has a melody, and Ray Charles is mentioned in the first stanza. In the original Russian, "Lullaby of Cape Cod" is composed of twelve parts, each containing five strophes of six verses. To the chagrin of the author, the English-language translation, by his friend the excellent poet Anthony Hecht, is ninety-three lines longer. In the same interview Brodsky declared that he wrote the poem because of the bicentennial—"I thought—well, why don't I do something?"[16] Its content, however, is not celebratory. And the poem does not start, like Miłosz's book, with "I am here." The author's presence is insistent but more oblique, as in the line of the fourth strophe: "It's strange to think of surviving, but that's what happened." Yet, right from the beginning we witness a realistic scene, as if he were indicating: Here is where I am. A small village on Cape Cod—"the eastern tip of the Empire." It is July, night is falling, the evening is hot and stifling. The poet sits by the window (it is a recurrent position of our poet in his poems); he is drinking whiskey, hoping it will let him sleep—the last apparition of the poem is a cod who comes to drink with him. The acceptance of emigration, the "I am here," is expressed, as always in Brodsky, with irony and pain:

> *On the deserted ground*
> *of a basketball court a vagrant bird has set*
> *its fragile egg in the steel hoop's raveled net.*
> *There's a smell of mint now, and of mignonette. (*CPE, *117)*

Emigration is described as the "switch" of empires. It happens gradually, first by crossing the line of "janissaries," then sailing into "muttony clouds" with the droning of a "turbine":

> *and space backed up like a crab, time surged ahead*
> *into first place and, streaming westwardly,*
> *seemed to be heading home, void of all light,*
> *soiling its garments with the tar of night. (*CPE, *117–18)*

The place of arrival is new, "No one is here / to set the proper focus of your eye" (*CPE*, 124), but the loneliness is the same as always:

> *the device in your hand is the same old pen and ink*
> *as before, the woodland plants exhibit no change*
> *of leafage, and the same old bombers range*
> *the clouds toward who knows what*
> *precisely chosen, carefully targeted spot.*
> *And what you really need now is a drink. (*CPE, *120)*

The poem is highly structured, but also very realistic, autoironic in the presentation of the author's loneliness, of his fight against illness and the passing of time, and also of his sober (though drinking is the motif

running throughout the poem) look at the new empire. The bombers
are the same:

> *the legions close their ranks*
> *and, leaning against cohorts, sleep upright.*
> *Circuses pile against fora. (*CPE, *122)*

He has arrived at the end of the world:

> *there's nowhere to go.*
> *Elsewhere is nothing more than a far-flung strew*
> *of stars, burning away. (*CPE, *122)*

It is a new place but both empires find themselves on the same globe,
like head and tails, and they are linked to each other beneath the sea.
There is no abyss between them, only the continuation of space.

> *Consisting of love, of dirty words, a blend*
> *of ashes, the fear of death, the fragile case*
> *of the bone, and the groin's jeopardy, an erect*
> *body at seaside is the foreskin of space,*
> *letting semen through. His cheek tear-silver-flecked,*
> *man juts forth into Time; man is his own end. (*CPE, *127)*

What can one say now about the attitude of Brodsky toward
America, toward emigration, empire? Right from the start, in his
early poems, where the topic of empire appeared, he thought about
the empire as an ahistorical, apolitical entity, a Moloch to be faced by
each of us alone — us who are defended only by our independence and
individualism. No sign of religiosity here as God's help is not expected.

A small state, Brodsky seems to be saying, forces a person to various kinds of solidarity, to complicity in history which hides the true nature of life, its radical loneliness and fragility. The empire consists of continuous decay, and there you see the nakedness of man and state. The only solidarity that the poet allows himself to feel is compassion. This is why he is singing a lullaby. But as for him, he is alone in

> *the land's vastness, your own minute*
> *size in comparison, swings you forth and back*
> *from wall to wall, like a cradle's rockabye. (*CPE, *128)*

He is tired, exhausted, lonely, his mind is attracted to death. The acceptance of the new place is not a victory—the place is not really new, and victory is not really possible. He hears "the soft song of the cod":

> *Time is far greater than space. Space is a thing.*
> *Whereas time is, in essence, the thought, the conscious dream*
> *of a thing. And life itself is a variety*
> *of time. The carp and bream*
> *are its clots and distillates. As are even more stark*
> *and elemental things, including the sea*
> *wave and the firmament of the dry land.*
> *Including death, that punctuation mark. (*CPE, *124)*

EIGHT

Poetry with a Foreign Accent

Both Czesław Miłosz and Joseph Brodsky passed the greater part of their lives in the United States. The English language played a large role in their creative work even before they arrived in America. Surrounded by English, they grew intimate with it. Gradually, they started to interfere in translations of their poems. By the end of his life, Miłosz translated most of his poems by himself, and in the last years of his life, Brodsky composed poems directly in English. For the poets "burdened" with romantic convictions about loyalties to their native tongue, these developments marked an evolution indeed.

Miłosz and Brodsky came from the same geographical part of Europe—the strip of land between the Baltic Sea and the Carpathian Mountains. Their main tool of self-identification was their language. But their family experiences were completely different: Miłosz grew up surrounded by many languages, Brodsky in a monolinguistic environment. Miłosz wrote that his loyalty to Polish led him to resist Lithuanian, Russian, and Belorussian—the languages he heard in his childhood. In that multilingual environment, for at least four hundred years, his family had continuously spoken Polish. It was a local Polish, a Polish with lexical and pronunciation specificities, different from the language of Warsaw or Kraków. He learned Russian early on, and for over seven years studied Latin in school. He considered these two languages opposite magnetic poles exerting their pressures on his Polish: the emphatic Russian "reinforcing his phrasing" and the classical Latin tending to make his tone more restrained.[1] The language of his childhood was his treasure and his self-defense, his "cocoon." That language had to be protected from standard Polish, and later, from English.

The case of Brodsky was almost opposite. Although his grandparents, some of whom he came to know in his childhood, probably knew Hebrew and Yiddish, his mother knew Latvian, German, and French, and his father, as he suspected, used to study Latin, the young Iosif grew up in a world of only one language. There were many reasons for this monolingualism, the most important one being the heavy price attached in Stalinist Russia to any kind of diversity. Brodsky grew up in the years of the "fight against cosmopolitanism"— as the anti-Jewish policies were described in government-speak—and his father lost his job owing to his Jewish origin. He does not say in his writings whether his parents understood Yiddish or Hebrew, although he must have heard some Yiddish, or a Yiddish version of German, judging by his poem "Dva chasa v rezerwuare" [Two Hours in a Reservoir] (1965). He never expressed any interest in Yiddish or in Hebrew, nor in any other Jewish matter. Russian was the sole language of his childhood. From his earliest youth he tried to escape from this "one-languageness."

The history of European literature has known many bilingual moments, and both poets were very much aware of them. "For a couple of centuries," wrote Miłosz, "in several European countries the literati were bilingual, their vernacular modified by their Latin and vice versa" (*TB*, 19). In Russia, the poets of romanticism, including Pushkin, wrote and conversed in French, and the Polish romantic bard, Adam Mickiewicz, was famous in Russia for his improvisations in French. Yet, it was romanticism itself that undermined that duality and turned poets into guardians of their national memory. East-Central European romantics were busy creating unified national cultures and fighting for nation-states, and a successful national culture depended on authenticity drawn from a people's customs, rites, and language. The poet-bard had to express that unique national essence. His Muse exchanged her antique tunic for a simple peasant garb. And she became more fickle: she easily denied him inspiration. His greatness was guaranteed by authenticity secured by constant contact with and fidelity toward his people. And by continuous presence within the community of national suffering.

The nineteenth and twentieth centuries sorely tested the stateless nations that had to place their essence in the hands of their poets. And the poets were forced to live in solidarity with the nations they served, protecting this alliance because the authenticity they needed stemmed from it. They were finding inspiration in their childhood, in burying themselves in their language, in remembering the family manor in which they passed their early days. Hence came about a deep fear of exile, a frequent fate of these poets. Exile meant writerly solitude: and what is a poet without readers? And there was a fear of barrenness, of being cut off from the sources of inspiration, from native soil, from living language. It is this fear that Czesław Miłosz addressed in his first letter to Brodsky. Exile does not stifle the voice of the Muse, he stated; but it did not follow that the poet could write in the language in which he did not grow up. Both Miłosz and Brodsky always declared their undivided loyalty toward their native tongue. But only Miłosz remained faithful to this conviction.

Even in his youth, Brodsky was fascinated by English-language poetry and poets. He felt limited by what he found around him, and kept looking for models beyond the borders of his language. One of his masters, Anna Akhmatova, knew and admired English poetry, but even before meeting Akhmatova, Brodsky and his contemporaries were fascinated by the culture of American film, literature, jazz, and technology. They were sensitive to the vitality of English, the language which, with two empires behind it, had a truly global reach. In his few years of schooling, Brodsky got an F in English, but soon he made great efforts to get English or American books or records. In Leningrad of the 1960s, the most important sources of foreign books were the few foreign students. The first time Brodsky placed a quotation in English in his poetry was already in 1961: it is the motto of his poem "Petersbursky roman." Two years later, in January 1963, he wrote his elegy for Robert Frost. Frost's poems were included in the anthology of the English-language poets that Brodsky owed to the Polish student Zofia Kapuścińska. In a letter dated October 11, 1963, he wrote to her that in this anthology he is reading "two great Irishmen," Yeats and Joyce, and that it is his "dearest book, although I understand only half of it." Among the portraits he kept on his desk were Akhmatova, Pasternak, and Robert Frost—along with Zofia Kapuścińska. As early as 1961, he was signing his letters to her in English (they corresponded in Russian): "Forever your [sic!] Joseph Brodsky." This was the name he used after settling in the United States. At this time, the new name was a funny pseudonym, a fantasy rather than a project of migration. The persistence of this vision—of life as Joseph Brodsky—is attested not only by the letters to Kapuścińska; he also signs a letter to Andrzej Drawicz in this way. Right after the elegy for Frost, he wrote a poem that marked a radical step forward in his finding of his own voice: "Bolshoya Elegya Dzhonu Donnu" [The Great Elegy for John Donne]. It was a tour de force, referring directly to the tradition of English metaphysical poetry. In a letter to Kapuścińska he wrote about this poem: "This is my best poem and the greatest, I believe, in contemporary poetry. God only knows how I was able to write it in such conditions" (March 15, 1963).

Many critics underline the influence of English-language poetry on the early works of Brodsky, though when he came to the United States his knowledge of English was still limited. It was good enough, however, to feel uneasy about the translations of his poems: some of them were excellent, but he did not recognize his tone of voice. This was not his poetry. He had a holistic vision of a poem. He did not accept a division into form and content—they were always inseparably intertwined for him. His works were formally complicated, rhymed, rhythmical, full of enjambments, dense with meaning that was often provoked by the rhymes. Right from the very beginning, he interfered in translations, demanding an exact rendering of content but not at the expense of form. His translators were faced with a very difficult, perhaps even impossible task. There were many tense moments and conflicts. Some of his translators were from among the best-known poets in the English language: Anthony Hecht, Howard Moss, Richard Wilbur; but Brodsky preferred people with less pronounced poetic personalities, so that in their translations his own voice would be more prominent.[2] Gradually, he started to translate his poems himself, crowding into the Russian metric form as much content as possible. He did not look for literal translations, but for the best rendition of the tension between the requirement of meter and the flow of thought. "Translation is a search for an equivalent, not for a substitute. It requires stylistic, if not psychological, congeniality" (*LTO*, 140). His own translations are soaked through and through with the tradition of Russian versification, linked to the Audenesque style of rhymed intellectual lyricism. He was trying to use English the way he used Russian, and he was creating his poems anew. In English, just as in Russian, he was moving in all registers of speech, placing them within a metrical form considered by many native English speakers as outdated or eccentric. In this way, what in effect were new poems undoubtedly came closer to the intent of the original than the translations, which fit well into the sound and history of Anglo-American poetry.

The problematic character of such an attitude to translations stems, obviously, from the very nature of poetic language. The poem needs to be comprehensible; therefore it has to be composed of words which can be comprehended. But in order to be poetic, it needs to contain words or formulations that are unusual. The poet has to say something new or in a new way, but what is new needs to be placed within what is well known. The Greeks already had pointed to this duality, and Aristotle had explained it in his *Poetics* (1458a). Countless generations of poets and critics have formulated the tension in ever different ways. It is exactly what Brodsky has in mind when he declares that he is writing to please the shadows of his ancestors, but at the same time that he dreads repetition. The language of poetry is a deviation, a detour from everyday speech, but this deviation or detour has to be kept within certain limits. Where these limits are situated is always a matter of negotiation: they are set anew by each new poem. "In literature," writes the superb Polish poet and translator Stanisław Barańczak, "a new thought cannot emerge except from a new way of speaking: in order to say anything relevant, you must break a norm. And this is precisely what an outsider cannot afford, since if breaking is to make any sense at all, you may break only the norms that bind you, not those that bind someone else. If a native writer purposely violates language, it's called progress; if an outsider does it, it's called malapropism."[3]

Brodsky faced a question: how to talk to his new reader? For the new reader was the one he was most interested in talking to, not his readers of the past. He felt oppressed by the too swift passage of time: he complained that the activity of translating by its very nature touched on works that were already old and distant. He felt forced so often to correct the texts translated by others, he said, that to avoid conflicts he started to translate his poems himself.[4] His translations were more rough, rhythmical, with more registers of speech than the translators' versions, which were easier for his American and, especially, his English readers to accept. Their content was less clear, more mysterious, and the rhymes more surprising, unusual. They sound authentic, truthful, and have a melody, an energy, the roughness of the originals. They are surprising and thrilling at the same time. His translators did not know how to replicate this specificity and power—it was all his own—so, finally, Brodsky translated his poems by himself. Each of them is akin to an explosion, though sometimes they do misfire.

The first volume of his poems that was edited solely by himself appeared in the United States in 1980, eight years after his settling there. It was called *A Part of Speech,* and out of thirty-seven poems in the volume only one, "Elegy for Robert Lowell," was written directly in English. It was the first poem he had written in English, a kind of homage, which turned out to be an initiation, composed in the language and style of the poet it was eulogizing. The volume also contains two poems translated by Brodsky himself, ten translations in which he participated, and twenty-four, that is a great majority, signed by different poets. It seems, however, that even then the intrusion of Brodsky was major. Derek Walcott, who is indicated as the only translator of the poem "Letters from the Ming Dynasty," has said on several occasions that he does not know Russian and that the translation was really by Brodsky, who prepared the line-by-line version and later accepted some minor changes Walcott suggested. These proportions are reversed in the following volume, *To Urania,* published eight years later. Out of forty-six poems, twelve were written directly in

English, and twenty-two were translated by Brodsky. Eight poems are signed by both a translator and the author, and only four are signed by a translator alone. The third and last volume prepared by Brodsky—*So Forth*—appeared right after his death in 1996. Only one of the poems included in this volume is signed by a translator, seven by the author and translator, and the remaining poems are either translated by Brodsky—thirty-five of them—or written in English. In this volume, Brodsky abandons the custom of placing the translator's name under a poem, instead mentioning translators' names on the copyright page. Thus he had finally ceased delegating responsibility for the English-language shape of his poems. Everything in the volume was to be read as if written by Brodsky himself.

We could say, then, that this was the moment in which Iosif Brodskij truly turned into Joseph Brodsky, a poet of the English language. The transformation is clearly visible in his *Collected Poems in English*, published four years after his death by his assistant and the executor of his estate, Ann Kjellberg. In a volume of over five hundred pages, she placed only poems that Brodsky had approved, translated, or written into English himself. The names of the cotranslators are printed at the end of the book. It is interesting that in the latest editions of his collected work, Czesław Miłosz took possession of his poems in the same way. Translators of poetry (the "coolies of literature"—as Hans Magnus Enzensberger called them) are very badly paid in America, but never really pushed aside in this way. In *A Part of Speech*, Brodsky, conscious of possible objections, addressed the issue in a note. "I would like to thank each of my translators for his long hours of work in rendering my poems into English," he declared. "I have taken the liberty of reworking some of the translations to bring them closer to the original, though perhaps at the expense of their smoothness. I am doubly grateful to the translators for their indulgence."[5]

In actuality, he met with little indulgence. On that, we have excellent testimony from one of the translators, the British poet Daniel Weissbort. His book *From Russian with Love: Joseph Brodsky in English* could just as well be titled, quoting Weissbort's words, "The Trouble with Brodsky." The British poet translated several of Brodsky's poems, and many stormy exchanges resulted. Shocked by Brodsky's death, Weissbort goes back over the points of their conflicts, comparing texts, asking questions, agonizing over positions he once took. Brodsky would ask him to translate such and such a poem, then would rework his translations, "plagiarizing" parts of them, or, sometimes, rejecting them altogether. A comparison of various versions, generously provided by Weissbort, shows clearly that Brodsky was *writing* in English, and that he compensated for his shaky "ear" by flair, energy, the sense of ownership of the text that no translator could ever approach. Part memoir, part meditation on the nature of translation, *From Russian with Love* is an important book on English-language poetry of the last part of the twentieth century.

Brodsky acted against a commonly held conviction—one also adhered to by himself, although merely verbally—that a poet can create only in the language of his childhood, and that, since poetry depends on a native "ear," translators have to find equivalents in the poetic history of the language into which the poem is transposed. The expectation is that the equivalent will "work out" within the tradition of the language of translation. But Brodsky's efforts were directed at something else: his own translations were very similar to their original versions in Russian, and to his own poems written in English, full of complex rhymes and rhythmical figures. He mixed high and low styles, irony and pathos, classical allusions and colloquialisms. What is more important, though, he transposed the forms of Russian poems onto his English-language verses, and vice versa.[6] "The trouble with Brodsky," Weissbort wrote, "was that he simply wouldn't understand that he was asking for the impossible, for the Russian text to be *imported* into English wholesale, English having to be Russianized to accommodate it."[7] His poetry was different from anything the Anglo-American reader was accustomed to: it was nonconfessional, intellectual, ironic, and, at the same time, hot, forcing submission to its internal movement. Its form was provocative: he used rhymes that were often bent to his pronunciation; he mixed Anglicisms with Americanisms. His English, rich and supple, was nevertheless all his own. He introduced his Russian tone into the Anglo-American language of poetry.

He went about this work in an uncompromising and extravagant way. During his poetry readings, he chanted his poems as if he were a rapper, or rather a cross between a rapper and cantor. At first, he wrote only his essays in English (their language was also very poetic), along with an occasional poem—the elegy for Lowell, angry and mournful poems about the fighting in Belfast, the war in Yugoslavia, the imposition of martial law in Poland. But his repertoire grew, enlarged by new genres: poetic "songs," poems for children, travelogues. Toward the end of his life—he died before his fifty-sixth birthday— he was writing his poetry mostly in English. He was in a hurry. As he said ironically in 1991, he did not want to be known by the translations of his old poems, because then "you shake hands with people who have formed their opinion about you on the basis of something that has been written five or ten years ago. That prompts you in a sense to write occasionally a poem in English to show the boys who you are or who's in charge."[8] He died too soon for us to see how far this audacious experiment would lead him.

Irritable and restless, he was in conflict with many representatives of the American literary establishment. Right at the beginning of his stay in the United States, he attacked the poets W. S. Merwin and Clarence Brown for their free-verse translations of Mandelstam. In a conversation with me, Robert Faggen said that Brodsky provoked his colleagues with his arrogance, his irony, and by attracting their girlfriends. One of these well-known poets confessed to Faggen that once he mailed to Brodsky a poem as a kind of gift or homage, and Brodsky sent it back to him with corrections. Faggen reported that Miłosz functioned in a very different way. He remained far from New York's tensions, and maintained a Californian serenity, without extravagance or rigid convictions. For American poets, he was far less controversial.[9]

The issue, however, was mostly the matter of poetry, not of personality. As the idiosyncratic tone of Brodsky's poetry became more pronounced, his critics grew in number. After his death, the chorus of reservations grew louder. Richard Eder wrote in the *New York Times*: "English is a cello, and doesn't take pounding." John Bayley claimed in the *New York Review of Books* that the poet was pushing, attacking his reader. Sven Birkerts, in an otherwise very positive review, pointed to "the clanking of some of the later poems." The English poet Craig Raine assured his readers, in an article under the ironic title "A Reputation Subject to Inflation," that Brodsky was a bad poet, a very banal thinker, as well as a careerist. His main argument was that Brodsky's "ear" displayed "foreign ineptitude." In a particularly scornful article, "Brodsky in Retrospect," John Simon said that "the English language has proved hospitable to foreign prose writers as diverse as Joseph Conrad, Isak Dinesen, and Vladimir Nabokov, but Brodsky wrote poetry and that . . . may require a finer ear." Yet there was a British critic who accused Joseph Conrad in 1908 of being a man "without either country or language."[10] This is the critic's only claim to fame.

Many reviewers compared the linguistic parameters of English and Russian, proving beyond doubt that what Brodsky attempted was impossible. Even some of his closest friends seemed to be unhappy about the results of his efforts. Seamus Heaney wrote in a poem "Audenesque," celebrating Brodsky after his death:

> *Nevermore that rush to pun*
> *Or to hurry through all yon*
> *Jammed enjambments piling up*
> *As you went above the top,*
>
> *Nose in air, foot to the floor,*
> *Revving English like a car.*

Brodsky was also criticized by Yves Bonnefoy, W. S. Merwin, and Robert Hass, the translator of Miłosz. Although Hass did not like what Brodsky was doing to English verse, he understood his dilemma well. How should Brodsky sound, he asked in his review of *A Part of Speech*—"like Lowell, Auden, Byron, Pope?"[11] Brodsky of course knew that he wanted to sound only like Brodsky.

Sometimes Brodsky's stubbornness seems to meet with some sort of understanding, if not exactly acceptance. In an influential posthumous review of Brodsky's essays and poems in the *Times Literary Supplement*, the poet-translator Michael Hofmann wrote that Brodsky's English-language poems have "less to do with translation than authorship," and that Brodsky made of himself "an anarchic gift to his adopted language. . . . Perhaps his unspoken reservations about American contemporary poetry produced a rather tepid and defensive response from that establishment," Hofmann wondered.[12] And Daniel Weissbort, in "Something Like His Own Language: Brodsky in English," went further, rejecting Brodsky's critics' reliance on their "ear": Brodsky's translations, he said, do have a musical integrity, "although the music is not a familiar one." These translations and poems written in English revolutionized expectations regarding the quality of texts in that language—the "world language" of today. "In fact," he wrote, "to produce a text which seems to have been written in English, which in that sense 'reads smoothly,' is no longer the sine qua non of good translation. At this time, there appears to be more interest in somehow capturing the foreignness of the foreign. Of course, it is all a matter of judgment, and of course the extent to which change can be tolerated itself changes. It is quite likely that many of Brodsky's linguistic moves, to which Raine and others object, will be less rebarbative to the average reader in the not so distant future."[13] The same thought was expressed by Brodsky in one of his interviews: "I have no ambition to become another Nabokov or another Joseph Conrad. I simply don't have the time or energy or the narcissism. But I could easily imagine someone else like me writing poetry in both languages, in both English and Russian. I think that something like that is bound to happen sometime in the future. It's very likely that twenty or thirty or forty years from now there will be people for whom writing bilingually will be perfectly natural."[14]

Weissbort ends his introduction with a thought that was shared by some other poets. "[Brodsky's translations] create audible links between [English and Russian], and only time will tell what effect they have had on English poetry and on English usage itself. So, the volume, just published here by Carcanet, may be a kind of time bomb. But it also provides a rare opportunity for non-Russian speakers to read one of the greatest Russian poets in something like his own language."[15] Derek Walcott expressed the same idea. He admired Brodsky's English and his self-translating; he felt a great affinity with his Russian friend. Another friend and translator of Brodsky, Alan Myers, is quoted by Weissbort as saying, "He felt his own rhymes were rather more enterprising than those of the natives, whose ear might be dulled by familiarity."[16] After Brodsky's death, during an evening panel at Columbia University, Mark Strand said that Brodsky had caused a renewal of poetic language in the United States. He enlarged the rhyming possibilities of English, creatively using the peculiarities of his own pronunciation: these rhymes "are delightful," Strand said. About Brodsky's English-language poem "Song" he said with a smile: "pretty damn masterful." When one is growing up in a language, one's attitude toward it is conventional. "Joseph had more options."[17]

Czesław Miłosz was highly critical of Brodsky's self-sufficiency in English. "I witnessed many times," he said in a conversation with me, "how Brodsky read his poems in English. It did not work out. He was reading in English with the sing-song of Russian poetry reading, and the rules of the language are totally different. . . . The fact that Brodsky wrote his poems in English was, I think, a mistake. He should have kept to his own language." In another part of that conversation, Miłosz declared that one can write poetry only in the language of one's childhood, and that Brodsky, toward the end of his life, was "'androgynous.' . . . I prefer his other poems."[18] Miłosz did not attempt to hide this opinion from Brodsky; at the end of a letter he wrote to the Russian poet on December 26, 1984, he admonished Brodsky: "After our evening for the Amnesty International I wanted to talk to you at length about your Russian way of reading your poetry and your 'American' way. It seems to me they should be kept separated. If we are sentenced to lead a dual life, let it be. With warm feelings, Czesław." Brodsky replied a few weeks later: "Your advice about my 'American' reading manner is taken. I don't know what got into me that night: perhaps I wanted to be more brutal than the poems allowed for. 'Ah, old complaints' says Beckett in one of his plays. 'Old complaints are the best.' Entirely yours, Иосиф."[19]

In his reply, Brodsky typically avoided controversy with Miłosz, but he did not agree with him. During the Katowice honorary-degree celebration (and while Miłosz was resting in his hotel room), Brodsky replied to a question about his "melo-recitation": "Today's poet is afraid of the sardonic laughter of his reader, and because of it he tries to soften his poems and clear from them the moments that are strongly emotional. In other words, the poet tries to fit with his public. This is a mistake. The poet should charge his public like a tank, so that the reader has no escape. Poetry is an act of metaphysical and linguistic attack, not of a retreat. If a poet wants to be modest and nonaggressive, he should stop writing" (*StS*, 43). For Brodsky, a poem was an inseparable union of sound and content, conveyed to listeners in a state of intense concentration and with a rhythm that should elate them. His poetry was not to be read in the polite, low-tension atmosphere so often present at American poetry readings. Some of his Russian colleagues, for example Lev Loseff, were opposed to his emphatic way of reading. But his Russian public in America appreciated it very much. This is how Ludmilla Shtern remembers his last reading for Russian-language listeners: "There was a sheer magic in the way Brodsky read his poetry. The tone of his voice, its loudness, the movement of his hands and torso—everything was beautiful and raised deep emotions. The manner of the presentation was almost as important as its content."[20]

His attachment to his native language was a constant in his life—this was the meaning of his delivering his Nobel lecture in Russian. But he always disagreed with those who maintained that writing can be done only in one language. In his essay "To Please a Shadow" he recounts how in 1977, five years after his arrival in the United States, he "purchased a portable *Lettera 22* in a small typewriter shop on Sixth Avenue and set out to write (essays, translations, occasionally a poem) in English" (*LTO*, 357). In 1993, English had already become his "second nature." " The ability to use two languages is a kind of human norm. I do not think that I am an exception. Ninety percent of great authors of Russian literature of the nineteenth century, such as Pushkin, Turgenev, Baratynsky, exchanged letters and often spoke among themselves in French. It did not interfere with the creation of their works in Russian. And if you are not convinced by the example of the poets, I will tell you, that the last czar of Russia was keeping his intimate diary in English" (*StS*, 124). And during a conversation with John Glad he said: "The idea that a writer must be monolingual is something of an insult to both the individual writer and, I would say, to the human mind. . . . The psychological processes that I go through when I write in Russian are often emotionally and acoustically identical to writing poetry in English."[21] He wrote in English because he wanted to and was able to do it.

It was not an easily acquired ability. People learn new languages and sometimes switch to them, but they pray or count only in the language of their childhood. And often it is the only language in which they can react to poetry. Miłosz said that only poetry in Polish, original or translated, was truly accessible to him. Isaiah Berlin, whose mother tongue was Russian, said the same thing about his own language. In his conversation with Diana Myers—they spoke in Russian—he declared that he understood English-language poetry but did not feel it; yet he has spent most of his life in England. Berlin and Myers asked themselves why by the end of his life Brodsky was switching over to English and decided that it was a language that opened new possibilities for him. Brodsky always wanted to do something new, to discover new worlds for himself. "Language was for him something more than a particular, concrete tongue," said

Diana Myers, "and English was a challenge for him . . . [it opened] new horizons. He wanted to start a new, second life in it, catch a second wind. . . . English was associated in his mind with normalcy, with a normal existence. . . . He was afraid that his daughter, if she learns Russian, will become similar to us . . . we were not normal, we were burdened with a curse of unhappiness, because we existed in Russian. It was the language of unhappiness."[22] Brodsky never described Russian in this way but by the end of his life English had become by choice the language of his domesticity.

It is not only the "natives" that defend their language from poets with a foreign accent; the poets' émigré communities expect them to be faithful to their mother tongues. That fidelity is a cliché of émigré literature: obviously, the writers who remain in their country are rarely tempted to switch into another language. Language is a means through which émigrés belong to their country and carry it with themselves: it is their history and national library. But Brodsky is distant from such an understanding of the mother tongue; it is not languages but Language that is of interest to him. In his idiosyncratic philosophical system, Time stands above Space, and Language, "with its caesuras, pauses, spondees, and so forth," restructures Time. He often quoted Auden:

> *Time . . .*
>
>   *. . .*
>
> *Worships language and forgives*
> *Everyone by whom it lives;*
> *Pardons cowardice, conceit,*
> *Lays its honours at their feet.*[23]

He interprets these lines, indeed builds a kind of metaphysics out of them. "It is characteristic of Brodsky," writes Jonathan Schell, "that he attributes the substance of his thinking to another writer's lines (as if everything that he subsequently worked out was nothing more than a protracted elucidation of what Auden had packed into the one word 'worships'), presenting his thinking as merely the continuation of a broader train of thought that, implicitly, neither began with him nor will end with him; but it's also characteristic that he persists in his elucidation until he has arrived at novel, and sometimes extreme, conclusions. For example, if language is 'greater' than time, and time 'absorbs deity,' then language must in some sense be greater than God. Linguistics here seems to have swallowed up theology."[24]

Brodsky does not mean concrete, historical time—"time (not *the* time)" (*LTO*, 363)—or concrete language, but Language as giving measure to Time, that is life and death. He once delivered a lecture that was titled "Language as Otherland."[25] On another occasion, in a conversation with Walcott, he said: "Basically, for each of us the language in which we write gave us our reality; it gave us indeed our identity—otherwise we would be still defining ourselves in the categories of either political, religious, or geographical belief systems. A man's job above all is to find out who he is. . . . Nothing helps to define oneself better than one's own language."[26] The words *identity* and *language* are not used here in their conventional sense. It was poetic language that defined Brodsky's and Walcott's identities. They both believed in the primacy of that language over national languages in which the poetic language was expressed. Walcott formulated it in the following way: "Shakespeare is such a visionary: he knew as a material fact that the language of poetry is radically not rooted in any geography, in any race, or in any historical, or any ironical situations."[27]

Similarly complex attitudes toward languages have characterized many other writers from the borderlands of empires, as the two Irishmen James Joyce and Samuel Beckett prove. Joyce's monumental *Finnegans Wake* is a multilanguage, associational creation, crossing all genre and language boundaries. Beckett went in the opposite direction: reduction rather than overabundance. For a part of his life he wrote poetry and plays in French, in his own, "foreign," strange, simplified, emphatically nonnative French. And when he returned to English, it also became "strange" in a similar way. Jean-Michel Rey claimed that Beckett gave the French people a new understanding of their language, because, while using it, he always had English in the back of his mind, and these two languages continuously pervaded each other.[28] Critics have considered the two Irish writers' choices a sign of alienation and resistance to the language that had pushed away the tongue of their ancestors. But perhaps it is more apt to say that their language was open, directed not toward the English but toward what Jacques Derrida, quoting Edouard Glissant, called "the lack"— the consciousness of the lack of the language of their ancestors, the defeated language they were cut off from. Their use of language was a search for that lost echo, a search that could never be fulfilled.[29]

Writing in a victorious language—the language of an empire or of a majority into which an author is assimilated—gives access to a vital culture, to a larger readership, to various possibilities which the defeated language cannot provide. But the victorious language rises by crushing all other linguistic possibilities, leaving those who use it both enriched and stranded. They have to be "authorized" to use the majority language, and that authorization is always uncertain. Not only do they "lack" a language of their ancestors, but they also "lack" the "ear" for the language into which they have settled. Brodsky and even Walcott "lacked" the ear for English.[30] Yet Russians too criticized Brodsky for his eclectic use of his native tongue, the Jewish pronunciation of *r*, the English influences on his Russian. Miłosz, who wrote in a provincial Polish, was criticized by some centrally born Poles, especially younger ones, proud of their contemporary ear and unaccustomed to linguistic diversity in pre–World War II Poland. Brodsky and Miłosz were doubly, triply uprooted, and this deracination showed in their language. And yet it was language itself that was to be their place, their native soil!

According to legend, in the last part of his life Ovid wrote poetry in the language of his place of exile on the Black Sea coast. Brodsky would be an heir to that tradition, although his exile was not as dramatic as that of the Roman poet. Of Miłosz, on the other hand, one can say that he continued the tradition of Dante, who till the end of his days wrote in his own "dialect." In one of his last texts, "Bilingualism," Miłosz declared: "The resistance against writing poetry in other languages should be considered a virtue. Marina Tzvetaeva remained till her death a Russian poet to the core [Tzvetaeva wrote poetry also in French], while Iosif Brodsky, who adored poetry, was inclining in his last poems towards English, without great success. . . . We are born in a concrete point of the Earth and we have to remain faithful to this point, restrained in our following of foreign fashions." But Miłosz would not be true to himself without introducing into this statement a dissonant note. He ends the text by quoting two poems of an émigré Polish poet, Bogdan Czaykowski, which, according to Miłosz, "depict resistance to ascription to just one tongue owed to one's place of birth. The quotes show the conflict between belonging to the human family on the one hand and being beholden to the specificity of a given language on the other. It is a dilemma that no amount of thinking can resolve." The first of the poems by Czaykowski is called "Bunt wierszem" [Rebellion by Poetry], which opens with the lines:

> *I was born there.*
> *I did not choose the place.*
> *I would gladly be born simply in the grass.*
> *Grass grows everywhere. (*SL, *89)*

Emigrating at the beginning of the 1950s, at the height of the Cold War, Miłosz was most afraid of the drying up of his creative powers, and he often returned to this fear in his essays and interviews.[31] The article "Nie" (No), which he had written in 1951 to make public his break with communist Poland, opened with the sentence: "What I'm going to tell now could well be called a story of a suicide." Toward the end of this text he clarifies this point: "Suicide, the end of a literary career (and what else is it for a poet to lose his fatherland?)."[32] He was convinced then, as he mentions for example in his conversation with Renata Gorczyńska, that in order to write, a poet has to remain in his country (*PŚ*, 76). Forty-five years later, he would still ask himself how it was possible that he had managed to remain a Polish poet "among foreigners."[33] It was one of the miracles of his life, though emigration remained the source of suffering and danger. In his Nobel lecture, he said: "A patron saint of all poets in exile, who visit their towns and provinces only in remembrance, is always Dante. But how the number of Florences increased!"[34] And if from 1989 on he stopped using such dramatic language, he continuously returned to the questions surrounding the identity of a man living outside his country. What nationality, he wondered, was his friend Konstanty Jeleński, if he "spoke fluently in English, French, and Italian and moved outside of Polish émigré circles?" (*SL*, 83). Three years after so convincingly reassuring Brodsky that the poet's fear of emigration is a superstition, he wrote about the fate of the émigré poet in the following way:

"Exile accepted as a destiny, in the way we accept an incurable illness, should help us see through our self-delusions.

"He was aware of his task and people were waiting for his words, but he was forbidden to speak. Now where he lives he is free to speak but nobody listens and, moreover, he forgot what he had to say" (*TB*, 13).

It is a variation on a thought that leads back to one of Miłosz's most important sources, the writings of Adam Mickiewicz, who had written in the prologue to part 3 of *Forefathers' Eve:*

> *An exiled singer, now condemned to go*
> *Where foreign and inimicable throngs*
> *Will take for rude and idle sounds my songs.*

. . .

Alive, I shall be dead to these dear lands,
And all I think shall lie within my soul,
A diamond locked within its shell of coal.[35]

The myth of the solitary exiled poet returns in the works of Miłosz, because "love and respect of [the writer's hometown is] the only kind of love and respect that is really worth seeking" (*TB*, 18). But even without exile, Miłosz felt he was a stigmatized loner, a kind of *poète maudit*. This is very natural: in Polish culture, a poet cannot be healthy, sociable, and diligent. Yet, Miłosz never leaves a cliché undisturbed, as his "Notes on Exile" attests. It is not a complaint, or a submission to a cruel fate, even though it opens with a quotation from Mickiewicz: "He did not find happiness, for there was no happiness in his homeland." Miłosz understood what a poet needs in order to overcome the "despair inseparable from the first stage of exile," and he writes about it in a way that is reminiscent of his first letter to Brodsky. That despair results "more from one's personal shortcomings than from external circumstances" (Brodsky may have been right that Miłosz's letter was more of a challenge than a consolation), and a writer needs "new eyes, new thought, new distance." He has to superimpose the place from which he came onto the new one, the one in which he is writing, so that "the two centers and the two spaces arranged around them interfere with each other or—and this is a happy solution—coalesce." And it is not true that in exile the poet's language withers. "The new aspects and tonalities of the native tongue are discovered, for they stand out against the background of the language spoken in the new milieu. Thus the narrowing down in some areas (street idioms, slang) is compensated for by a widening in others (purity of vocabulary, rhythmic expressiveness, syntactic balance)." He can also change the language in which he is writing, "either literally, by writing in the tongue of the country of his residence, or [by using] his native tongue in such a manner that what he writes will be understandable and acceptable to a new audience. Then, however, he ceases to be an exile." In any case "he must either condemn himself to sterility or undergo a total transformation" (*TB,* 13–19).

Toward the end of his stay in Berkeley, Miłosz stopped being an exile. The word *exile* itself belonged to the Cold War epoch; after the collapse of the Iron Curtain it could not be applied any longer to Miłosz or Brodsky—instead it denoted Ovid, Dante, and Mickiewicz, poets who had been unable to return. Remaining faithful to his native tongue, Miłosz was gradually accepted into the company of American poets, and he was aware of it, as his conversation at the end of the 1970s with Renata Gorczyńska attests. He adds, however, that he never planned to write in English—he did not feel able to and such an option did not appeal to him anyway (*CCM,* 93). He was therefore still enmeshed in the theory of the link of the poet to the soil of his youth, although by his own efforts he proved it wrong. He passed most of his life outside of his country but it did not harm him as a poet. For decades, he was cut off from the daily life of the Polish language but did not lose contact with it. And, what is most important: although for years and years he was immersed in English—teaching, writing, translating into it—this immersion did not muffle the voice of his Muse. Quite the opposite; the constant company of English enriched him, opened him to new models and traditions, allowing him to write within "the main current" of Polish poetry and, at the same time, to enter into the domain of the foreign language. He possessed an unusual capacity for openness to outside influences, with steady loyalty to what was his own. He took what he needed, not a drop more.

Miłosz was not only translated into English; he was continuously translating others' works into Polish and into English. It is difficult to overestimate what translations mean for the very essence of a culture, any culture: they are the place in which the world gathers and meets. Miłosz, one could say, worshiped through translation. He started to translate when very young, and continued as long as he was able to. He called his passion for translation "the devotion of the translator." Renata Gorczyńska wrote: "If one were to measure life work by the number of written pages, Miłosz-translator would surpass Miłosz-poet" (*PŚ1*, 365). Translating meant openness for him, a dialogical stance, curiosity, continuous enrichment of technique and imagination. It was a process of learning, an attentive studying of poetry of many languages and historical periods, a close reading. No other poet in the history of Polish literature was so strongly grounded both in the Polish language and in world poetry. He enjoyed translating and described it beautifully in the already quoted poem about Anna Swir, as being "submerged / In the murmuring Polish, in meditation" (*NCP*, 598). The range of authors he translated was very large; among his contemporaries only Stanisław Barańczak surpassed him. Miłosz's translation of the Bible was a special event in the history of the Polish language; it is difficult to overestimate its importance. "When we reach for the biblical texts," he said in one of the interviews, "we are reaching for the principal tropes of all poetry."[36] To be able to do it, he had learned Hebrew, treating the task of translating from that language as an effort to cleanse Polish soil of the sin of the genocide that had been committed on its territory.[37]

He worked on the translations of biblical texts during his stay in California, when his exile seemed destined to last till the end of his life. Although that translation was carried out into Polish, he was also strongly drawn to translating into English. During his stay in the United States in 1946–50, when he was a diplomat for the Polish government and judged his English to be very poor, he had translated some poems of Tadeusz Różewicz into English, and later some of Zbigniew Herbert's. For years he did not translate his own poems, for they seemed to him untranslatable. As we can see in his Nobel lecture, Miłosz considered the entire body of Polish literature untranslatable, but that never stopped him from trying to overcome such an obstacle; he always felt responsible for "the estate of Polish poetry." In the 1960s he started to translate more Polish poets, and in 1965 he published the anthology *Postwar Polish Poetry*. Many American poets remember the encounter with this volume as one of the most important moments in their poetic development. The book started what Clare Cavanagh called "the East-European invasion of Anglo-American poetry." In an article significantly titled "The Americanization of Czesław Miłosz," she describes the influence of Miłosz's translations on English-language poetry, including such poets as Walcott, Heaney, and the Americans Robert Hass, Robert Pinsky, Edward Hirsch, Mark Strand, Rosanna Warren, Jonathan Aaron, and Carolyn Forché.[38] I enumerate here only those poets who recognize this influence and have spoken of it with gratitude. And how many more were influenced without their knowledge or ours?

At a certain moment, Miłosz felt compelled to start translating his own poems. It happened, as with Brodsky, when he encountered versions he did not like. It soon appeared that the only translations he did like were his own, even if they were imperfect. He translated his cycle "The World," for example. "Several translators have tried their hands at it," he writes in a letter to Bogdan Czaykowski (May 29, 1975), and "a fine version by Robert Hass and Robert Pinsky was published. . . . [But] I opted for a version done by myself, less ambitious but literal" (*NCP,* 749). In English-language versions of his poems Miłosz wanted to hear "the rhythmical tone" of the original, his own tone.[39] It is clear that, thanks to his total control over translations and publishing of English-language versions of his poems, his tone, rhythm, and "diction" are maintained and do not change as they necessarily would with the changes of translators. His voice is as recognizable in English as it is in Polish.

As in the case of Brodsky, Miłosz's intervention into translations of his work met with severe criticism. It is well known that translations are never perfect, can always be made anew, and therefore are never finished, which in turn leaves the original always open. Brodsky's and Miłosz's translations created new originals, interfering in that way in the traditional relation between the original and the translation (or copy), and also between the (foreign) author and the critic. According to convention, those who do not have the competence of a native speaker are not permitted, not "authorized," to write poetry in the new language, to translate poetry into it, or even to judge the adequacy of translation. Prose writing is as far as they can go. But who has more right than the author to change his text, write it anew, even in a language of translation? Like Brodsky, Miłosz does not place himself in the hands of his translators, who could find equivalents for his poems within the styles of English-language poetry. Theoretically, Miłosz agreed that a nonnative speaker lacks the feel for nuances, the depth that one can acquire only in childhood. We have seen how sternly he admonished Brodsky for refusing to submit to the requirements of English-language poetry, with its open form and weakened rhythm. And how badly he reacts to Brodsky's way of reciting his poetry as if it were a song or a prayer. He praises the fluid and suave translations of Brodsky's poems prepared by well-known American poets. But, in his own case, everything he does is in conflict with these proscriptions. Miłosz translates his poems by himself, always having them read by a native speaker, but "the participation of the cotranslator," he wrote in the letter to Czaykowski, "is limited to some corrections in grammar and style *within* [emphasis in original] the rhythmical shape which I impose."[40] The practice of living in a language was stronger than long-standing cultural proscriptions.

Like Brodsky, he is unable to accept even the most "successful" translations if they do not reflect his voice and are in the style of another poet or another tradition. And there was no tradition within English-language poetry with which he could truly identify. Submitting to the voice of the translator or to another style is of course common, but it is very difficult to do if the destination language is well known to the author of the translated work. And for both poets

English was a second home. Gradually they became less and less able to accept somebody else's versions of their poems. They start to translate-write their poems in English, introducing into their new tongue their own way of talking, their "accent." The difference between them was that, even if both Polish and Russian poetry deal with the highest levels of spirituality, Polish poets tend to use a quiet, understated voice. This is why Miłosz, without acting against the spirit of his own poetry, sounds much "easier" in English.

In the last years of his life, Miłosz depended more and more on the translations made or revised by Robert Hass. In the 2001 commentary to his "Treatise on Poetry," Miłosz wrote that Hass's translation of the work was "unusual, and in the eyes of the connoisseurs a masterpiece of translation." But in the previous sentence he wrote that it was *he himself* who had translated the work in its entirety into metric verse and "in this form [had] entrusted it to Hass."[41] As far as I know, Hass's knowledge of Polish is limited—a situation that would give Miłosz an even stronger voice in the choice of the final form of his work. But there is in any case a great, perhaps overwhelming, disparity between translating a poem, even one's own, and creating it. Creation arises from the first impulse, from the whisper of the Muse, from the "ear" reacting to that whisper. By teaching Polish literature, by writing its history, and, most of all, by translating the Bible into Polish, Miłosz was working within the very heart of the Polish language. He believed in mimesis and suffered chronically from a feeling of the inadequacy of his language for capturing the reality that he wanted to communicate. During World War II, when he still lived in Poland, he translated Eliot's "The Waste Land" and prepared an anthology of English and American poetry, abandoning, as was already mentioned, French poetry, which he used to love very much. Now he had come to think that French poetry focused excessively on formal values, limiting the possibilities of its content. Anglo-American poetry, on the other hand, appealed to him because of "its descriptiveness," and for him, as for Brodsky, English was extremely poetic. Also, he was always looking for "a more spacious form," which he often found in various models of English-language poetry. By its versification, themes, and didacticism, his "Moral Treatise" refers to Auden's "New Year Letter." His "Treatise on Poetry"—a work without any precedent in Polish literature—was inspired by Karl Shapiro's "Essay on Rime." The choice of the form of the treatise was a rebellion against the then dominant avant-gardist rejection of form. Miłosz was very proud of this work, and said in 2001 that "a great part of the regard that Brodsky had for me I attribute to his reading of the Treatise, which convinced him of the value of my poetry."[42] While Miłosz confesses to these inspirations and influences stemming from English-language poetry, he also declares that he wrote both treatises to—and here he uses an expression borrowed from Brodsky—"please the shadow" of Adam Mickiewicz.[43] Brodsky's words serve to describe the essence of his poetic work.

Clare Cavanagh writes that W. H. Auden and Karl Shapiro showed Miłosz the way to resist history, to maintain an equilibrium between lyricism and civic poetry. She cites the Polish literary critic Jerzy Kwiatkowski, who has described Miłosz as an "amplifier" of modern Polish culture. Miłosz's "'rehabilitation of discourse, of the long discursive poem,' was achieved partly through the influence of the

Anglo-American poets—Blake, Whitman, Yeats, Eliot, and others— whose work Miłosz had read and translated. A contemporary Anglophone poet might be surprised at this," Cavanagh continues, "for one of Miłosz's gifts to this adopted country has been seen as precisely the same kind of 'rehabilitation of discourse' that Kwiatkowski ascribes in part to his reading of Anglo-American poetry." Cavanagh quotes several opinions of various Anglophone poets, adding: "Since his Nobel Prize in 1980 and the publication of his Harvard Norton lectures as *The Witness of Poetry* (1983), he has come to serve as a kind of de facto poet laureate not just to the States, but to the English-speaking world at large."[44] Miłosz, Herbert, Różewicz, and Szymborska were taken by Anglophone poets as models of how to write poetry that is both personal and civic. Their poems are steeped in history, which they at the same time keep at a distance. These poets have been influential thanks to the talent and devotion of their translators. Only in that way can cultures become fruitfully intertwined.

Miłosz often declared his resistance to romantic poetry; his immersion in the English-language culture had kept him from the automatic literary impulses that governed Polish poetry. He needed models of discursive poetry; he wanted to talk about everything, from the most concrete description to the most abstract reflections. Brodsky's needs were similar. Of course, the search for form was not formal. The Polish verse line, syllabic because of the constancy of accentuation, resulted from imitation of medieval Church Latin. Its most frequent length was eleven or thirteen syllables with a caesura after the fifth or seventh syllable. Miłosz used these and other traditional lines, usually without rhyming. But as early as during his first postwar stay in America, he adopted as a basic structure of his poems something that he called "a little line": one that corresponds to the unit of meaning. As his model, Miłosz frequently mentioned Walt Whitman. He was enchanted by the capacity, spaciousness, and dignity of Whitman's phrase, which Miłosz could hear clearly since it was derived from the Bible. He calls his wish "to embrace everything, to contain everything in a verse," his "Whitmanian temptation." And it was this temptation, linked to the search "for a new formula outside of the models of the traditional syllabic versification," that was one of the motives for his translation of biblical texts.[45] Gradually, biblical verse became the most common metrum of Miłosz's poetry. When he was reading his poems in English, the biblical cadence sounded American, native. For Americans, his accent was thick, but his tone was not foreign. Leonard Nathan expressed the point succinctly: "Even in translation, his poetry is simply shining . . . the long verses, which in Polish are so rhythmical, do not sound in English like a translation."[46]

As we have seen, Miłosz underlined that his exile, while purifying his language, did not erode his grasp of his "mother tongue." His friend, the Kraków literary critic Jan Błoński, described this "tongue" as a language of the prewar, Vilnius intelligentsia, with a "spoken" style, a melody of its own, and a rather antiquated vocabulary.[47] It was definitely a language of the provinces. This is the language about which Miłosz wrote: "Faithful mother tongue . . . you were my native land; I lacked any other" (*NCP*, 245). The language is faithful because it stays with him in exile, and his own faithfulness toward the language is a sign of alienation from the West, his scar and his pride, like

Mickiewicz's faithfulness toward the suffering motherland.[48] Brodsky did not speak of defending his language; he readily acknowledged that English influenced his Russian and his way of writing poems. But Miłosz steadily rejected "foreign fashions." He did not like what he considered to be Brodsky's poetic "dogmatism," his rigid commitment to certain forms, his overall lack of moderation and tendency to overrate the role of poetry and language. But most of all, he did not like the poems Brodsky was writing in English.

In his book *Prywatne obowiązki* (Private Duties), Miłosz declares that writers who perfectly absorb a foreign language, such as Conrad or Nabokov, have "a secret taint."[49] A similar attitude toward the acquisition of a foreign language was expressed by Hannah Arendt, who remained in the United States after the war and did not return to her native Germany. Her German accent in English was a source of pride for her, as was the fact that German remained her *Muttersprache.* In a conversation with Günter Gauss titled "What Remains? It Is the Mother Tongue That Remains," she declared that those who speak very well in a foreign language use "a language in which one cliché expels the other because the productivity that one shows in one's own language has been neatly cut off, as one forgets that language." Jacques Derrida, from whom I take these words of Arendt, juxtaposes them to an attitude toward language shown by Emmanuel Lévinas, a multilingual person if there ever was one. "A different experience, indeed," Derrida writes about him, "for someone who wrote, taught, and lived almost all his life in the French language, whereas Russian, Lithuanian, German, and Hebrew remained his other familiar languages. There seems to be little solemn reference to a mother tongue in his works and no self-assurance assumed in proximity with it, except for the gratitude he expressed, on behalf of someone who declared that 'the essence of language is friendship and hospitality,' to the French language on each occasion, to French as an adopted or elected language, the welcoming language, the language of the host." The difference, Derrida says, is Lévinas's suspicion toward the "sacrality of the root. . . . [For him] language is 'expression' rather than [as for Heideggerian Arendt] generation or foundation."[50] This juxtaposition describes well the difference between Miłosz and Brodsky. By his way of writing and his loyalty to Polish, Miłosz affirms the foundational value of the language of childhood—a romantic, Mickiewiczean attachment to his roots. Brodsky feels gratitude toward the friendliness and hospitality of the language of the host. Miłosz was faithful to the language that was a memory. Brodsky was in search of his own language, while remaining faithful to what he called the Language.

I think that these two directions of faithfulness were not a matter of free choice. We should reach back to both poets' family histories—histories that were a result, of course, of the pressures of the European past. Miłosz was better settled in the world and in his language; even if that language was imposed long ago on his ancestors by colonization (as he suggested many times), now it was his own language, especially because it was linked to the Catholic faith, of which Miłosz was a deep believer. All the changes in his life took place within this homeostasis, this somewhat painful but often very delicious tension between being very Polish and being not-so-Polish after all. His past, his family, and his history made him stronger. An exclusive devotion to Russian could only weaken Brodsky. He was radically cut off from the history of his family, from the language and culture of his ancestors. A dislike of that history is written into Russian, starting with the very word "Jew"—*Jewriej*. It was a word that described him in his own language, a word for himself that he could hardly force himself to pronounce. In the language that Miłosz used, no hostility toward his ancestors was inscribed. Brodsky's otherness was present in his native language. When he was speaking in this language about himself, the violence of the effacement and replacement of that other, previous language had to be felt. Perhaps that hostility inscribed in the Russian kept reminding him of the "lacking" language, and this was the reason for his continuous search, for reaching for other languages and other ways of being in a language. Burdened, as he was, by the "monolingualism of the Other," he felt entrapped within the tongue of his childhood, the only one, the loved one, the language that kept him from that other, replaced, unloved language or languages. Derrida wrote about this "lack," analyzing his own total devotion to French and the assimilation into it of his own ancestors, the Jews of Maghreb. He would love to write, he says, a text which would have the title "The Jews of the Twentieth Century: The Monolingualism of the Guest." In it, he would write about assimilation, about "a certain mode of loving and desperate appropriation of language and through it of a forbidding as well as forbidden speech" (33). Switching, however partially, into English, Brodsky becomes "a guest" of the world.

These are then two different strategies of "linguistic disobedience." Miłosz, who at the beginning was a traditional exile, separated from his reader, chose faithfulness to his native tongue and resistance against the speech of "the host." He worked in English, but his main activity—writing poetry—was done only in Polish. Brodsky did not take on the role of the exile—in the era of mass migration, global connections on land, air, and seas, that role had been exhausted. Miłosz was still an exile, Brodsky was only an immigrant. And he decided to enter into the new language just like an enterprising immigrant, with an immigrant's audacity and accent. When asked how one has to change in order to be able to write poetry in an acquired language, Brodsky replied: "One does not have to change, it is enough to fall in love with the language in which one writes" (*StS*, 30). Writing poetry was for him an ability independent from the language in which it takes place. And, just as Miłosz could become the patron saint of exiled poets, Brodsky should be declared the patron of immigrant poets—of those whose faces are turned not only toward their native Florence but who see as well the tree outside their window. And this is why they write poetry with a foreign accent.

Epilogue

NINE

Death and Friendship

Miłosz was a prodigious worker, felicitously productive. He died after a long and fruitful life—having been active as a writer for no less than seventy-five years. At his funeral, August 27, 2004, in Kraków, Rabbi Sacha Pecaric declared: "Miłosz was a poet of plenitude, and his life attained such fullness that, like old patriarchs, he left us sated with his days." Brodsky died too early, knocked down while still rising. After the deaths of the two poets, wakes, masses, memorial services proliferated around the world: for Miłosz in Kraków, New York, Berkeley, and Vilnius, among other places; for Brodsky in New York, Moscow, St. Petersburg, and Venice. In both cases obituaries, articles, and poems were printed in scores of newspapers, their deaths unleashing enormous poetic energy. The death of a poet demands to be recorded in poems, to be transformed into words. Although by now there already have been numerous commemorations in books, articles, and documentaries, the work of mourning is far from completed. It has been said that, by dying, our poets entrust themselves to us, their readers. This book is one of the steps in this commemorative effort.

Elegiac lyric poetry is the basic mode used by contemporary poets to record a passing moment, the transitoriness of life, one's own or somebody else's. Both Brodsky and Miłosz practiced this type of poetry, attracted by its openness to autobiography. Mikhail Lotman has written that in the works of Brodsky, death is almost an obsession; Lotman makes his point by enumerating poems about the deaths not only of people but also of birds, centaurs, and butterflies.[1] David Bethea expresses the same opinion in his important book *Joseph Brodsky and the Creation of Exile.*[2] The poet lived in the shadow of death, constantly reminded of it by his unsound heart. In 1981, in an essay on Tsvetaeva's poem on the death of Rainer Maria Rilke, Brodsky summarized his thoughts regarding poetic elegy. Poems "on the death of" a poet, he wrote, create an occasion for the author to express the feelings caused by that loss as well as for general musings related to "death per se." But "the tragic timbre is always autobiographical. . . . Any 'on the death of' poem contains an element of self-portrait." Using tragic intonation, the author always mourns himself, his own loss, the passing of his own life and "the sense of loneliness . . . intrinsic to a writer." But the death of a poet is "something more than a human loss. Above all, it is a drama of language as such: that of inadequacy of linguistic experience vis-à-vis existential experience." Funeral lament is not due to the fact that "existence without the poet is unthinkable but precisely in that such an existence *is* thinkable.

And as a consequence of this conceivability, the author's attitude toward herself, still living, is more merciless, more uncompromising" (*LTO*, 190, 198, 205).

Brodsky and Miłosz both wrote so many "poems on the death of poets" that it was hardly surprising that elegies were written on the occasion of their own deaths. In their writings, they commemorated lives and deaths of other writers; now it was their turn to be remembered and praised. Besides, Miłosz had been solemnly celebrated even during his lifetime; his birthdays were an occasion for great festivities, for example, especially after he returned to Kraków, a city that loves to pay homage to its poets and knows how to enjoy it, too. In an article commemorating Miłosz's ninetieth birthday, Adam Zagajewski, who also has returned to Kraków from exile, wrote that, like Cavafy and Auden, he is "a poet of great intelligence and great ecstasy and reason."[3] Another member of that poetic family, Seamus Heaney, celebrated the eighty-fifth birthday of Miłosz with the poem "The Master"; and, after the Old Poet's death, he dedicated to him an adaptation of Sophocles. The first lines of this work speak of the role Miłosz played for younger poets:

> *His instruction calmed us, his company and voice*
> *Were like high tidings in the summer trees,*
> *Except this time he turned away and left us.*[4]

In a long obituary of the Polish poet called "The Door Stands Open," Heaney explained what made him associate Miłosz with Oedipus.[5] Miłosz was a Wise Man who Returned—obviously Heaney himself thought about life's cycle as exile and return. When he visited Miłosz in Kraków, he found him sitting in his living room by the bust of his late wife Carol, "being ministered to by his daughter-in-law, and perhaps it was her hovering attentions as much as his translated appearance that brought to mind the aged Oedipus being minded by daughters in the grove at Colonus, the old king who had arrived where he knew he would die. Colonus was not his birthplace, but it was where he had come home to himself, to the world, and to the otherworld; and the same could be said of Miłosz in Kraków." The Master who chooses how and where he is going to die: this is how Heaney inscribed Miłosz into literary tradition. A classical gesture of commemoration, of endowing the poet's death with dignity and even majesty.

Heaney traveled to Kraków for Miłosz's funeral and participated in the solemn poetry reading that followed it. In *New Republic* article from which the above quotation comes, he associated Miłosz with several other figures from antiquity: Orpheus, Tiresias, and Socrates; he also caught there the uniqueness of Miłosz's poetry: it is "the speech of the whole man." While he mentioned Miłosz's numerous friends, it remained unclear whether he considered himself to be among them; the tone of the article is one of distance and respect. He used a different voice to commemorate the death of Joseph Brodsky, whom he also invoked in the same article about Miłosz. Brodsky, in fact, was frequently mentioned in Miłosz's obituaries—an obvious result of the persistent repetition of "my friend" by the Polish poet. Heaney was a poetic "contemporary" of Brodsky; their friendship was an association of equals, of brothers. The poem "Audenesque," from which I quoted in the last chapter, speaks of Brodsky on a first-name basis, criticizes him (through tears), bows in sorrow and love in front of his poetic obsessions, especially the one that David Bethea called his "Audentic-ity," that is, his adoration of the work of the English poet. During the memorial service for Joseph Brodsky in the Cathedral of St. John the Divine in New York, Heaney read "Reveille," probably the mourned Russian's most Audenesque poem. And in a long commemorative ar-ticle, published in the *New York Times Book Review*, Heaney declared: "Having to speak of him in the past tense feels like an affront to gram-mar itself" (quoting from Brodsky's sentences from his elegies of both Auden and Stephen Spender).[6] No classical comparisons for Brodsky, no Orpheus or Socrates, rather the lament of a bereaved friend. He considered Brodsky "a verifying presence," while Miłosz formed a kind of model or aspiration. He believed both of them to be poetic geniuses. Miłosz was a king, while Brodsky was his fellow traveler in the world of poetry.

This difference is important, because in the remembrances writ-ten for both of our poets the words *friend* and *friendship* appear with an insistence and frequency that is truly remarkable. Sometimes I feel that, out of gratitude, the readers themselves consider the poets their friends. But these words are used most frequently by writers, journal-ists, and poets, as if *friend* meant a member of the same guild, "a fel-low writer." The elegies devoted to poets build the pedigree for those who write them. This praise is a reciprocal operation: a written work creates its own antecedents, and if literature is to continue to exist, this process of creation has to be constantly renewed. The circularity of literary witnessing has been described in the stories of Jorge Luis Borges, who was of course an excellent poet. An example of such operation can be found in the anthology *Lament for the Makers: A*

Memorial Anthology, composed by the poet W. S. Merwin out of works of twenty-three poets who, he says, influenced him. He chooses as his predecessors Eliot, Auden, James Merrill, and similar poets. Each death changes this hierarchy, the place in the long line. The dead poet is moved into a new category: from a competitor he can turn into a patron. But the process of commemoration is part of an effort to combat death. And loneliness. Time is illiterate, as Adam Zagajewski has written. As long as the poets remember their predecessors, they don't stop being alive.

The death of Joseph Brodsky caused an outpouring of writings about him. The authors, some of whom have been mentioned in this book, constitute a dense network in the "republic of poets." Among them were the Russians Lev Loseff, Yevgeny Rein, Anatoly Nayman, Jakov Gordin, Ludmilla Shtern, Natalia Gorbanevskaya; and, from the members of the international brotherhood of poets, Mark Strand, Derek Walcott, Seamus Heaney, and Daniel Weissbort, as well as Susan Sontag and Miłosz. A former student of Brodsky, Małgosia Krasowska, wrote in an e-mail that circulated on the occasion of the fourth anniversary of his death: "A great Master, Poet, Reader, Writer, Friend. He often mentioned that to commemorate a poet one should either write or read a poem." She recommended that his poems be read on that day. The same message was given in a poem written for Brodsky by his friend and translator the poet Anthony Hecht: "He now dwells in the care of each of us. / Reader, dwell with his poems." This poem, called "A Death in Winter," was one of several published in a minianthology commemorating Brodsky that appeared in the *New Yorker* in late 1996. Many more poems were published in numerous periodicals.

Brodsky's devotion to the cause of poetry, his promotion of poets' work and standing in society, were among the reasons to mourn and celebrate him. In the elegies written for him, it is his voice, the intensity of his conversation that is most often recalled. The poet's voice contains the essence of his work, his "spiritual frequency" or wavelength, to use Zagajewski's formulation. It is what remains when his physical presence has ended. "Poets' real biographies," wrote Brodsky in a text about Walcott, "are like those of birds, almost identical— their real data are in the way they sound" (*LTO*, 164). In the texts and poems written after his death, his friends complained both that no new poems would be created and that the physical voice had been silenced. Loseff mentioned both things in his remembrance, as did Heaney. In the poem "Conversation with a Seagull," Carol Rumens goes so far as to "quote" a (I assume imaginary) sentence of Brodsky with his Russian inflection. Another poet, Glyn Maxwell, wrote in the poem "Under These Lights": "Your voice is hung in the heights of the ballroom / A flex of vowels slung on a crown of hooks." And Mark Strand in his poem "Et Cetera, Et Cetera" tries to capture and retain the energy and hurry with which Brodsky hurled himself into conversation, with words too slow to follow the quickness of his thinking, and sentences abandoned to move to a higher point of argument.[7]

It was not only his American and Russian friends who wrote about him. Many of Tomas Venclova's poems from 1996 deal with the death of Brodsky, thereby continuing a poetic dialogue that had begun at least as early as 1972. Polish poets seem to have been especially affected by his death. First came many declarations. Miłosz said that as long as Brodsky was alive, his fellow poets felt safe. Wisława Szymborska recalled that Brodsky was the only person who proudly pronounced the word *poet* "without any shyness, with a kind of provocative freedom."[8] Poems for him were written by many well-established poets, including Ryszard Krynicki, Julia Hartwig, Anna Frajlich, and Adam Zagajewski. In the poem "A Morning in Vicenza," Zagajewski captured the moment of learning about the death of two of his friends, Brodsky and the Polish filmmaker Krzysztof Kieślowski. About his Russian friend he wrote: "you lived two times as strongly as the rest, on two continents, / In two languages, in the world and in imagination."[9]

A separate place should be made for the poems in which Derek Walcott recalled the Russian poet. Walcott remembers him in a beautiful poem "A Blessing Rain," but especially in his "Italian Eclogues," dedicated to Brodsky. The six-part "Italian Eclogues" was a reply to Brodsky's Italian poems—a similar use of a traditional literary form with its pastoral aura and dialogue. It is a conversation with "Joseph," or, at least, a long apostrophe. The poem—a trip through Italy—follows the Russian poet, seeing in him similarities to Ovid, mentioning Montale and Quasimodo, and, of course, Auden. Walcott is performing for Brodsky the same service Heaney accomplished for Miłosz: he inscribes him into classical landscape and tradition. Searching for him in Venice, Walcott writes: "Off the ferry, your shade turns the corners / of a book and stands at the end of perspective, waiting for me." Brodsky embodies for Walcott the very tradition of poetry.[10]

Miłosz was not commemorated by people his own age, since most of them had died. But the number of those who grieved after his death was very great. The most frequent words of mourning were of course those from fellow Poles. Again, the feeling expressed was that they had lost a friend. Sometimes the word *friend* appeared in his obituaries in surprising contexts. In Poland, he was called friend by publishers and editorial houses, by newspapers and embassies; the Society for the Defense of the Białowieża Forest mourned him as a friend of that forest. In the last years of his life, he signed many appeals and protest letters, participated in public debates and worried about many causes. He inspired deep gratitude in his collaborators and acquaintances. Brodsky softened in his last years, but not as much as Miłosz, who became cordial and patient. It was a pleasure to work with him; he was quick, nonpedantic, to the point. At his funeral, Adam Michnik spoke of a magnetism and greatness that did not interfere with his friendliness and simplicity in his relations with friends. "I say farewell to the friend who joyfully greeted his friends and liked to laugh with his great, Gargantuan laughter," wrote Zagajewski.[11] His deep and truly unique laughter acted on his interlocutors like a vitamin of life. This laughter, mourned as much as Brodsky's voice and intense conversation, is difficult to describe: deep, explosive, with a very large range of sounds, profoundly infectious. When Miłosz gradually lost his hearing, this laugh started from another place on the scale, it was not as well tuned as before. Its infectiousness was its strongest side: it cordially pulled in the people who were within its range. It expressed in a primordial way Miłosz's attitude to life, which he found wonderful, although somewhat ridiculous or comical. There was nothing ironic, sardonic, bitter in his laughter; rather, it expressed his appetite and vitality. It was healthy, approving, and wise.

Tomas Venclova wrote in his remembrance of Miłosz: "I am happy and proud to have been a fellow-citizen and contemporary of Czesław Miłosz." That fellow-citizenship must have meant their common American passports, and Venclova's testimony has been printed in a volume in which other American citizens—Edward Hirsch, Leonard Nathan, Robert Pinsky—declared that Miłosz was for them an American poet, as well as a poet of the world. Their claim was not a denial of his Polishness, but an acknowledgment of the range of his poetry, of its impact. Miłosz did not feel to them to be a translated, adapted, exotic voice: he was one of them, their very own. In a poem for him, Jane Hirshfield recalled their common interest in Zen Buddhism. Leon Wieseltier called him a friend and "an indispensable man."[12]

Friendship is the thread that links the reminiscences about both of the poets. But where do these many friends come from? Some of the reminiscences were written by people who were intimate with our poets; however, to cite Aristotle, friendship is a rare union and one can have only a few true friends. In its highest form, friendship is a kind of love, and even of affiliation with God: Miłosz's apokatastasis is an overcoming of the loneliness into which we are thrown by death—it is a return not so much to our corporeality as to "God's friendship." Even the simplest act of mourning is a rite of friendship, the bringing back of the dead, because death does not end friendship but turns it into vigil and memory. In his treatise on friendship, Cicero wrote that it permits a continuation of life after one's own death—it guarantees posthumous existence as long as our friends' lives last. *Mortui vivunt*: the dead are alive, he wrote, because the sorrow and respect of their friends continues.[13] Because friendship is an activity, it expresses itself in action, in memorializing. This is exactly what Miłosz and Brodsky did when they were bending over their dead.

Miłosz, Brodsky, and the poets who mourn their deaths share a conviction that their tasks set them apart and that they are linked by the sense of community, a kind of fraternal love—*philia*—that we can only call friendship. This feeling of fraternity with other poets was well expressed by Miłosz in his poem "Report," calling his writing of poetry not a lonely pursuit but one in which he is "a companion in an expedition that never ceases," devoted to "the same unnamed service" (*NCP,* 590, 613). This service, and it is important, consists in giving voice to those who cannot speak themselves, who suffer, who are not here anymore. In a 1948 poem, "To Tadeusz Różewicz, the Poet," Miłosz wrote: lucky is the nation that has a poet, the nation that in its toil does not march in silence. Brodsky, too, mentioned luck: Poland was lucky to have three great poets. Yet neither Miłosz nor Brodsky directed their poetry to a nation, or to any other community. Their poetry was destined directly and separately to each one of us. And in this I find the explanation of the friendship that their readers bestow upon these poets.

TEN

Return and Death

There was no greater difference between Brodsky and Miłosz than the ways in which they passed away. Brodsky died suddenly, alone, at night. Miłosz had been gravely ill, dying for a long time. After his death, Brodsky was buried several times, provisionally, until finally he found his place of rest on a small funerary island overlooking Venice. Miłosz's funeral procession was led through Kraków crowds by the highest Church authorities to a place of rest for Meritorious Poles. Brodsky escaped, slipped away; the Kraków funeral ceremony was Miłosz's final return. Both places of rest—the grave and the tomb—are temporary. The cemetery of San Michele is threatened by rising waters and could be submerged for good before long. The crypt in which Miłosz has been housed is already deemed too modest, so that his remains may be moved to the Wawel castle, the place of bards and kings. The apotheosis of Miłosz would then be accompanied by the literal sinking of Brodsky.

Joseph Brodsky died during the night of January 28, 1996, in his Brooklyn apartment—in May of that year he would have turned fifty-six. After a dinner and evening conversation with his wife, Maria, his collaborator, Ann Kjellberg, and her husband, Eric Zerof, he went upstairs to his study where he was felled by a heart attack. He had been getting ready for a third round of heart surgery, but he was not rushing into it, as it was known to be risky. Everybody who was in contact with him around that time was aware of his illness, yet his death was a horrible surprise. In the minds of his friends, Heaney wrote, he existed as "some kind of principle of indestructibility" because of his intensity, boldness, of the "immediate vertical takeoff" of his conversation, with "no deceleration possible."[1] When he was feeling at his worst, and in his last years he had difficulty even walking, he would take a pill, smoke more intensely, drink a cup of coffee, all the time intensely concentrated on the topic at hand. Listening to him was an extraordinary experience—his was perhaps the liveliest intelligence in New York, a city hardly lacking in intelligent people.

The shock of his death provoked an eruption of sorrow and bitterness. Resentful gossip and accusations circulated among the Russian diaspora in the United States: his health had been neglected, he was killed by bad doctors, by critical book reviews. In Russia, the expressions of sorrow were even stronger, though Brodsky—a Jew and an émigré—was scarcely loved by everybody. The state and the representatives of the literary organizations recognized his greatness and took steps to get him back. A group of writers appealed to President

Yeltsin to bring the body to Russia and organize a state funeral. They were convinced—this was one of the pieces of gossip, entirely false, then circulating—that this is what he had requested in his testament. Yeltsin and the prime minister, Victor Chernomyrdin, agreed to this proposal. The newspaper *Izvestia* announced a couple of days after Brodsky's death that the mayor of St. Petersburg, Anatoly Sobchak, at the instigation of Yevgeny Yevtushenko, had sent a letter to the widow proposing the funeral in that city. Brodsky's posthumous return was considered completely obvious. But Brodsky did not leave any instructions in this matter. Although well aware of the state of his health, he never said where he wanted to be buried. "I don't know anymore what earth will nurse my carcass," he wrote in "The Fifth Anniversary" (*CPE*, 244). In a television interview, he said that he could rest in South Hadley, Massachusetts, where he had a house—the surrounding nature there reminded him of Russia. He also said in a conversation with Sven Birkerts that he would like to die in Venice. But one thing was clear: he had always repeated that he did not want to return to Russia.

He was often asked about returning, especially after receiving his Nobel Prize. And he had a standard reply to that question: the impossibility of any return as such, the irreversibility of going away. In one of the interviews he said: "I am not a pendulum, Lyuba. To swing one's self back and forth . . . I don't think I would ever do that. It's just that a person moves in only one direction. And only AWAY. Away from a place, away from that thought which has occurred, away from one's self. It's impossible to enter the same river twice. And you can't step twice on the same pavement. It has changed with each new wave of cars . . . with the passage of time you become more and more an autonomous body, you become a capsule, released towards an unknown destination. For a certain amount of time, the force of gravity is still active, but at some point you pass beyond a certain boundary and a different system of gravity arises—on the outside."[2] He expressed the same thought in "December in Florence," a poem written only four years after leaving Russia, which opens with a motto from Akhmatova: "He has not returned to his old Florence, / even after having died." The motto echoes the opening line of the last stanza of his poem: "There are cities one won't see again" (*CPE*, 130–32). There is no doubt that the city in question was St. Petersburg. At most, he wanted to appear, as in the immaterial visit in the poem for Tomas Venclova, for one moment, just to see and touch. Yevgeny Rein said that after Brodsky's death, he dreamed about a one-evening incognito visit in "Piter"—St. Petersburg's nickname. That did not happen; Lev Loseff titled the last chapter of Brodsky's biography "The One Who Did Not Return."

A model Return from Exile was performed by Aleksander Solzhenitsyn who, in 1994, left behind his Vermont retreat and traveled by train from the Far East to Moscow, stopping among the crowds greeting him to hear about their problems and sorrows. Such a return, even in a simplified version, did not fit the poetics of Brodsky's life. Pressed by questioners and, after the collapse of the Soviet Union, by invitations, he would explain that he did not want to expose himself to celebrations and awards, did not want to be a diva. This refusal was also linked to his gradual move into English. If I exchanged one empire for the other, he seemed to be saying, the role of

National Poet is not for me. He consciously rejected all the elements that were part of that role. He was ironic and antinostalgic, did not revel in his childhood memories; he demythologized his early literary friendships and the greatest love of his youth. He did not agree to play the role of a victim of the regime, or that of the persecuted poet. He was devoted to his craft, to language, not to a nation or a fatherland. Perhaps he was also blocked by his fragile health, by the fear of an effort that could kill him, although he was not in the habit of avoiding exertion. It is more likely that he did not contemplate return because he was cut off from religion. He was self-taught not only in matters of culture but also in matters of faith, including his acquaintance with the Bible. In a conversation with David Bethea, he said that he grew up in an atheistic state, where "Christianity wasn't available."[3] This lack of religious perspective may have left him insensitive to the ideas of Beginning and Return. Reading the Bible for the first time when he was already twenty-three left him "shepherdless. . . . I wouldn't really know *what to return to,*" he said, "I don't have any notion of paradise . . . [or] afterlife."[4] It is unclear to what degree one can compensate in later life for such an upbringing. In the case of Miłosz, his return had an explicitly religious dimension. Brodsky approached Time in a different way. He was conquering it through Language.

Time constitutes the basic theme of Brodsky's work, and in his hierarchically structured mind it is more important than space. Time submits only to language—that is, the rhythm of poetry. "Time, conscious of its monotony, calls forth men to tell its yesterday from its tomorrow," he writes, "[but] what the past and the future have in common is our imagination, which conjures them. And our imagination is rooted in our eschatological dread: the dread of thinking that we are without precedence or consequence" (*OGR*, 291–92, 269). He makes that claim in an even stronger form in his text about Tsvetaeva: "A poetic 'paradise' is not limited to 'eternal bliss,' and it is not threatened with the overcrowding of a dogmatic paradise. In contrast to the standard Christian paradise that is presented as a kind of last instance, the soul's dead end, poetic paradise is, rather, a peak, and a bard's soul is not so much perfected as left in a continual state of motion. The poetic idea of eternal life on the whole gravitates more toward a cosmogony than toward theology. . . . Dante's paradise is much more interesting than the ecclesiastical version of it" (*LTO*, 203–4).

One has to approach these declarations without being literal-minded. Brodsky is a poet of philosophical irony, of provocative panache. But these passages do express his thoughts about life and death. He did not expect an encounter with God or a resurrection. The soul of the poet embodies itself in his creations, so it does not make sense to juxtapose it to his physical existence. Not only is the poet's biography contained in his work but so too is the materiality of his soul. "The poet lives in Language—the element of human subjectivity," Adam Pomorski summarized.[5] And after death, he remains in language. Perhaps this explains why he was not concentrating on his place of burial: his shadow, as Walcott wrote, was resident in books. His afterlife is in his poems, guarded in the memory of those who are still alive, and in the memory of the poets who want to please his shadow, just as he pleased the shadow of his "beloved" Auden. The readers and poets to whose memory he was entrusting his poems were not only Russian, of course. And this could have been still another reason why he did not want to be buried in his motherland.

The extreme cold which gripped New York after his death reminded mourners of Leningrad winters. His open casket was on view in the funeral home on Bleecker Street, in the Village, not far from Morton Street, where he lived for many years before he moved to Brooklyn Heights. His favorite coffee shop—Caffe Reggio—was on the neighboring street. The long line to see his body was composed of mourners covered in furs and scarves. They were coming and going, some sitting on the benches in the room in which the coffin stood. In the Beinecke archive one can find the signing book, but the list there is far from complete as not everybody stopped to sign in. He rested in the coffin in his brown velvet jacket, with a small cross placed between his hands. Many Russians kissed him good-bye. A New York Russian-language newspaper wrote that Czesław Miłosz, who flew in from California with his wife, touched his forehead with his lips.

The bitter cold continued on March 8, the day of the memorial service in the Cathedral of St. John the Divine. There was a mass, music, and a poetry reading of Brodsky's poems, all in the gigantic space full of people holding slim candles in mournful dusk. The readers included Jonathan Aaron, Seamus Heaney, Anthony Hecht, Lev Loseff, Mark Strand, Yevgeny Rein, Derek Walcott, Tomas Venclova, Melissa Green, and Rosanna Warren. The first to speak was Miłosz, who was the only one to read a poem of his own rather than a poem by Brodsky or one of his favored dead poets. At the end, we heard the voice of Brodsky himself, floating in the space above the mourners. Several people wrote accounts of the ceremony—it was an extremely literary event from many points of view. *Zeszyty Literackie,* the Polish quarterly with which he used to collaborate, paid attention to the winterly, Leningrad-like atmosphere of the evening. Miłosz chronicled the magnificence of the occasion. Daniel Weissbort expressed his and his Jewish friends' puzzlement at the very Christian nature of the celebration. For New York newspapers it was part social page— three Nobel Prize laureates—part reminiscence.

A smaller group of mourners met a year and a half later—on June 21, 1997—for Brodsky's final burial on the island of San Michele in Venice. There was no cold, of course, on this occasion. Although Venice was overflowing with tourists, the cemetery of San Michele and the church in which the mass was held were cool and relatively empty. Miłosz flew in this time as well; disembarking from the plane he said to Robert Faggen: "I have to finish this." The cemetery of San Michele is Catholic, but there are parts of it that are devoted to Protestants and to Christian Orthodox believers. Igor Stravinsky and Sergey Diaghilev are buried there. Brodsky's grave is in the Protestant part of the cemetery, and the funeral service over his grave was led by a woman-pastor of the Waldensian church. Originally, a place was reserved for Brodsky close to the ornate tomb of Ezra Pound and his wife, Olga Rudge, but then another location was found. Brodsky did not like Pound, and in his *Watermark* he had written without sympathy about his widow. He had visited her once in Venice together with Susan Sontag, one of the mourners present at his own funeral. Also present in Venice were Adam Zagajewski with his wife,

Maja, as well as Rein, Nayman, Venclova, Aaron, and Strand. After the Americans and Russians, the largest group was from Poland, among them Zofia Kapuścińska Ratajczakowa. After the lowering of the coffin, the mourners proceeded to the church. A Catholic mass followed, even though Brodsky had not been baptized. Here, just as in his life, he remained different, barely fitting in with his surroundings. After the mass, several of his poems were read by Mark Strand, Adriana Vianello, and Lev Loseff. His family was represented by his son, Andrei Basmanov; his four-year-old daughter, Anna; and his widow, Maria. In the evening, during the common supper of the "friends of Joseph"—as we were called in the invitation—Miłosz, mindful of his seniority, spoke at length to Andrei Basmanov, accompanying him in his "son's job." The fresh grave was covered by flowers; by now it has become a site of pilgrimages and is covered regularly by offerings left by visitors. The last time I was there, I saw tokens for the St. Petersburg subway, a bottle of vodka, a container full of writing pens, some manuscripts in plastic covers, Russian candy, and little stones placed on the tombstone, just as in Jewish cemeteries. Brodsky's readers: poets, drinkers, Petersburg dwellers . . .

Miłosz mentioned the Venice funeral in a poem published in *Second Space,* the last volume of poems he himself prepared and translated into English with the help of Robert Hass. The city of Venice, like everything in the poems of the "late" Miłosz, is embedded in his life:

> *I often think of Venice, which returns like a musical motif,*
> *From the time of my first visit there before the war,*

When I saw on the beach at Lido
The goddess Diana in the form of a German girl,
To the last when, after burying Joseph Brodsky,
We feasted at the Palazzo Mocenigo, the very one
In which Lord Byron had lived.

In these few lines we can hear the music of Vivaldi, the echoes of Thomas Mann, Mozart, the romantics. He also goes on to mention Oskar Miłosz, and then continues:

Venice sets sail like a great ship of death,
On its deck a swarming crowd of people changed into ghosts.
I said my farewell at San Michele to Joseph's grave and Ezra
    Pound's.
The city was ready, of course, to receive the crowds of the unborn
For whom we will be just an enigmatic legend.[6]

Venice is, as we know, one of the most literary places in the world, a work of art, a postmodern city, occupied only with expressing itself. Brodsky found himself in Venice during his first émigré winter, and after that spent most of his winter vacations there. He wrote a great deal about the city, most memorably a long essay called *Watermark* that was commissioned by the Venice city council. Dated 1989, it is a somewhat perverse memoir-as-tourist guide combination. The official objective of the book was to help the city to mobilize public opinion to save that sinking *meraviglia*. Brodsky was attracted to Venice by its water, an element, he said, in which he recognized himself. His Venice is different from the city inundated each summer by hordes of visitors—it is a winter city, gray and misty, and always flooded by water—an unstable, "temporary city" (Lotman), just like Leningrad.[7] *Aqua alta,* covering San Marco square each evening, continuously reminds one of the passing of time. Besides instability and water, Brodsky was attracted by Venice's liminal, borderline character: between nature and art, between existence and sinking, between Christianity and elements of the East. Venice was powerless yet remembering its imperial past. The embankments, monuments, the smell of "freezing seaweed"—all of this reminded him of his childhood and youth. In the poem "In Italy" he wrote: "I, too, once lived in a city whose cornices used to court / clouds with statues, . . . / and an infinite quay was rendering life myopic" (*CPE,* 340).

Perhaps this was his Return, his yearly, winterly repetitive return. After all, he did write, in *Watermark,* of his first trip to Venice: "It all felt like arriving in the provinces, in some unknown, insignificant spot—possibly one's own birthplace—after years of absence."[8] He did not expect any other kind of return.

Venice was not the only place in Italy that interested him. Italian art and poetry, Italian cities and landscapes were a constant motif of his poetry. He thought that his love for Italy was rather typical for a representative of the Russian tradition. "Everything of value in Russian art for the past two centuries," he wrote with typical emphasis, "has owed a great debt to, and shown the unmistakable influence of, the great Italian culture with which Russian painters, architects, musicians, and writers were during [the eighteenth and nineteenth] centuries in constant contact. The dependence of Russian culture on these contacts cannot be overstated." Brodsky was worried that the seventy years of the Soviet Union had severed this relation between "the mother of Russian aesthetics" and her child. This is why, in the last part of his life, he devoted some time to the creation of the Russian Academy in Rome. The above quotations are from his project submitted in the fall of 1995 to Francesco Rutelli, the mayor of Rome at that time, with the request that the city devote a building for a seat of the academy.[9] Hence a rather one-sided description of the dependence between the two cultures. Italian literature, for example, owes a lot to the translations, mostly via French, of nineteenth-century Russian prose. Brodsky's death slowed down and complicated the creation of the academy, but it has been functioning, although in a less ambitious form than Brodsky had hoped; it is supported by donations from Brodsky's friends, who help in the implementation of his ideas.

The Russian Academy in Rome was for Brodsky an aspect of his broader devotion to tending the estate of Russian poetry and paying his debt to Russian literature and language. In his last years, his activities on behalf of that estate became more intense. But for him Italy was also a place of imperial culture, and imperial Rome became increasingly central in his work. Armless, marble torsos and fragmentary centaurs reminded him of his Leningrad youth, yet they were also a sign of an unchanging present. They made the past contemporary. His last volume of poetry, *So Forth*, moves in two directions: toward the English, or rather American language, and toward the Roman tradition. In the poems "Anti-Shenandoah: Two Skits and a Chorus," "Blues," "In Memory of Clifford Brown," and "To My Daughter" one can hear the tones of American streets. In the poems "Venice: Lido,"

"Porta San Pancrazio," or "Via Funari" we see the second part of his "familiar" landscape—Italy and its past, the Roman empire. The same growing attraction to Italy as empire is palpable in his last essays. This is the otherland in which, toward the end of his life, he was finding his place. Italy was opening up to him both space and time.

One of the last essays Brodsky wrote was "Letter to Horace." Like its sister-essay, "Homage to Marcus Aurelius," it is an "oblique" show of erudition, as if Brodsky wanted to prove to his readers that classics are his homeland. But the approach is ironic, in a way anti-classical; he makes fun of himself, ridicules (only to a certain extent) his reading of Roman authors in Russian. Parts of these essays are pastiches from the works of the classical authors he debates. Tradition, as he understands it and forcefully conveys to his readers, is a continuation of the work and attitudes of certain poets, not a belief in concrete culture. "Letter to Horace" is a perverse epistle addressed to one poet—Horace—but praising another poet, his rival Ovid. As usual, Brodsky says more here about himself, about his *ars poetica,* than about the manifest theme of his text. Autoirony is undermined by the seriousness of the matter—literature—and the worry that he may be misunderstood as promoting himself as today's Ovid. He denies this repeatedly: Ovid's banishment from Rome is incomparable to the luxuries of Brodsky's emigration; he will never be able to write something similar to *The Metamorphoses;* and, unlike Ovid, he witnessed the collapse of his own empire: "I saw my Terza Roma crumble. I have my vanity," he writes about himself, "but it has its limits. Now that they are drawn by age, they are more palpable than before. But even as a young pup, kicked out of my home to the Polar Circle,

I never fancied myself playing his double. Though then my empire looked indeed eternal, and one could roam on the ice of our many deltas all winter long" (*OGR*, 433). He has in mind the ice on the Danube, about which Ovid wrote, but also the British empire, over which the sun never set. It is one of many asides that show Brodsky's Anglophilia, expressed also in his manner of dressing.

Publius Ovidius Naso stands here for Brodsky's ironic literary self-portrait, for the description of his literary "genotype." He taught me practically everything, Brodsky declares.

Naso insists that in this world *one thing is another* . . . a man evolved into an object, and vice versa, with the immanent logic of grammar, like a statement sprouting a subordinate clause . . . the tenor is the vehicle . . . and the source of it all is the ink pot. So long as there was a drop of that dark liquid in it, he would go on—which is to say, the world would go on. . . . To him, language was a godsend; more exactly, its grammar was. More exactly still, to him the world was the language: one thing was another, and as to which was more real, it was a toss-up. . . . Small wonder that he eventually came to compose in the local dialect. As long as vowels and consonants were there, he could go on, Pax Romana or no Pax Romana. In the end, what is a foreign tongue if not just another set of synonyms. Besides, my good old Geloni had no *écriture*. And even if they had, it would be only natural for him, the genius of metamorphosis, to mutate into an alien alphabet. (*OGR*, 452–53)

"My good old Geloni" are the ancestors of Brodsky, as he indicated at the beginning of the essay. When you were writing, Brodsky says to Horace, "we didn't have a language. We weren't even we; we were Geloni, Getae, Budini, etc.: just bubbles in our own future gene pool" (*OGR*, 430). "We" therefore are nomads from the north of Scythia, otherwise called Hyperborea. Toward the end of his life, Brodsky's narrator, as in his early poems "Ex Ponte" or "Lithuanian Nocturne," is a man of the border, from the provinces of an empire. This is where he was looking for his ancestors, even if they only had the form of bubbles, and where he was finding his literary predecessor, the exiled Ovid. His true country, his real family was the timeless Elysium of poets. In his Nobel lecture, he pointed to his tradition and his family. That family lives in an open time, in the permanent present—Horace was lately embodied in Auden. They do not die. This is what the inscription on Brodsky's grave says: *Letum non omnia finit*. Death does not end everything.

When Miłosz learned about the death of Brodsky, he was shocked. "I have lost a dear friend," he said. "He was uncommonly faithful in friendship and I felt he gave me generous gifts."[10] Miłosz often repeated that although we don't know if Brodsky was religious, he was definitely a man of faith, a pious man.[11] Yet the two men's attitudes toward religion were diametrically opposed. Brodsky declared that if he did believe in God, it was the austere God of the Old Testament; Christianity was for him a part of culture. Miłosz was a Catholic poet, and he thought about religion and worried about his place in Catholicism throughout his life. He respected the religious dogmas and the pre–Vatican II liturgy. Yet he considered himself a kind of heretic. In a letter to Renata Gorczyńska, he wrote: "I am *the only* Polish writer with a metaphysical temperament and this makes me totally un-Polish."[12] And we remember his poem celebrating the memory of his wife Janina, with its refusal to accept the wall separating the dead from those who are alive, a step only from embracing a version of the doctrine of apokatastasis. Miłosz himself pointed to the paganlike closeness in Polish Catholicism between the living and the dead. He calls his deviation from orthodoxy Manicheism, and explains it as a reaction dictated by the ubiquity of suffering and evil. At the same time, he considers suffering a part of God's plan, of the "incomprehensible Mystery of Redemption." Only faith can endow our existence with meaning. This is why he supports the Church, the institutional existence of faith and its rituals, which, focusing on individual salvation, limit the evil present in human nature. Moreover, the social presence of Christianity equals for Miłosz not only an ethical heritage but also an aesthetic one. And here his thinking meets Brodsky's, who chose the Catholic tradition as one of the pillars of his art. For both of them, the Christian poetic imagination imposes an order on the world, gives it a hierarchical moral structure. For Miłosz it also gives him hope that he can escape from "the land of disinheritance—the Land of Ulro." And the hope of the Return to the Land of Before.

Miłosz died in Kraków on August 24, 2004, thus surviving Brodsky by more than eight years. Although, like Brodsky, he did not say where he would like to be buried, he treated his death in a way very different from his Russian friend: he prepared for it and died as he wanted to die, in agreement with God and the rites of the Catholic

Church. This agreement, submission to the will of God, was for him linked with gratitude. Toward the end of his life, his poems became more and more like prayers. His "Treatise on Theology" ends with his giving himself to the care of the "Beautiful Lady"—the one "who appeared to the children at Lourdes and Fatima." The "Treatise" sums up his thinking about religion; it speaks of thanksgiving and the search for truth, that is for meaning which does not exist without an absolute point of reference. It speaks as well of his conflict with his fellow believers, whom he "suspected [of] an inveterate lesion of humiliation / which had issued in this compensatory tribal rite"; and it addresses his "wandering on the outskirts of heresy." Away from the serenity of faith, he is searching for the language in which to talk seriously about serious things, because there was no such language among his fellow believers, and Catholic dogmas are "armored against reason." He calls upon his great predecessor, Adam Mickiewicz, and debates with him about original sin and redemption.[13]

In his search, he turned to the pope and found consolation in Catholic orthodoxy. In May 2000, four years before his death, he wrote "Ode for the Eightieth Birthday of Pope John Paul II," in which he declares:

> *We come to you, men of weak faith,*
> *So that you might fortify us with the example of your life*
> *And liberate us from anxiety*
> *About tomorrow and next year. (NCP, 709)*

He exchanged letters with the pope, copies of which John Paul II sent in a telegram, after Miłosz's death, to Franciszek Cardinal

Macharski. The Polish Church hierarchy agonized over how and where to bury the poet, and the pope's gesture was meant to end the Church's hesitation. Allow me to quote the fragment of Miłosz's letter that John Paul II himself found important:

The age changes perspective and when I was young it was considered inappropriate for a poet to ask for papal benediction. Yet this is what preoccupies me now, because during these last years I wrote my poems with the thought of not straying from Catholic orthodoxy and I don't know what the result was. I am therefore asking for a word confirming my striving towards our common goal. Let Christ's promise of the Day of the Lord's Resurrection be fulfilled.

John Paul II responded:

You write that in Your writings You were preoccupied "not to stray from Catholic orthodoxy." I am convinced that such an attitude of the Poet is decisive. In this sense I am glad to be able to confirm Your words about "striving towards our common goal."[14]

The telegram to Cardinal Macharski was publicized in daily newspapers, together with a memorandum of Miłosz's confessor, who declared that the poet "left this world after having received holy sacraments, reconciled with God and with the Church." The confessor assured the public that during the last years of his life Miłosz took communion regularly, and "when the state of His health did not allow Him to go to church (when his wife was alive they went together to the St. Giles Church in Kraków), He received the Holy Eucharist at home."[15] The declaration was pinned to the door of the Crypt of the Pauline Fathers, where Miłosz's body was laid to rest. These declarations, press releases, and certifications of proper religious behavior were prompted by public opposition—a vocal minority—against a state and church funeral for the poet. The same minority was later clamoring against a Kraków monument to Miłosz. In the end, a solemn mass was celebrated in the main Kraków cathedral by Cardinal Macharski, who also led the funeral cortège through the streets of the city. The funeral procession was accompanied by what seemed to have been the entire population of Kraków, along with many visitors, several of them the poets who later that day read Miłosz's poems to the public. The last journey of the poet consisted, then, of three church stages: the mass in St. Mary's Cathedral, the laying of the body in the Crypt of the Pauline Fathers, and an evening of poetry in St. Catherine's Church. Miłosz returned to a Kraków that was not only the city of his friends, but also the city of Cardinal Wojtyła and of the Catholic Church.

So, even though both funerals—Brodsky's and Miłosz's—took place in Catholic churches, their nature was totally different. The funeral of Brodsky was basically extraterritorial, almost literary. The funeral of Miłosz constituted a total return to the bosom of the Catholic Church. Brodsky was buried by his friends, Miłosz was buried by the Nation. Brodsky lies in an out-of-the-way graveyard, far from the land of his birth, on a little island undermined by rising tides; Miłosz is in his hometown, in a crypt above the city. He himself said that in Poland the sacrum of religion is united with the sacrum of the nation. All his life he protested this joining, this "nationalizing" of religion, only to embrace it voluntarily at the end of his days.

Many "true" patriots and "true" Catholics protested vehemently against placing Miłosz in the Crypt of the Meritorious Poles—the first step toward becoming the National Poet. He had to be vetted, to pass moral, national, and religious examination. The "true" Poles reminded the nation of Miłosz's Lithuanian origin, his religious unorthodoxy, and his leftist past. Miłosz's poem "A Nation" was recalled on this occasion, and considered scandalously critical of Poland. So were his accusations against the Polish style of Catholic religiosity: the lack of theological interests, its functioning as national self-justification, its particular form of animism—the cult of ancestors with its rites to celebrate them. In 1999, he published in the Kraków Catholic weekly a "Letter to Denise [Levertov]," which contained a straight critique of Poles as "practicing nonbelievers." I wonder, he wrote, if it makes sense to translate into Polish, Denise, your Catholic poetry, since here "the language of Gospels serves to mask national phobias and the cross is changed into the sign of hate."[16] And in matters of literature, he was resented as the one who received the Nobel Prize and unseated Zbigniew Herbert, whom the "true" Poles considered the "true" Polish national poet. The Church authorities worried about the reactions of their brethren, some of whom threatened protests and scandals.

Miłosz was on the side of religion, but against the shallow, habitual religiosity of the Polish Church. He was continuing, as he himself understood, the traditional critical attitude of the Polish prewar intelligentsia. So one could say that not much was new in his attitude.

Also, the attacks against him had precedents in Polish history, with Miłosz's model, Adam Mickiewicz, a prime target of such accusations and protests. Mickiewicz's contemporary, the poet Cyprian Norwid, wrote about the ordeal in his poem "What Did You Do to Athens, Socrates?" in which he (rightly) prophesized that Mickiewicz's tomb would be reopened and his merits proclaimed with different words. Today, the then-maligned Mickiewicz lies side by side with the Polish kings in Wawel Castle. The vision of Wawel could have been the reason why Miłosz did not indicate the place of his burial: he knew Polish literary history, he knew his worth, but could not nominate himself for such an honor. Marek Zaleski, Polish literary critic and author of books about Miłosz, formulated the possibility openly: "The burial of Miłosz at the Crypt and not on Wawel, by Mickiewicz's side, is for me a sorry mistake. If he did not give us any disposition about the place for his grave, it means that he gave us a sign, a chance, to part in dignity with something that constituted an epoch in Polish culture. . . . Here we have some miserable compromise, which proves that we are unable to recognize not only our littleness but also our greatness."[17]

These words form a part of an essay in which Zaleski convincingly shows that Miłosz modeled his biography in such a way as to make it harmonize and respond to the biography of the Polish arch-poet Mickiewicz. "What is the myth of the arch-poet in the culture of a community and to what degree does that myth have a capacity to model the literary behavior of its members?" asks Zaleski at the beginning of his essay.[18] And he goes on to enumerate several moments in which Miłosz's biography was very Mickiewiczean. Both poets came from the vicinity of Vilnius, and that fact conditioned their admiring attitude toward an idea of multiethnic Poland. Other similarities consist of the greatness and volume of their work, the steadiness and intensity of their self-commentary; and common biographical facts: a happy, carefree childhood, the miracle of early rescue from death, youthful poetic friendships, exile, attachment to the mother tongue, anti-Western rebellion, interest in matters Russian. One could add other similarities, such as the illnesses of both poets' wives.

Although in the "Treatise on Theology" Miłosz quotes the mystical visions of Mickiewicz, he was really interested in the Mickiewicz of the Enlightenment—reasonable, attentive to reality, satirical, very much unlike the late, heretical Mickiewicz obsessed by the ideas of Towiański. This choice of the early, healthy, productive Mickiewicz helped Miłosz to continue to write, to avoid the defeats of emigration that in the end destroyed the romantic bard. As if his position as the national poet were decided already, Miłosz had many triumphs: his words ended up on monuments. During Solidarity movement strikes, the workers of Gdańsk Shipyard quoted Miłosz on a monument built quickly to celebrate slain colleagues:

> *You who wronged a simple man . . .*
>
> . . .
>
> *Do not feel safe. The poet remembers.*
> *You can kill one, another is born.*
> *The words are written down, the deed, the date. (NCP, 103)*

Such use of his words meant that he belonged to the nation, that his work and his life will be remembered and scrutinized. He was therefore treated as Mickiewicz was, with adoration and with calumnies. And this also explains the creation of two camps, of those who decided that he indeed was the national poet, and those who opted for Herbert. They were repeating the conflict between Adam Mickiewicz and Juliusz Słowacki, because in Poland there is not enough room for two, three, four national poets. This paucity of space and repetitiousness of history was caught well in a 1997 cartoon by the playwright Sławomir Mrożek. At the top of the drawing two long-haired men are flying, one following the other, and one of the two other men, standing in the lower right corner, comments: "Słowacki is chasing Mickiewicz."[19] This unending chase seems to be inscribed into the DNA of Polish culture.

No Polish romantic poet returned from nineteenth-century exile, and this is how Miłosz was thinking about his future. The exceptional, almost miraculous possibility of return was due of course to the collapse of the Soviet empire. In a beautiful text, Krzysztof Czyżewski marveled at the character of that return: "I encountered the Returning One, the one who overcame Exile and was coming back with the Book in which memory, knowledge, and faith are saved. For us, the 'new barbarians,' it was a gift, the link in the chain."[20] But before Miłosz was able to come back in person, he returned, so to speak, immaterially, in his poems. As he expected to die in exile, he had deposited his papers in the Beinecke Library, at Yale University, and he wrote:

> *He had his home, posthumous, in the town of New Haven,*
> *In a white building, behind walls*
> *Of translucent marble like a turtle shell,*

Which seep yellowish light on ranges of books,
Portraits and busts in bronze. There precisely
He decided to dwell when nothing any more
*Would be revealed by his ashes. (*NCP, *523)*

He lived much longer, accumulating many more papers. His only visit to Poland before the collapse of communism—it was owed to his Nobel Prize and the short legal existence of the Solidarity movement—was celebrated in the Polish press with articles about his return. But he did not feel at home in communist Poland, and the return referred rather to his books, now by necessity permitted publication. In 1987, in *A Year of the Hunter,* he wrote that Vilnius was for him like Atlantis, and that he was unable to imagine his life in Poland. Even after 1989, when communism was no more, he did not plan at first to return. In 1992, during the conference at Rutgers, he declared that he remained in the United States for personal reasons, and added, laughing, that his return would be difficult because being a Nobel Prize laureate in Poland would be "very restricting, whereas in California, in the Bay area where I live, there are, I think, some sixteen Nobel laureates, so it alleviates the burden." Brodsky jumped right in, observing that he did not see a place for himself in the new Russia.[21]

In the mind of Miłosz, still another, poetic version of return was present, but he did not apply it to himself. In 1980 he wrote a poem describing a return that had occurred one hundred years previously. It was a story of Julian Klaczko (1825–1906), an art historian, literary critic, and polyglot, who returned to Kraków from exile. The title of the poem is "Return to Kraków in 1880," from which I have already quoted, discussing "the shadow of the empire." The poem presents the city presciently as it felt when Miłosz himself came back to it later:

> *So I returned here from the big capitals,*
> *To a town in a narrow valley under the cathedral hill*
> *With royal tombs.*
>
> . . .
>
> *My country will remain what it is, the backyard of empires,*
> *Nursing its humiliation with provincial daydreams.*
> *I leave for a morning walk tapping with my cane.*
> (NCP, *427*)

If it is true that nothing is accidental in literature, this poem would constitute a "dry" tryout of return, an imagining of a return. The actual return happened gradually, and without special celebration. Miłosz first came to Kraków with his wife for summers only, then for summers and falls, and finally they remained permanently. Berkeley became difficult; the stairs to and from Grizzly Peak Road were more and more challenging for Miłosz. So it was a slow, long returning, not one Return, and it started with visits to places of childhood and youth. This is how Krzysztof Czyżewski met Miłosz in Krasnogruda, a place of his childhood vacations, since Krasnogruda was a name of Miłosz's mother's family manor. The poet also visited Lithuania, and wrote beautiful poems about these voyages in space and time. As early as 1990, in the poem "Return," he wrote: "In my old age, I decided to visit places where I wandered long ago in my early youth" (*NCP,* 562). The lines of this poem are long and calm; it is a cross between a prayer and a confession. The next trip, in 1992, brought a short poetic cycle called "Lithuania after Fifty-Two Years," and the poem "In Szetejnie." About that stay in Lithuania he said: "Such a return is almost unimaginable . . . it is a very difficult and complex experience, in which joy is mixed with sorrow. Memory brings forth faces, a multitude of human faces, which don't exist anymore, but whose presence I feel almost physically."[22] He recorded the same feeling in the poem "City of My Youth":

> *It would be more decorous not to live. To live is not decorous,*
> *Says he who after many years.*
> *Returned to the city of his youth. There was no one left*
> *Of those who once walked these streets. (*NCP, *596)*

But this trip was not only a source of sadness: as often in Miłosz, it was transformed into happiness. The last poem of this cycle, "A Meadow," ends with the words: "And the scent garnered me, all knowing ceased. / Suddenly I felt I was disappearing and weeping with joy" (*NCP,* 597).

What did the friendship between Miłosz and Brodsky consist of? Weren't they too different, separated as they were by age, nationality, language, sensibility, fate? In the introduction to his translation to the Book of Job, Miłosz wrote about himself: "There is a burden that is particularly difficult to carry, it is the consciousness that is too sharp. Nobody who is educated on Polish literature can get rid of the image of a poet as a prophet or a bard. I did try, however, to get rid of it, because of shame. But I noticed early on that I am marked in a particular way, and if anyone suspects me of megalomania, I can assure, that in such marking there is nothing pleasant and that it is accepted as a kind of crippling disability. I have in mind moments, flashes of consciousness so bright, that they merit the name of clairvoyance, felt as coming from outside, not from inside. So not a talent, but a particular sharpness of sensuous perception, not a sensitivity to words, but the wrestling with a force that catches us like an attack of illness, ruins our life, pushes people away."[23] Miłosz saw himself as a bard, and the weight and size of his work cannot be enclosed in a few sentences. His was a rare talent, but he was also characterized by masterly craft, versatility, diligence, fecundity, all-encompassing curiosity, sureness of pitch, continuous development, capacity for many genres, unshakeable dignity linked to a sense of humor. Repetitions that characterize his work are like musical motifs, reiterations, the same but always new. Yes, we had an unusual guest.

"He was Lithuanian, from the prewar period, from the times of German occupation, from his stay in Paris, from emigration; he was American, a Nobel laureate, then from Kraków," wrote Jerzy Pilch.[24] But long before, in 1975, Sławomir Mrożek had felt that only Miłosz among the Poles was a True Writer. "In Miłosz, I adore a writer who is *truly* a writer, who is not an accident, a perturbation, a mistake in the central administration of culture, but a magnificent regularity, a fruit of Polish, Lithuanian, European, World tradition, who was born as a mind authentically higher, with a magnificent trail of genes, without mental and psychological disabilities that I ascribe to myself, and that leave me unable to work, learn, see, remember, and truly create."[25] The bar of accomplishment set up in Polish culture by Miłosz's work is very, very high.

Miłosz was a poet of being, the poet of "yes," "Praising, renewing, healing,"—"Grateful because the sun rose for you and will rise for others" (*CNP,* 697). Brodsky was totally different—negation and contestation were his elements. Lavishly talented, diligent, proud of his craft, ferociously individual and productive, he saw himself as an antibard. Here is how he presents himself in a lecture delivered in 1988:

The [author] belongs to the category of people (alas, I can no longer use the term "generation," which implies a certain sense of mass and unity) for whom literature has always been a matter of some hundred names; to the people whose social graces would make Robinson Crusoe or even Tarzan wince; to those who fall awkward at large gatherings, do not dance at parties, tend to find metaphysical excuses for adultery, and are finicky about discussing politics; the people who dislike themselves far more than their detractors do; who still prefer alcohol and tobacco to heroin or marijuana—those who, in W. H. Auden's words, "one will not find on the barricades and who never shoot themselves or their lovers." If such people occasionally find themselves swimming in their blood on the floor of prison cells or speaking from a platform, it is because they rebel against (or, more precisely, object to) not some particular injustice but the order of the world as a whole. (*OGR,* 99–100)

So how one can classify Brodsky? The best attempt, I think, is to be found in the words of Susan Sontag, pronounced after the poet's death at a reading at the Miller Theatre, at Columbia University, on October 29, 1996. Like Auden, he was perhaps not American, she said, but he was definitely a New Yorker. And I found the best definition of what it means to be a New Yorker in an article describing William Kapell, a pianist who died at the age of thirty-one in a plane accident: "He was a stereotype of a native New Yorker: bright, brash, tactless, competitive, funny, cocky, and thin-skinned. He could be exceptionally generous and also nasty. He was a nervous, obsessive person, and meticulous." Even the title of this article—"The Undefeated"—fits Brodsky very well.[26] He was considered to be a poet of dialogue, but the dialogue was rather a quarrel. In a continuous fight against time and banality, holding always a contrarian view, escaping forward, toward the future, he left behind a body of work that is difficult to embrace even knowing both languages in which he worked. His posthumous career will be more strewn with obstacles than that of Miłosz, whose creative path is perfectly clear to a Polish reader. Both were poets of genius and both led their followers into the as-yet-unknown terrains of world poetry. There, they will feast together with those whose shadows they pleased.

Their friendship was above guild solidarity or intimate fraternity. They were united by the similarity of their life situation—a poet in exile, a man with a double, Janus-like face, turned toward the past and the future, toward fatherland and otherland. They were also united by the consciousness of the greatness of the talents that were given to them and of the responsibility linked to these talents. And by the similarity of their attitude toward poetic challenge: life is a debt, paid off by work and friendship. And friendship consists of an attentive acceptance of every person, of help to those who are unknown and friendless, so that they do not go through life without words, in silence.

Notes

PROLOGUE

1. Jan T. Gross and Irena Grudzińska-Gross, "A Conversation with Tomas Venclova," *Aneks* 28 (1982): 152.

2. All the passages from Joseph Brodsky's works are quoted here with the permission of his estate. He did not want his letters to be published, which is why I am using only fragments of them. The letter to Miłosz is in the Miłosz archive at the Beinecke Rare Book and Manuscript Library, Yale University. All translations are mine, unless indicated otherwise.

3. Czesław Miłosz, "Czy poeci mogą się lubić?" [Can Poets Like Each Other?], interview with Irena Grudzińska-Gross, *Gazeta Wyborcza*, September 5–6, 1998, 12–13.

4. Czesław Miłosz, *Piesek przydrożny* [Roadside Dog] (Kraków: Znak, 1997), 162.

5. Both quotations from Valentina Polukhina, *Brodsky through the Eyes of his Contemporaries* (London: Palgrave-Macmillan, 1992), 326.

6. "Nie moralnością, lecz smakiem: Rozmowa z Josifem Brodskim" [Not by Morality but by Taste: Conversation with Joseph Brodsky], interview with Grzegorz Musiał, *NaGłos* 2 (1990): 205.

7. The reading, in Russian, took place at Boston University, April 9, 1995; Brodsky died nine months later. Quoted after Ludmilla Shtern, *Brodsky: A Personal Memoir* (Fort Worth, TX: Baskerville Publishers, 2004), 360.

8. Czesław Miłosz, ed., *A Book of Luminous Things: An International Anthology of Poetry* (New York: Harcourt Brace, 1996), 115. This poem was translated from the Russian by George Kline.

CHAPTER 1. PAN CZESŁAW AND IOSIF

1. Wiktor Woroszylski wrote about it in his diary; photocopies of the quoted pages are in the possession of the author.

2. Ryszard Matuszewski, *Alfabet: Wybór z pamięci 90-latka* [Alphabet: From the Memory of a Ninety-Year-Old] (Warsaw: Iskry, 2004), 28.

3. Tadeusz Konwicki, *Bohiń* (Warsaw: Czytelnik, 1987), 154.

4. During the Cold War many Poles remained in the West, settling predominantly in England, France, and the United States. Among the émigrés there were writers, editors, and critics publishing in several newspapers and periodicals.

5. Aleksander Fiut, *W stronę Miłosza* [Toward Miłosz] (Kraków: Wydawnictwo Literackie, 2003), 242.

6. Yuri Slezkine, *The Jewish Century* (Princeton, NJ: Princeton University Press, 2004).

7. *Reszty nie trzeba: Rozmowy z Josifem Brodskim* [Never Mind: Conversations with Joseph Brodsky], ed. Jerzy Illg (Katowice: Książnica, 1993), 127.

8. Svetlana Boym, *The Future of Nostalgia* (New York: Basic Books, 2002).

9. See the analysis of the poem about Brodsky's mother in Willem G. Weststeijn, "The Thought of You Is Going Away . . . ," in *Joseph Brodsky: The Art of a Poem,* ed. Lev Loseff and Valentina Polukhina (New York: St. Martin's Press, 1999), 177–90.

CHAPTER 2. POETRY, YOUTH, AND FRIENDSHIP

1. Joseph Brodsky, foreword to *An Age Ago: A Selection of Nineteenth-Century Russian Poetry*, ed. Alan Myers (New York: Farrar, Straus and Giroux, 1988).

2. W. H. Auden, "Thanksgiving for Habitat," pt. 9, *Collected Poems*, ed. Edward Mendelson (New York: Random House, 1991), 707.

3. Volkov's *Conversations with Joseph Brodsky* (cited here as *CJB*) caused serious controversies, as most of its chapters were not authorized by Brodsky and were printed against the wish of his executors. Volkov admitted to reshaping the material and did not allow access to transcripts or recordings of his original interviews.

4. Anatoly Nayman, in conversation with the author, New York, October 18, 1996.

5. An unusual testimony of the invasion of the state into the most intimate family relation can be found in an undervalued novel by Lydia Chukovskaya, *The Deserted House* (known also as *Sofia Petrovna*).

6. See the chapter "The Spoiler State" in Jan T. Gross, *Revolution from Abroad* (Princeton, NJ: Princeton University Press, 1988).

7. During public meetings in the last years of his life he read his prose as if to finish as soon as possible, as if it was only poetry that was worthy of slower reading.

8. Anatoly Nayman, *Rasskazy o Annie Achmatowoj* [On Anna Akhmatova] (Moscow: Khudozhestvienna Literatura, 1989), 72–73; from there also the fragments about the formation of their group and the words of Akhmatova about Gorbanevskaya.

9. Czesław Miłosz, "Myśląc o Brodskim: Kilka uwag" [Thinking about Brodsky: A Few Remarks], in *O Brodskim: Studia, szkice, refleksje* [On Brodsky: Studies, Essays, Reflections], ed. Piotr Fast (Katowice: Śląsk, 1993), 5–8.

10. Czesław Miłosz, "Czy poeci mogą się lubić?" [Can Poets Like Each Other?], interview with Irena Grudzińska-Gross, *Gazeta Wyborcza*, September 5–6, 1998, 12–13.

11. Dmitry Bobyshev, "Achmatowskie sieroty" [Akhmatova's Orphans], trans. K. Pietrzycka-Bohosiewicz, *Zeszyty Literackie* 30 (Spring 1990): 114–19.

12. Joseph Brodsky, "Fate of a Poet," *New York Review of Books,* April 1, 1976.

13. Czesław Miłosz, letters to Joseph Brodsky, in Brodsky Papers, Beinecke Rare Book and Manuscript Library, Yale University.

14. Jan T. Gross and Irena Grudzińska-Gross, "A Conversation with Tomas Venclova," *Aneks* 28 (1982): 151.

15. Tomas Venclova, "'Divertimento litewskie' Josifa Brodskiego" [Joseph Brodsky's 'Lithuanian Divertissement'], in Tomas Venclova, *Niezniszczalny rytm: Eseje o literaturze* [Indestructible Rhythm: Essays on Literature] (Sejny: Pogranicze and Fundacja Zeszytów Literackich, 2002), trans. Stanisław Barańczak, 189–209.

16. Tomas Venclova, "Lithuanian Nocturne," in *Joseph Brodsky: The Art of a Poem,* ed. Lev Loseff and Valentina Polukhina (New York: St. Martin's Press, 1999), 107–49.

17. Venclova, "Niezniszczalny rytm," 253–58.

18. Anatoly Nayman, *Roman s Samovarom* (New York: Novyi Medved, 2006).

19. "Czy poeci mogą się lubić?"

20. Alina Witkowska, *Mickiewicz: Słowo i czyn* [Mickiewicz: Word and Deed] (Warsaw: PIW, 1975); see the chapter "Filomata i Gustaw."

21. Czesław Miłosz, *Miłosz's ABC's,* trans. Madeline G. Levine (New York: Farrar, Straus and Giroux, 2001), 3.

22. Madeline G. Levine, "*Abecadło* i trzecia powieść Czesława Miłosza, jak dotąd nie napisana" [*ABC* and the Third Novel of Miłosz, So Far Unwritten], in *Poznawanie Młosza, Część Druga* [Understanding Miłosz, Part Two], ed. Aleksander Fiut (Kraków: Wydawnictwo Literackie, 2001), 305–12. See also conversation of Elżbieta Sawicka with Czesław Miłosz, "Ameryka poetów" [America of Poets: Elżbieta Sawicka Speaks to Czesław Miłosz], *Plus-Minus,* May 16–17, 1998.

23. Miłosz speaking during the Claremont McKenna International Czesław Miłosz Festival: *International Czesław Miłosz Festival,* special section of *Partisan Review* 66, no. 1 (1999): 151.

24. The reply Czesław Miłosz wrote on January 17, 1959, to Thomas Merton's letter about his reading of *The Captive Mind.* See *Striving Towards Being: The Letters of Thomas Merton and Czesław Miłosz,* ed. Robert Faggen (New York: Farrar, Straus and Giroux, 1997), 6–7, 11.

25. Czesław Miłosz, "Nie" [No], *Kultura* (May 1951): 3–13.

26. *International Czesław Miłosz Festival,* 50.

27. See Maria Janion, "Kroński-Miłosz," in *Do Europy tak, ale z naszymi umarłymi* [To Europe, Yes, but with Our Dead] (Warsaw: Sic! 2000); and Aleksander Fiut, "W objęciach Tygrysa," in *W stronę Miłosza* [Towards Miłosz] (Kraków: Wydawnictwo Literackie, 2003).

28. Czesław Miłosz, *The Captive Mind* (New York: Vintage Books, 1981), 82.

29. This is not always well understood. See for example the review of Miłosz's *Legends of Modernity,* by Timothy Snyder, *The Nation,* January 9–16, 2006, 26–30.

30. Robert Louis Stevenson, quoted in Ronald A. Sharp, *Friendship and Literature: Spirit and Form* (Durham, NC: Duke University Press, 1986), 35.

31. "Ameryka poetów" [America of Poets: Elżbieta Sawicka Speaks to Czesław Miłosz], *Plus-Minus,* May 16–17, 1998.

CHAPTER 3. FRIENDSHIP AND THE ESTATE OF POETRY

1. Czesław Miłosz, *Życie na wyspach* [Living on Islands] (Kraków: Znak, 1998), 192.

2. Joanna Pyszny, "Sprawa Miłosza, czyli poeta w czyścu" [L'Affaire Miłosz, or the Poet in Purgatory], in *Poznanie Miłosza Drugie, 1980–1998* [Understanding Miłosz, 1980–1998], ed. Aleksander Fiut (Kraków: Wydawnictwo Literackie, 1998), 53–81.

3. Czesław Miłosz, *Człowiek wśród skorpionów* [Man among Scorpions] (Kraków: Znak, 2000), 9.

4. In the introduction to the 1993 *Wilson Quarterly* issue devoted to Zbigniew Herbert's poems.

5. Nicola Chiaromonte, "Albert Camus," in *The Worm of Consciousness and Other Essays,* trans. Miriam Chiaromonte, intro. Mary McCarthy (New York: Harcourt Brace Jovanovich, 1976), quotations from pp. 51, 52.

6. Conversation with Mark Strand, Rome, June 14, 1997.

7. "Introduction to Mark Strand" (1987), Brodsky Papers, Beinecke Rare Book and Manuscript Library, Yale University.

8. A copy of this unpublished poem is in the Brodsky Papers.

9. Adam Zagajewski wrote that "if in the United States there existed the Republic of Poets, Derek Walcott would be not only one of its founders, its pillar and president, but also minister, messenger, and driver, because he is ready to do much for his friends, not only deliver speeches." In "Derek Walcott," *Zeszyty Literackie* 41 (1993): 59.

10. *Conversations with Derek Walcott,* ed. William Baer (Jackson: University Press of Mississippi, 1996), 30.

11. Both the poem and the introduction are in the Brodsky Papers.

12. Valentina Polukhina, *Brodsky through the Eyes of his Contemporaries* (London: Palgrave-Macmillan, 1992), 314.

13. *Conversations with Derek Walcott,* 119.

14. Quoted after Clare Cavanagh, "The Unacknowledged Legislator's Dream," in *The Other Herbert,* ed. Bożena Shallcross, special issue of *Indiana Slavic Studies* 9 (1998): 97–120.

15. Seamus Heaney to Joseph Brodsky, June 20, 1983, in the Brodsky Papers.

16. Seamus Heaney, quoted in Hilton Als, "The Islander," *New Yorker,* February 9, 2004, 49.

17. Askold Melnyczuk, "Killing the Common Moth," in *Seamus Heaney: A Celebration,* ed. Stratis Haviaras (Cambridge, MA: Harvard Review Monograph, 1996), 108–11; quotation p. 108.

18. From Czesław Miłosz, "Czy poeci mogą się lubić?" [Can Poets Like Each Other?], interview with Irena Grudzińska-Gross, *Gazeta Wyborcza,* September 5–6, 1998, 12–13; quotation p. 13. The Neustadt Inter-

national Prize for Literature is a biennial award established in 1969 and sponsored by the University of Oklahoma. It was established, together with the periodical *World Literature Today,* by Estonian poet Ivar Ivask. The award gained great respect when its laureates Gabriel Garcia Marquez, Czesław Miłosz, and Octavio Paz received literary Nobels. A grateful Miłosz repaid Ivask by translating into Polish (from English) his Baltic elegies.

19. Joseph Brodsky, "Presentation of Czesław Miłosz to the Jury," *World Literature Today,* no. 3 (1978): 364.
20. Joseph Brodsky: "Poet's View: A True Child of the Century," *New York Times,* October 10, 1980.
21. Sven Birkerts, interview with Brodsky. The transcript of the interview is in the Brodsky Papers at Beinecke. The edited version was published in the *Paris Review*: "The Art of Poetry: Conversation with Joseph Brodsky," *Paris Review* 83 (Spring 1982): 83–126.
22. The draft letter is from the early 1980s, in Renata Gorczyńska Papers Relating to Czesław Miłosz, General Collection of Rare Books and Manuscripts, Beinecke Rare Book and Manuscript Library, Yale University.
23. Renata Gorczyńska, *Jestem z Wilna i inne adresy* [I am from Vilnius, and Other Addresses] (Kraków: Wydawnictwo Krakowskie, 2003), 102 and 107.
24. Elżbieta Sawicka, *Przystanek Europa: Rozmowy nie tylko o literaturze* [The Europe Stop: Conversations Not Only about Literature] (Warsaw: Most, 1996), 6.
25. Joseph Brodsky to Zofia Kapuścińska Ratajczakowa, August 26, 1993, in the Brodsky Papers.
26. Czesław Miłosz, "Myśląc o Brodskim: Kilka uwag" [Thinking about Brodsky: A Few Remarks], in *O Brodskim: Studia, szkice, refleksje* [On Brodsky: Studies, Essays, Reflections], ed. Piotr Fast (Katowice: Śląsk, 1993), 5–8. The comedy Miłosz refers to is Aleksander Fredro's *The Vengeance.*
27. Ibid.

28. Jerzy Illg, in *Tygodnik Powszechny,* July 4, 1993; quoted after *StS,* 25–26.

29. *New York Review of Books,* August 14, 1980, 23–25.

30. Brodsky figures on the list together with Akhmatova, Mandelstam, Cavafy, and the French poets Apollinaire, Cendrars, Claudel, Péguy, Saint-John Perse, and Valéry. Miłosz included also the poems of Zbigniew Herbert and Oskar Miłosz.

31. Brodsky's "The Elegy for John Donne" illustrated Miłosz's reference to metaphysical poets; the religious poems were "The Halt in the Desert," "Nunc Dimittis," and "Dominicans" (a fragment of the "Lithuanian Divertissement"); as for classical poems, Miłosz taught "Odysseus to Telemachus" and "Torso." From Miłosz's notes (in Miłosz Papers) one can see that he took into consideration also a fragment without a title, "1972," and "Lullaby of Cape Cod."

32. Liam McCarthy, e-mail to author, April 22, 2002.

33. "Czy poeci mogą się lubić?" 12.

34. Czesław Miłosz, ed., *Postwar Polish Poetry,* 3rd ed. (Berkeley: University of California Press, 1983), xiii.

35. Czesław Miłosz, "Święto przyjaźni, rodzaj cudu" [Celebration of Friendship, Kind of Miracle], *Plus-Minus,* May 16–17, 1998.

36. *Gazeta Wyborcza,* October 30–November 1, 2004.

37. Miłosz, "Święto przyjaźni, rodzaj cudu."

38. "Przyszli tlumacze: Z Adamem Zagajewskim rozmawia Joanna Gromek" [Future Translators: Conversation with Joanna Gromek], *Gazeta Wyborcza,* July 10, 2003.

CHAPTER 4. WOMEN, WOMEN WRITERS, AND MUSES

1. Unpublished transcript of "Robert Silvers Speaks with Czesław Miłosz and Joseph Brodsky," New York Institute for the Humanities, September 22, 1981, Beinecke Rare Book and Manuscript Library, Yale University.

2. The phrase just quoted is from an untitled poem of 1962, the first in the series devoted to the main addressee of Brodsky's love poetry,

M.B. See Joseph Brodsky, *Novoye Stanci k Avguste* [New Stanzas for Augusta] (Ann Arbor, MI: Ardis, 1983), 3.

3. Czesław Miłosz, *Inne Abecadło* [Another Alphabet] (Kraków: Wydawnictwo Literackie, 1998), 90.

4. Jan Błoński and Sławomir Mrożek, *Listy, 1963–1996* [Letters], ed. Tadeusz Nyczek (Kraków: Wydawnictwo Literackie, 2004), 542.

5. Anna Swir, *Talking to My Body,* trans. Czesław Miłosz and Leonard Nathan (Port Townsend, WA: Copper Canyon Press, 1996), 157.

6. Ibid.

7. Letter in the Beinecke Library, Renata Gorczyńska Papers Related to Czesław Miłosz, General Collection of Rare Books and Manuscripts, Beinecke Rare Book and Manuscript Library, Yale University.

8. "Hurry sickness," a note of Aleksander Perski, Hotel "Mälardal," September 8, 1994. In the possession of the author.

9. Brodsky in conversation with H. Jangfeld-Jakubovitch (1993), quoted after Piotr Fast, *Spotkania z Brodskim* [Encounters with Brodsky] (Wrocław: Wirydarz, 1996), 120, 122.

10. Venclova counted that Brodsky dedicated nine poems to Akhmatova, four of which begin with epigraphs taken from her poetry; she also appears in person in some of them. Tomas Venclova, "Petersburskie spotkania: Achmatowa i Brodski" [Petersburg Encounters: Akhmatova and Brodsky], *Zeszyty Literackie* 83 (2003): 168.

11. The poem can be found in Roberta Reeder, *Anna Akhmatova: Poet and Prophet* (New York: St. Martin's Press, 1994), 373.

12. Venclova, "Petersburskie spotkania," 167.

13. Isaiah Berlin, *Personal Impressions* (New York: Viking Press, 1981), 193.

14. Nadezhda Mandelstam, *Mozart and Salieri,* trans. Robert A. McLean (Ann Arbor, MI: Ardis, 1973), 19–20, 23, 69.

15. Ibid., 83.

16. Anna Akhmatova, *Selected Poems,* ed. and intro. Walter Arndt (New York: Ardis/Overlook, 1976), 75. The "veil tossed overhead" is a reference, as she herself suggests in "A Word about Dante," to

the presentation of Beatrice in *Purgatorio* canto XXX, lines 31–33. See Anna Akhmatova, *My Half-Century: Selected Prose,* trans. Ronald Meyer (Evanston, IL: Northwestern University Press, 1992), 266.

17. Julia Hartwig, "Najwieksze szczęście, największy ból" [The Greatest Happiness, the Greatest Pain], interview with Jarosław Mikołajewski, *Wysokie Obcasy,* March 26, 2005.

18. Joseph Brodsky, *Novoye Stanci k Avguste* [New Stanzas for Augusta] (Ann Arbor, MI: Ardis, 1983). See also Lev Loseff, *Iosif Brodskij: Opit Literaturnoy Biografii* [Joseph Brodsky: A Literary Biography] (Moscow: Mołodaya Gvardia, 2006), 72–73.

19. Gerry Smith, "A Song without Music," in *Joseph Brodsky: The Art of a Poem,* ed. Lev Loseff and Valentina Polukhina (New York: St. Martin's Press, 1999), 22.

20. "Debiut," in Iosif Brodsky, *Konets Prekrasnoy Epokhi* [The End of a Beautiful Era] (New York: Slovo/Word, 2000), 100. The poem was written in 1971.

CHAPTER 5. IN THE SHADOW OF EMPIRE: RUSSIA

1. Czesław Miłosz, "Looking for a Center: On the Poetry of Central Europe," *Cross Currents: A Yearbook of Central European Culture* 1 (1982): 1–11; and Milan Kundera, "The Tragedy of Central Europe," *New York Review of Books,* April 26, 1984, 35–38.

2. Ludmilla Shtern, *Brodsky, A Personal Memoir* (Fort Worth, TX: Baskerville Publishers, 2004), 220.

3. The article by Kundera appeared on January 6, 1985, in the *New York Times Book Review.* It was an introduction to his play, a variation on Diderot's "Jacques le Fataliste." Brodsky's response appeared there on January 17, 1985.

4. "The Lisbon Conference on Literature: Central European and Russian Writers" (May 7–8, 1988), ed. Ladislav Matejka, *Cross Currents: A Yearbook of Central European Culture* 9 (1990): 120–21.

5. *Intellectuals and Social Change in Central and Eastern Europe,* proceedings of a conference at Rutgers University, April 1992, ed. William Phillips, special issue of *Partisan Review* 59, no. 4 (Fall 1992): 547.

6. Faulty transcript of Venclova's words. Giedroyć was born in Minsk, in Belarus, and Venclova was mentioning the little town of Giedroyce, once belonging to the family of the editor.

7. For the debate on the rise and fall of the concept of Central Europe, see the Ph.D. dissertation of Jessie Labov, "Reinventing Central Europe: *Cross-Currents* and the Émigré Writer in the 1980s," Department of Comparative Literature, New York University, 2003.

8. Per-Årne Bodin, "Miłosz i Rosja, z perspektywy szwedzkiej" [Miłosz and Russia, from a Swedish Perspective], *Teksty Drugie* 5 (1997): 9. See also Luigi Marinelli, "Miłosz et l'autre Europe," manuscript in possession of Irena Grudzinska Gross; and his "Ricerca di una patria: L'Europa familiare di Miłosz fra Seteinai e la baia di San Francisco" [Search for a Homeland: Miłosz's Europe from Šeteinai to San Francisco Bay], in *I Nobel letterari polacchi* [Polish Nobels in Literature] (Milan: Mimep-Docete, 2004), 49–65.

9. About Custine's attitude to Russia, see Irena Grudzinska Gross, *The Scar of Revolution: Custine, Tocqueville, and the Romantic Imagination* (Berkeley: University of California Press, 1991). For an analysis of the similarities between the Russia of Mickiewicz and Custine, see Irena Grudzinska Gross, "Adam Mickiewicz: A European from Nowogrodek," *East European Politics and Society* 2 (Spring 1995): 295–316.

10. Wojciech Karpiński, *Książki zbójeckie* [Dangerous Books] (Warsaw: Biblioteka Narodowa, 1996), 161.

11. Witold Gombrowicz, *Dziennik, 1961–1966* [Diaries, 1961–1966] (Paris: Instytut Literacki, 1982), 152.

12. Clare Cavanagh, *Osip Mandelstam and the Modernist Creation of Tradition* (Princeton, NJ.: Princeton University Press, 1995), 297.

13. Osip Mandelstam, "Ode to Stalin," trans. Gregory Freidin, quoted after J. M. Coetzee, *Giving Offense: Essays on Censorship* (Chicago: University of Chicago Press, 1996), 107–8.

14. Czesław Miłosz, "Komentarz do 'Ody do Stalina' Osipa Mandelsztama" [Commentary on the "Ode to Stalin" by Osip Mandelstam]. *NaGłos* 22 (August 1996): 82. Reprint, with cuts and changed title:

"Bez wstydu ni miary" [Without Shame or Measure], *Gazeta Wyborcza,* November 23–24, 1996.

15. The date of the conversation was December 5, 1996.

16. Though the Poet attempts to offend God by naming Him the Czar. See Adam Mickiewicz's *The Forefathers' Eve.*

17. James Rice, review of two books on Osip Mandelstam (*Osip Mandel'shtam i ego vremia,* comp. and preface Vadim Kreid [Kreyd] and Evgenii Necheporuk; and *Mandel'shtam i stalinskaia epokha: Ezopov iazyk w poezii Mandel'shtama 30-kh godov,* by Irina Mess-Beier [Mess-Baher]), *Slavic Review* (Summer 1998): 482.

18. J. M. Coetzee, *Giving Offense: Essays on Censorship* (Chicago: University of Chicago Press, 1996), 106, 112, 116.

19. *Washington Post,* June 4, 1972; W. H. Auden liked this text very much, as his letter to Brodsky affirms (letter in Brodsky Papers, Beinecke Rare Book and Manuscript Library, Yale University).

20. Lev Loseff, "O lubvi Ahmatovoj k 'Narodu'" [About Akhmatova's Love of "Narod"], in *Iosif Brodskij: Un crocevia fra culture* [Joseph Brodsky: A Crossroads of Culture], ed. Alessandro Niero and Sergio Pescatori (Milan: MG Print on Demand, 2002), 159–81.

21. Valentina Polukhina, *Joseph Brodsky: A Poet for Our Time* (Cambridge: Cambridge University Press, 1989), 212.

22. "Żyć w historii" [To Live in History], conversation with Jerzy Illg, in *Reszty nie trzeba: Rozmowy z Josifem Brodskim* [Never Mind: Conversations with Joseph Brodsky], ed. Jerzy Illg (Katowice: Książnica, 1993), 127.

23. He said this in a conversation in 1988, published in the periodical *Akiračiai.* See Tomas Venclova, *Niezniszczalny rytm: Eseje o literaturze* [Indestructible Rhythm: Essays on Literature] (Sejny: Pogranicze and Fundacja Zeszytów Literackich, 2002), 255.

24. "Po obu stronach oceanu: Adam Michnik rozmawia z Iosifem Brodskim" [On Both Sides of the Ocean: Adam Michnik Talks with Joseph Brodsky], *Gazeta Wyborcza,* January 20, 1995, 6–11. The encounter was registered by Jacek Kucharczyk, transcribed by Irena

Lewandowska, and edited by Joanna Szczęsna. The original tape was discarded.

25. Interview with Jane Ellen Grasser, in *Joseph Brodsky: Conversations,* ed. Cynthia L. Haven (Jackson: University Press of Mississippi, 2002), 41.

26. "Po obu stronach oceanu," 8.

27. Transcript of his statements during the debate "Whether and How History Speaks," Mount Holyoke College, October 16, 1985. Brodsky participated in that debate with Czesław Miłosz and Peter Viereck. (Transcript in possession of the author.)

28. Polukhina, *Joseph Brodsky,* 225.

29. Maurice Bowra, *The Greek Experience* (Oxford: Oxford University Press, 1967), 132.

30. Agata Araszkiewicz, *Wypowiadam wam moje życie: Melancholia Zuzanny Ginczanki* [I Take My Life Away from You: Melancholy of Zuzanna Ginczanka] (Warsaw: Ośka, 2001), 106.

31. Jadwiga Szymak-Reiferowa, "*Anno Domini* Josifa Brodskiego" [*Anno Domini* of Joseph Brodsky], in *O Brodskim: Studia, szkice, refleksje* [On Brodsky: Studies, Essays, Reflections], ed. Piotr Fast (Katowice: Śląsk, 1993), 119–32. See also Tomas Venclova, "Lithuanian Nocturne," in *Joseph Brodsky: The Art of a Poem,* ed. Lev Loseff and Valentina Polukhina (New York: St. Martin's Press, 1999), 107–49.

32. Czesław Miłosz, "O Josifie Brodskim" [On Joseph Brodsky], in *Życie na wyspach* [Living on Islands] (Kraków: Znak, 1998), 269.

33. Czesław Miłosz, "A Struggle against Suffocation," *New York Review of Books,* August 14, 1980, 23–24.

34. Czesław Miłosz, *Wiersze* [Poems] (Kraków: Znak, 2004), vol. 4, 162.

35. Shtern, *Brodsky,* 310.

36. Lev Loseff [Losiev], "O lubvi Ahmatovoj k 'Narodu,'" [About Akhmatova's Love of "Narod"], in *Iosif Brodskij: Un crocevia fra culture,* 159–81.

37. Sylvia Molloy, "Bilingualism, Writing, and the Feeling of Not Quite Being There," in *Lives in Translation: Bilingual Writers on Identity*

and Creativity, ed. Isabelle de Courtivron (New York: Palgrave-Macmillan), 74.

38. Mikhail Lotman, "On 'The Death of Zhukov,'" in *Joseph Brodsky: The Art of a Poem,* 57.

39. *Progułki s Brodskim* [Walks with Brodsky], film (DVD), produced and directed by Elena Yakovich, Aleksey Chichov, and Evgeny Rein (Drugoye Kino, 2004).

CHAPTER 6. IOSIF BRODSKIJ AND POLAND

1. Tomas Venclova in conversation with Jan T. Gross and Irena Grudzińska-Gross, *Aneks* 28 (1982): 124–25. The titles enumerated by Venclova and Brodsky (in the following paragraph) refer to a propaganda publication *Polska* [Poland], literary monthly *Twórczość* [Creativity], satirical weekly *Szpilki* [Needles], intellectual and artistic weekly *Przekrój* [Cross-Section], and even dailies, *Życie Warszawy* [The Life of Warsaw] and *Trybuna Ludu* [People's Tribune; the organ of the Polish Communist Party].

2. Brodsky, "A Talk with Joseph Brodsky," with Anna Husarska, *New Leader,* December 14, 1987, 8.

3. Brodsky, "Żyć w historii" [To Live in History], conversation with Jerzy Illg, in *Reszty nie trzeba: Rozmowy z Josifem Brodskim* [Never Mind: Conversations with Joseph Brodsky], ed. Jerzy Illg (Katowice: Książnica, 1993), 122.

4. Piotr Fast, "Josif Brodski a Polska" [Joseph Brodsky and Poland], *Panorama Polska* (Edmonton, Ont.), no. 37 (November 1996): 4; Irina Adelgeim, "'Rasshireniye rechii': Iosif Brodskij i Polsha" ["The Enlargement of Speech": Joseph Brodsky and Poland], in *Polyaki i Russkyje w glazah drug druga* [Poles and Russians in Each Other's Eyes], ed. V. A. Horev (Moscow: Idrik, 2000), 144.

5. Quoted by Husarska in her interview, and by Irina Adelgeim, "Iosif Brodskij i Polsha," 145.

6. Tomas Venclova, "Josifo Brodskio Atminimui," in *Josifas Brodskis: Vaizdas i jura* [With the View of the Sea], ed. Lilija Tulyte and Konstantas Markevicius (Vilnius: Vyturys, 1999), 355–62; p. 357.

Venclova believes that Lithuania had for Joseph Brodsky the same importance as Georgia for Pasternak and Armenia for Mandelstam; see p. 359.

7. Fragment of "September the First," in Joseph Brodsky, *Selected Poems*, trans. and intro. George L. Kline, foreword by W. H. Auden (London: Penguin Books, 1973), 90.

8. A. V. Issatschenko, "Russian," in *The Slavic Literary Languages: Formation and development*, ed. Alexander M. Schenker and Edward Stankiewicz (New Haven: Yale Russian and East European Publications, 1980), 126–27.

9. As reported by Nina Perlina in a conversation with the author, Bloomington, Indiana, September 2000.

10. See the discussion of Brodsky's poem "Sofyia" in chapter 4.

11. "To nie wzięło się z powietrza: O Josifie Brodskim z Zofią Ratajczakową rozmawia Jerzy Illg" [It Did Not Come from Nowhere: Conversation with Zofia Ratajczakowa], in *Reszty nie trzeba: Rozmowy z Josifem Brodskim* [Never Mind: Conversations with Joseph Brodsky], ed. Jerzy Illg (Katowice: Książnica, 1993), 9.

12. These letters are in the Brodsky Papers, Beinecke Rare Book and Manuscript Library, Yale University.

13. "Po obu stronach oceanu: Adam Michnik rozmawia z Iosifem Brodskim" [On Both Sides of the Ocean: Adam Michnik Talks with Joseph Brodsky], *Gazeta Wyborcza*, January 20, 1995, 7. The encounter was registered by Jacek Kucharczyk, transcribed by Irena Lewandowska, and edited by Joanna Szczęsna. The original tape was discarded.

14. This last definition of Polish was given by Brodsky in 1981, during the panel discussion with Miłosz and Robert Silvers in the New York Institute of Humanities. Unpublished transcript, "Robert Silvers Speaks with Czesław Miłosz and Joseph Brodsky," New York Institute for the Humanities, September 22, 1981, Brodsky Papers, General Collection of Rare Books and Manuscripts, Beinecke Rare Book and Manuscript Library, Yale University, 36.

15. Asar Eppel is quoted in Anna Bikont and Joanna Szczęsna, *Pamiątkowe rupiecie* [Memorabilia] (Warsaw: Prószyński, 1997), 16.

16. Quoted after Piotr Fast, in Piotr Fast, ed. *Poezja polska w Przekładach Josifa Brodskiego* (Katowice: Wydawnictwo Uniwersytetu Śląskiego, 2004), 138.

17. "Patrząc bardzo smutnym wzrokiem / w strony świata te i owe / Joseph Brodsky z NOWYM ROKIEM / Was pozdrawia / DRAWICOWE." In *StS*, 19 and 14.

18. Conversation with Zofia Ratajczakowa, 20. See also, in Nayman's book about Anna Akhmatova, her letter to Brodsky, written from Komarovo on February 15, 1965.

19. *Iosif Brodskij,* ed. Victor Kulle, bibliography of his publications in Russian (St. Petersburg: Russian National Library, 1999).

20. See conversation with Husarska in the *New Leader.*

21. As can be seen on the tape of the TV program "Z Brodskim o zmierzchu" [With Brodsky at Dusk] ed. Andrzej Drawicz. Woroszylski did not attend this occasion, as he was sick. He died in 1996. Dąbrowski was no longer alive. Drawicz died in 1997.

22. Interview with Ludmiła Bołotowa and Jadwiga Szymak-Reiferowa in *Przekrój,* July 4, 1993. The newspaper he mentioned must have been the *New York Review of Books* (March 17, 1983) and the poem in English, as the Polish translation by Stanisław Barańczak appeared in *Zeszyty Literackie* in the summer of 1983, when, I believe, both writers were already free. Barańczak's translation could have been published in a Polish underground newspaper, but I was unable to find any proof of it. Perhaps it was just a typed version. Woroszylski describes that telephone conversation in his private diary (in author's possession) in exactly the same way as Brodsky's recollection.

23. Katowice speech, English original, dated New York, May 31, 1993, Beinecke Rare Book and Manuscript Library, Yale University.

24. "Po obu stronach oceanu," 7.

25. Brodsky's introduction, called "Lettera al lettore italiano" [Letter to the Italian Reader], to Zbigniew Herbert, *Rapporto dalla città assediata,* trans. Pietro Marchesani (Milan: Adelphi, 1983).

26. Gustaw Herling-Grudziński, *Dziennik pisany nocą, 1997–1999* [Diary Written by Night, 1997–1999] (Warsaw: Czytelnik, 2000), 38.

27. Author's conversation with Anatoly Nayman, New York, November 1997.

28. In 1964, Anna Akhmatova received for translation three poems of Wisława Szymborska. She translated one of the poems herself, and gave two to be translated to Anatoly Nayman, her then otherwise unemployed secretary. The three poems signed by Akhmatova appeared in the May 1964 issue of *Polsza*. Information comes from Nayman himself. Bikont and Szczęsna, *Pamiątkowe rupiecie*, 217.

29. Ludmilla Shtern, *Brodsky: A Personal Memoir* (Fort Worth, TX: Baskerville Publishers, 2004), 25.

30. Ann Kjellberg, letter to author, September 17, 2000.

31. *Conversations in Exile: Russian Writers Abroad,* ed. John Glad (Durham, NC: Duke University Press, 1993), 112–13.

32. Expression he used while writing about Auden. This is how Irina Adelgeim characterized the influence Polish culture had on Brodsky, in Adelgeim, "Iosif Brodskij i Polsha," 152.

33. "Po obu stronach oceanu," 11.

34. George F. Kennan, "Russia's International Position at the Close of the War with Germany (May 1945)," in *Memoirs, 1925–1950* (Boston: Little, Brown, 1967), 534–35.

Chapter 7. Loneliness as Always: America

1. Ewa Bieńkowska, "Lekcja wygnania: Miłosz, Herling-Grudziński" [The Lesson of Exile: Miłosz, Herling-Grudziński], *Zeszyty Literackie* 67 (1999): 101.

2. "Robert Silvers Speaks with Czesław Miłosz and Joseph Brodsky," New York Institute for the Humanities, September 22, 1981, Brodsky Papers, General Collection of Rare Books and Manuscripts, Beinecke Rare Book and Manuscript Library, Yale University.

3. Jan Błoński and Sławomir Mrożek, *Listy, 1963–1996* [Letters], ed. T. Nyczek (Kraków: Wydawnictwo Literackie, 2004), 80.

4. Czesław Miłosz, *Aleksander Hertz* (Kraków: Judaica Foundation, 2000), 25, 24.

5. Peter Viereck, poet and translator, and Brodsky were long-time friends, and Brodsky dedicated to him his poem "The Berlin Wall Tune." Both were on the faculty of Mount Holyoke College and occasionally co-taught a class on poetry "between Hitler and Stalin"; they called that class "Rime and Punishment." Daniel Weissbort, "Peter Viereck," *Modern Poetry in Translation*, no. 18 (2001): 236–40.

6. Transcript of the tape of the discussion, in the possession of the author.

7. Czesław Miłosz, *The Captive Mind* (New York: Vintage Books, 1981), 223.

8. I will leave out, no doubt unjustly, the intervention of Peter Viereck, long and full of anecdotes, in which he spoke about how historians' biographies influenced their view of history.

9. "Intellectuals and Social Change in Central and Eastern Europe," Conference, Rutgers University, April 1992; in *Intellectuals and Social Change in Central and Eastern Europe*, ed. William Phillips, special issue of *Partisan Review* 59, no. 4 (Fall 1992): 525–750; p. 552.

10. Leif Sjöberg, "An Interview with Derek Walcott," in *Conversations with Derek Walcott*, ed. William Baer (Jackson: University Press of Mississippi, 1996), 79–85.

11. Quoted in Daniel Weissbort, "Peter Viereck," 236.

12. William Logan, "The Poet of Exile," *New York Times Book Review*, April 8, 2007, 1, 8–9.

13. "The Lisbon Conference on Literature: Central European and Russian Writers" (May 7–8, 1988), ed. Ladislav Matejka, *Cross Currents: A Yearbook of Central European Culture* 9 (1990): 75–124; p. 115.

14. "Intellectuals and Social Change," 552.

15. M. J. Orski, "Spotkanie z Brodskim" [Encounter with Brodsky], *Znak* 12 (1990): 18; quoted in Jadwiga Szymak-Reiferowa, "*Anno Domini* Josifa Brodskiego" [*Anno Domini* of Joseph Brodsky], in *O Brodskim: Studia, szkice, refleksje* [On Brodsky: Studies, Essays, Reflections], ed. Piotr Fast (Katowice: Śląsk, 1993), 204.

16. David Montenegro, conversation with Joseph Brodsky, in *Joseph Brodsky: Conversations*, ed. Cynthia L. Haven (Jackson: University

Press of Mississippi, 2002), 13. In the *Collected Poems in English* the poem is dated 1975, not 1976.

CHAPTER 8. POETRY WITH A FOREIGN ACCENT

1. Czesław Miłosz, *Ziemia Ulro* [The Land of Ulro] (Paris: Instytut Literacki, 1980), 50.

2. About Brodsky's conflicts with his translators, and the critical reaction to his own translations of his poetry, see Bożena Karwowska, *Miłosz i Brodski. Recepcja krytyczna twòrczości w krajach anglojęzycznych* [Miłosz and Brodsky: Critical Reception of Their Work in English-Language Countries] (Warsaw: IBL, 2000), 118–42. See especially Daniel Weissbort, *From Russian with Love: Joseph Brodsky in English* (London: Anvil Press, 2004), about which I will write more later, and the conversation of Valentina Polukhina with Derek Walcott in the already quoted *Joseph Brodsky through the Eyes of his Contemporaries* (London: Palgrave-Macmillan, 1992).

3. Stanisław Barańczak, "Tongue-Tied Eloquence: Notes on Language, Exile, and Writing," in *Breathing under Water and Other East European Essays* (Cambridge, MA: Harvard University Press, 1990), 238.

4. See "Joseph Brodsky: An Interview with Mike Hammer and Christina Daub," in *Joseph Brodsky: Conversations*, ed. Cynthia L. Haven (Jackson: University Press of Mississippi, 2002), 163.

5. Joseph Brodsky, *A Part of Speech* (New York: Farrar, Straus and Giroux, 1980), copyright page.

6. "Morton Street 44," interview with Joseph Brodsky, by Bożena Shallcross, in *Reszty nie trzeba: Rozmowy z Josifem Brodskim* [Never Mind: Conversations with Joseph Brodsky], ed. Jerzy Illg (Katowice: Ksiąźnica, 1993), 166–79.

7. Weissbort, *From Russian with Love*, 31.

8. Interview with Mike Hammer and Christana Daub, 163.

9. Author's conversation with Robert Faggen, Los Angeles, April 2005.

10. Richard Eder, *New York Times*, December 19, 2001; John Bayley, *New York Review of Books*, October 19, 2000; Sven Birkerts, *New York Times Book Review*, September 17, 2000; Craig Raine, *Financial*

Times, November 16, 1996; John Simon, *New Leader,* September 9–21, 1996.

11. Robert Hass, *New Republic,* December 20, 1980.

12. Michael Hofmann, *Times Literary Supplement,* January 10, 1997, 6–8.

13. Daniel Weissbort, "Something Like His Own Language: Brodsky in English," reprinted in *Iosif Brodskij: Un crocevia fra culture* [Joseph Brodsky: A Crossroads of Cultures], ed. Alessandro Niero and Sergio Pescatori (Milan: MG Print on Demand, 2002), 279.

14. *Conversations in Exile: Russian Writers Abroad,* ed. John Glad (Durham, NC: Duke University Press, 1993), 110.

15. Weissbort, "Something Like His Own Language," *Un crocevia fra culture,* 286.

16. Ibid., in Joseph Brodsky, *Collected Poems in English,* ed. Ann Kjellberg (Manchester, Eng.: Carcanet Press, 2001), 55.

17. The remembrance evening took place on October 29, 1996, in Miller Theatre, Columbia University. Besides Strand, Derek Walcott, Susan Sontag, and Tatyana Tolstaya spoke.

18. Czesław Miłosz, "Czy poeci mogą się lubić?" [Can Poets Like Each Other?], interview with Irena Grudzińska-Gross, *Gazeta Wyborcza,* September 5–6, 1998, 12–13; quotation p. 12.

19. Miłosz Papers, Beinecke Rare Book and Manuscript Library, Yale University.

20. Ludmilla Shtern, *Brodsky: A Personal Memoir* (Fort Worth, TX: Baskerville Publishers, 2004), 359.

21. *Conversations in Exile,* ed. Glad, 109–10.

22. Isaiah Berlin, "My guljali s nim po niebiesach" [We Wandered with Him in the Skies], conversation with Diana Myers, 34, no date, Brodsky Papers, Beinecke Rare Book and Manuscript Library, Yale University.

23. Edward Mendelson, *Later Auden* (New York: Farrar, Straus and Giroux, 2000), 8.

24. Jonathan Schell, "Paradise," *Granta* 21 (Spring 1987): 201–18; quotation p. 203.

25. Mentioned in Polukhina, *Brodsky through the Eyes,* 339.

26. *The Power of Poetry: Joseph Brodsky and Derek Walcott in Discussion,* ed. Raoul Granqvist, special issue of *Moderna Språk* 1 (1995).

27. Ibid.

28. Jean-Michel Rey, "Sur Samuel Beckett," *Café Librairie* 1 (1983): 63–66.

29. Jacques Derrida, *Monolingualism of the Other; or, The Prosthesis of Origin,* trans. Patrick Mensah (Stanford, CA: Stanford University Press, 1998). See the opening pages.

30. This is what allows a person from "the center" like John Bayley, Thomas Warton Professor of English Emeritus at the University of Oxford, to say that Brodsky is "like a bear playing the flute" (*New York Times Book Review,* September 1, 1996); and William Logan, also a professor and a poet, to say that Walcott has no ear, and that he has remained "a figure of divided loyalties and a double tongue" (*New York Times Book Review,* April 8, 2007).

31. Elżbieta Kiślak, *Walka Jakuba z aniołem: Czesław Miłosz wobec romantyczności* [Jacob's Fight with the Angel: Czesław Miłosz and Romanticism] (Warsaw: Prószyński, 2000); see especially the chapter on "Exile and Heritage," 157–90.

32. "Nie" [No]. *Kultura* (May 1951): 3–13.

33. Czesław Miłosz, *Życie na wyspach* [Living on Islands] (Kraków: Znak, 1998), 124.

34. Czesław Miłosz, *Nobel Lecture* (New York: Farrar, Straus and Giroux, 1980), 13.

35. Adam Mickiewicz, *Forefathers' Eve,* pt. 3, in *Polish Romantic Drama: Three Plays in English Translation,* ed. Harold B. Segel (Ithaca, NY: Cornell University Press, 1977), 82.

36. Interview in *Tydzień Polski,* November 1–2, 1981.

37. So explained Miłosz during the unpublished "Robert Silvers Speaks with Czesław Miłosz and Joseph Brodsky," New York Institute for the Humanities, September 22, 1981, Brodsky Papers, General Collection of Rare Books and Manuscripts, Beinecke Rare Book and Manuscript Library, Yale University.

38. Clare Cavanagh, "The Americanization of Czesław Miłosz," *Literary Imagination: The Review of the Association of Literary Scholars and Critics* 3 (2004): 332–55; quotation p. 340.

39. This is a quotation from Miłosz's letter to Bogdan Czaykowski, May 29, 1975, cited in Bożena Karwowska, *Miłosz i Brodski: Recepcja krytyczna twórczości w krajach anglojęzycznych* [Miłosz and Brodsky: Critical Reception of Their Work in English-Language Countries] (Warsaw: IBL, 2000), 121. The quotation from the previous sentence is also from Karwowska, p. 125.

40. Ibid.

41. Czesław Miłosz, *Traktat poetycki z moim komentarzem* [Poetic Treatise with My Commentary] (Kraków: Wydawnictwo Literackie, 2001), 6.

42. Ibid.

43. Czesław Miłosz, *Traktat moralny i traktat poetycki: Lekcja literatury* [Moral Treatise and Poetic Treatise: Literature Lesson], ed. Aleksander Fiut and Andrzej Franaszek (Kraków: Wydawnictwo Literackie, 1996); quotation comes from the introductory conversation with Aleksander Fiut and Andrzej Franaszek; see also chapter "Letters from America," in Kiślak, *Walka Jakuba z aniołem,* 120–56.

44. Clare Cavanagh, "The Unacknowledged Legislator's Dream," in *The Other Herbert,* ed. Bożena Shallcross, special issue of *Indiana Slavic Studies* 9 (1998): 100.

45. Czesław Miłosz, *Ogród nauk* [The Garden of Science] (Kraków: Znak, 1998), 250.

46. Leonard Nathan, "On przynosi ratunek" [He Rescues Us], *Tygodnik Powszechny,* June 9, 1996. I am sorry to be forced to translate the words of this American poet from Polish back into his native English.

47. Jan Błoński, *Miłosz jak świat* [Miłosz as a World] (Kraków: Znak, 1998), 6.

48. Marek Zaleski, "Arcywzór biografii poetry" [Arch-Model of Poet's Biography], in *Zamiast: O twórczości Czesława Miłosza* [Instead: On the work of Czesław Miłosz] (Kraków: Wydawnictwo Literackie, 2005), 259.

49. Czesław Miłosz, *Prywatne obowiązki* [Private Duties] (Paris: Instytut Literacki, 1972), 81.
50. Jacques Derrida, *Monolingualism of the Other*, 91, 90.

CHAPTER 9. DEATH AND FRIENDSHIP

1. Mikhail Lotman, "On 'The Death of Zhukov,'" in *Joseph Brodsky: The Art of a Poem*, ed. Lev Loseff and Valentina Polukhina (New York: St. Martin's Press, 1999), 33–57.
2. David Bethea, *Joseph Brodsky and the Creation of Exile* (Princeton, NJ: Princeton University Press, 1994), 27, 165–66.
3. Adam Zagajewski, "Miłosz: Rozum i róże" [Miłosz: Reason and Roses], *Gazeta Wyborcza*, June 29, 2001.
4. Seamus Heaney, "What Passed at Colonus," *New York Review of Books*, October 7, 2004.
5. Seamus Heaney, "The Door Stands Open," *New Republic*, September 13, 2004.
6. Seamus Heaney, "The Singer of Tales: On Joseph Brodsky," *New York Times Book Review*, March 3, 1996.
7. The poems by Hecht, Strand, Rumens, and Maxwell are from the *New Yorker*, November 4, 1996.
8. Miłosz's declaration from *Gazeta Wyborcza*, January 30, 1996; Szymborska's from the same newspaper, December 9, 1996.
9. Adam Zagajewski, "A Morning in Vicenza," trans. Clare Cavanagh, *New Republic*, December 27, 1999.
10. Derek Walcott, "The Italian Eclogues," *New York Review of Books*, August 8, 1996.
11. *Czesław Miłosz: In Memoriam*, ed. Joanna Gromek (Kraków: Znak, 2004), 45. This is an anthology of reactions to Miłosz's death; all the quotations below come from this volume, unless otherwise indicated.
12. Leon Wieseltier, "Czesław Miłosz, 1911–2004," *New York Times Book Review*, December 12, 2004.
13. Cicero, cited several times in Jacques Derrida, *Politiques de l'amitié* (Paris: Galilée, 1994), 9–64.

CHAPTER 10. RETURN AND DEATH

1. Seamus Heaney, "The Singer of Tales: On Joseph Brodsky," *New York Times Book Review,* March 3, 1996.

2. Interview with Liubov Arkus, 1988; quoted in *Joseph Brodsky: The Art of a Poem,* ed. Lev Loseff and Valentina Polukhina (New York: St. Martin's Press, 1999), 210.

3. David Bethea, *Joseph Brodsky and the Creation of Exile* (Princeton, NJ: Princeton University Press, 1994), 163.

4. Sven Birkerts, "The Art of Poetry: Conversation with Joseph Brodsky," *Paris Review* 83 (Spring 1982): 111.

5. Adam Pomorski, "Los i wola" [Fate and Will], in *O Brodskim: Studia, szkice, refleksje* [On Brodsky: Studies, Essays, Reflections], ed. Piotr Fast (Katowice: Śląsk, 1993), 63.

6. Czesław Miłosz, "Apprentice," *Second Space,* trans. Czesław Miłosz and Robert Hass (New York: HarperCollins, 2004), 74, 78.

7. Quoted after Tomas Venclova, *Niezniszczalny rytm: Eseje o literaturze* [Indestructible Rhythm: Essays on Literature] (Sejny: Pogranicze and Fundacja Zeszytów Literackich, 2002), 239.

8. Joseph Brodsky, *Watermark* (New York: Farrar, Straus and Giroux, 1992), 5, 8.

9. After his death, the proposal was published in the *New York Review of Books,* March 21, 1996.

10. Czesław Miłosz, "Straciłem przyjaciela" [I've Lost a Friend], *Gazeta Wyborcza,* January 30, 1996.

11. *Czesław Miłosz: Conversations,* ed. Cynthia L. Haven (Jackson: University Press of Mississippi, 2006), 196.

12. Renata Gorczyńska Papers Relating to Czesław Miłosz, General Collection of Rare Books and Manuscripts, Beinecke Rare Book and Manuscript Library, Yale University, letter from October 18, 1987; in another letter in this archive he wrote: "My conflict with the Polishness is as tiring as an abscess" (February 5, 1988).

13. Czesław Miłosz, "Treatise on Theology," *Second Space,* 47–64.

14. The Pope's telegram to Franciszek Cardinal Macharski was sent from Castel Gandolfo and dated August 25, 2004; it was given to

the press by the cardinal himself. Quoted after *Gazeta Wyborcza*, August 27, 2004.

15. Quoted after *Gazeta Wyborcza*, August 27, 2004.

16. Czesław Miłosz, "List do Denise" [Letter to Denise], in *O podróżach w czasie* [On Travels in Time] (Kraków: Znak, 2004), 152–53.

17. Marek Zaleski, "Arcywzór biografii poety" [The Model Poet's Biography], in *Zamiast: O twórczości Czesława Miłosza* [Instead: On the Work of Czesław Miłosz] (Kraków: Wydawnictwo Literackie, 2005), 269.

18. Ibid., 249.

19. *Rzeczpospolita*, October 4–5, 1997.

20. Krzysztof Czyżewski, "Linia powrotu" [The Line of Return], *Tygodnik Powszechny*, August 22, 2004.

21. *Intellectuals and Social Change in Central and Eastern Europe*, proceedings of a conference at Rutgers University, April 1992, ed. William Phillips, special issue of *Partisan Review* 59, no. 4 (Fall 1992): 553–54.

22. Elżbieta Sawicka, *Przystanek Europa: Rozmowy nie tylko o literaturze* [The Europe Stop: Conversations Not Only about Literature] (Warsaw: Most, 1996), 23.

23. Czesław Miłosz, *Księgi bibilijne* [The Books of the Bible] (Kraków: Wydawnictwo Literackie, 2003), 283–84.

24. Jerzy Pilch, "Czesław Miłosz," *Polityka*, August 28, 2004.

25. In a letter to Błoński, in Jan Błoński and Sławomir Mrożek, *Listy, 1963–1996* [Letters], ed. Tadeusz Nyczek (Kraków: Wydawnictwo Literackie, 2004), 539.

26. Michael Kimmelman, "The Undefeated," *New York Review of Books*, March 24, 2005.

Bibliography

Joseph Brodsky: Works

An Age Ago: A Selection of Nineteenth-Century Russian Poetry. Foreword and bibliographical notes by Joseph Brodsky. Ed. Alan Myers. New York: Farrar, Straus and Giroux, 1988.

Brodsky Papers. General Collection of Rare Books and Manuscripts, Beinecke Rare Book and Manuscript Library, Yale University.

Collected Poems in English. Ed. Ann Kjellberg. New York: Farrar, Straus and Giroux, 2000; Manchester, Eng.: Carcanet Press, 2001.

"Fate of a Poet." *New York Review of Books,* April 1, 1976.

Introduction to special issue devoted to Zbigniew Herbert's poems. *Wilson Quarterly* 1 (1993).

Konets Prekrasnoy Epokhi [The End of a Beautiful Era]. New York: Slovo/Word, 2000.

Less Than One: Selected Essays. New York: Farrar, Straus and Giroux, 1986.

Letter to Leonid Brezhnev. *Washington Post,* June 4, 1972.

Lettera al lettore italiano [Letter to the Italian Reader]. Introduction to Zbigniew Herbert, *Rapporto dalla città assediata,* trans. Pietro Marchesani. Milan: Adelphi, 1983.

Nativity Poems. New York: Farrar, Straus and Giroux, 2001.

Novoye Stanci k Avguste [New Stanzas for Augusta]. Ann Arbor, MI: Ardis, 1983.

On Grief and Reason: Selected Essays. New York: Farrar, Straus and Giroux, 1995.

A Part of Speech. New York: Farrar, Straus and Giroux, 1980.

"Poet's View: A True Child of the Century." *New York Times,* October 10, 1980.

"Presentation of Czesław Miłosz to the Jury." *World Literature Today,* no. 3 (1978).

Selected Poems. Trans. and intro. George L. Kline. Foreword by W. H. Auden. London: Penguin Books, 1973.

Watermark. New York: Farrar, Straus and Giroux, 1992.

"Why Kundera Is Wrong about Dostoyevsky." *New York Times Book Review,* January 17, 1985.

Joseph Brodsky: Interviews

Birkerts, Sven. "The Art of Poetry: Conversation with Joseph Brodsky." *Paris Review* 83 (Spring 1982): 83–126.

"Conversation with Joseph Brodsky." In *Conversations in Exile: Russian Writers Abroad.* Ed. John Glad, 102–13. Durham, NC: Duke University Press, 1993.

Joseph Brodsky: Conversations. Ed. Cynthia L. Haven. Jackson: University Press of Mississippi, 2002.

"Nie moralnością, lecz smakiem: Rozmowa z Josifem Brodskim" [Not by Morality but by Taste: Conversation with Joseph Brodsky]. Interview with Grzegorz Musiał. *NaGłos* 2 (1990): 196–208.

"Po obu stronach oceanu: Adam Michnik rozmawia z Josifem Brodskim" [On Both Shores of the Ocean: Adam Michnik Talks with Joseph Brodsky]. *Gazeta Wyborcza,* January 20, 1995, 6–11.

Progułki s Brodskim [Walks with Brodsky]. Film (DVD). Produced and directed by Elena Yakovich, Aleksey Chichov, and Evgeny Rein. Drugoye Kino, 2004.

Reszty nie trzeba: Rozmowy z Josifem Brodskim [Never Mind: Conversations with Joseph Brodsky]. Ed. Jerzy Illg. Katowice: Książnica, 1993.

"A Talk with Joseph Brodsky." With Anna Husarska. *New Leader*, December 14, 1987, 8.

"Wywiad z Josifem Brodskim" [Interview with Joseph Brodsky]. Interview with Ludmiła Bołotowa and Jadwiga Szymak-Reiferowa. *Przekrój*, July 4, 1993.

"Żyć w historii" [To Live in History]. Conversation with Jerzy Illg. In *Reszty nie trzeba: Rozmowy z Josifem Brodskim* [Never Mind: Conversations with Joseph Brodsky], ed. Jerzy Illg, 113–27. Katowice: Książnica, 1993.

Czesław Miłosz: Works

Aleksander Hertz. Kraków: Judaica Foundation, 2000.

Antologia osobista [Personal Anthology]. Kraków: Znak, 1998.

A Book of Luminous Things: An International Anthology of Poetry. Ed. Czesław Miłosz. New York: Harcourt Brace, 1996.

The Captive Mind. New York: Vintage Books, 1981.

Człowiek wśród skorpionów [Man among Scorpions]. Kraków: Znak, 2000.

Gdzie wschodzi słońce i kędy zapada [From the Rising of the Sun]. Paris: Instytut Literacki, 1974.

Inne Abecadło [Another Alphabet]. Kraków: Wydawnictwo Literackie, 1998.

Jakiegoż to gościa mieliśmy: O Annie Świrszczyńskiej [What a Guest We Had: About Anna Świrszczyńska]. Kraków: Znak, 1996.

"Komentarz do 'Ody do Stalina' Osipa Mandelsztama" [Commentary on the "Ode to Stalin" by Osip Mandelstam]. *NaGłos* 22 (August 1996): 77–83. Reprint, with cuts and changed title: "Bez wstydu ni miary" [Without Shame or Measure]. *Gazeta Wyborcza*, November 23–24, 1996.

Bibliography

Księgi bibilijne [The Books of the Bible]. Kraków: Wydawnictwo Literackie, 2003.

Letters of Czesław Miłosz to Joseph Brodsky. *Zeszyty literackie* 65 (1999). Ed. and trans., with a note by Irena Grudzińska-Gross.

"Looking for a Center: On the Poetry of Central Europe." *Cross Currents: A Yearbook of Central European Culture* 1 (1982): 1–11.

Miłosz Papers. General Collection of Rare Books and Manuscripts, Beinecke Rare Book and Manuscript Library, Yale University.

Miłosz's ABC's. Trans. Madeline G. Levine. New York: Farrar, Straus and Giroux, 2001.

"Myśląc o Brodskim: Kilka uwag" [Thinking about Brodsky: A Few Remarks]. In *O Brodskim: Studia, szkice, refleksje* [On Brodsky: Studies, Essays, Reflections], ed. Piotr Fast, 5–8. Katowice: Śląsk, 1993.

Native Realm: A Search for Self-Definition. Berkeley: University of California Press, 1981.

New and Collected Poems. New York: Ecco, 2001.

"Nie" [No]. *Kultura* (May 1951): 3–13.

Nobel Lecture. New York: Farrar, Straus and Giroux, 1980.

"O Josifie Brodskim" [On Joseph Brodsky]. In *Życie na wyspach* [Living on Islands], 266–77. Kraków: Znak, 1998.

O podróżach w czasie [On Travels in Time]. Kraków: Znak, 2004.

Ogród nauk [The Garden of Sciences]. Kraków: Znak, 1998.

Piesek przydrożny [Roadside Dog]. Kraków: Znak, 1997.

"Poeta i Państwo" [The Poet and the State]. *Rzeczpospolita,* December 7–8, 1996.

Postwar Polish Poetry. Ed. Czesław Miłosz. 3rd ed. Berkeley: University of California Press, 1983.

Prywatne obowiązki [Private Duties]. Paris: Instytut Literacki, 1972.

Second Space. Trans. Czesław Miłosz and Robert Hass. New York: HarperCollins, 2004.

Spiżarnia literacka [Literary Bounty]. Kraków: Wydawnictwo Literackie, 2004.

Striving Towards Being: The Letters of Thomas Merton and Czesław Miłosz. Ed. Robert Faggen. New York: Farrar, Straus and Giroux, 1997.

"A Struggle against Suffocation." *New York Review of Books,* August 14, 1980, 23–24.

"Święto przyjaźni, rodzaj cudu" [Celebration of Friendship, Kind of Miracle]. *Plus-Minus,* May 16–17, 1998.

To Begin Where I Am: Selected Essays. Ed. and intro. Bogdana Carpenter and Madeline G. Levine. New York: Farrar, Straus and Giroux, 2001.

Traktat moralny i traktat poetycki: Lekcja literatury [Moral Treatise and Poetic Treatise: Literature Lesson]. Ed. Aleksander Fiut and Andrzej Franaszek. Kraków: Wydawnictwo Literackie, 1996.

Traktat poetycki z moim komentarzem [Poetic Treatise with My Commentary]. Kraków: Wydawnictwo Literackie, 2001.

Visions from San Francisco Bay. Trans. Richard Lourie. New York: Farrar, Straus and Giroux, 1975.

Wiersze [Poems]. Kraków: Znak, 2004.

The Witness of Poetry. Cambridge, MA: Harvard University Press, 1983.

Wyprawa w dwudziestolecie [Foray into the 1920s]. Kraków: Wydawnictwo Literackie, 1999.

A Year of the Hunter. Trans. Madeline G. Levine. New York: Farrar, Straus and Giroux, 1994.

Ziemia Ulro [The Land of Ulro].Paris: Instytut Literacki, 1980.

Życie na wyspach [Living on Islands]. Kraków: Znak, 1998.

CZESŁAW MIŁOSZ: INTERVIEWS

"Ameryka poetów" [America of Poets: Elżbieta Sawicka Speaks to Czesław Miłosz]. *Plus-Minus,* May 16–17, 1998.

Czesław Miłosz: Conversations. Ed. Cynthia L. Haven. Jackson: University Press of Mississippi, 2006.

"Czy poeci mogą się lubić?" [Can Poets Like Each Other?]. Interview with Irena Grudzińska-Gross. *Gazeta Wyborcza,* September 5–6, 1998, 12–13.

Ewa Czarnecka and Aleksander Fiut. *Conversations with Czesław Miłosz.* Trans. Richard Lourie. New York: Harcourt Brace Jovanovich, 1987.

Renata Gorczyńska [Ewa Czarnecka]. *Podróżny świata: Rozmowy z Czesławem Miłoszem* [World Traveler: Conversations with Czesław Miłosz]. 1st ed., with commentaries. New York: Bicentennial Publishing, 1983. Reprint, Kraków: Wydawnictwo Literackie, 2002.

OTHER SOURCES

Akhmatova, Anna. *My Half-Century: Selected Prose.* Trans. Ronald Meyer. Evanston, IL: Northwestern University Press, 1992.

———. *Selected Poems.* Ed. and intro. Walter Arndt. New York: Ardis/Overlook, 1976.

Adelgeim, Irina. " 'Rasshireniye rechii': Iosif Brodskij i Polsha" ["The Enlargement of Speech": Joseph Brodsky and Poland]. In *Polyaki i Russkyje w glazah drug druga* [Poles and Russians in Each Other's Eyes], ed. V. A. Horev, 144–53. Moscow: Idrik, 2000.

Als, Hilton. "The Islander." *New Yorker,* February 9, 2004, 43–51.

Araszkiewicz, Agata. *Wypowiadam wam moje życie: Melancholia Zuzanny Ginczanki* [I Take My Life Away from You: Melancholy of Zuzanna Ginczanka]. Warsaw: Ośka, 2001.

Auden, W. H. *Collected Poems.* Ed. Edward Mendelson. New York: Random House, 1991.

Barańczak, Stanisław. *Breathing under Water and Other East European Essays.* Cambridge, MA: Harvard University Press, 1990.

———. *Poezja i duch Uogòlnienia.* Kraków: Znak, 1996.

Berlin, Isaiah. "My guljali s nim po niebiesach" [We Wandered with Him in the Skies]. Conversation with Diana Myers, 34. No date. Brodsky Papers, General Collection of Rare Books and Manuscripts, Beinecke Rare Book and Manuscript Library, Yale University.

———. *Personal Impressions.* New York: Viking Press, 1981.

Bethea, David. *Joseph Brodsky and the Creation of Exile.* Princeton, NJ: Princeton University Press, 1994.

Bieńkowska, Ewa. "Lekcja wygnania: Miłosz, Herling-Grudziński" [The Lesson of Exile: Miłosz, Herling-Grudziński]. *Zeszyty Literackie* 67 (1999): 99–105.

Bikont, Anna, and Joanna Szczęsna. *Pamiątkowe rupiecie* [Memorabilia]. Warsaw: Prószyński, 1997.

Błoński, Jan. *Miłosz jak świat* [Miłosz as a World]. Kraków: Znak, 1998.

Błoński, Jan, and Sławomir Mrożek. *Listy, 1963–1996* [Letters]. Ed. Tadeusz Nyczek. Kraków: Wydawnictwo Literackie, 2004.

Bobyszew, Dmitrij [Bobyshev, Dmitry]. "Achmatowskie sieroty" [Akhmatova's Orphans]. Trans. K. Pietrzycka-Bohosiewicz. *Zeszyty Literackie* 30 (Spring 1990): 114–19.

Bodin, Per-Årne. "Miłosz i Rosja, z perspektywy szwedzkiej" [Miłosz and Russia, from a Swedish Perspective]. *Teksty Drugie* 5 (1997): 5–23.

Bowra, Maurice. *The Greek Experience.* Oxford: Oxford University Press, 1967.

Boym, Svetlana. *The Future of Nostalgia.* New York: Basic Books, 2002.

Cavanagh, Clare. "The Americanization of Czesław Miłosz." *Literary Imagination: The Review of the Association of Literary Scholars and Critics* 3 (2004): 332–55.

———. *Osip Mandelstam and the Modernist Creation of Tradition.* Princeton, NJ.: Princeton University Press, 1995.

———. "The Unacknowledged Legislator's Dream." In *The Other Herbert,* ed. Bożena Shallcross, special issue of *Indiana Slavic Studies* 9 (1998): 97–120.

Chiaromonte, Nicola. "Albert Camus." In *The Worm of Consciousness and Other Essays,* trans. Miriam Chiaromonte, intro. Mary McCarthy, 50–57. New York: Harcourt Brace Jovanovich, 1976.

Coetzee, J. M. *Giving Offense: Essays on Censorship.* Chicago: University of Chicago Press, 1996.

Conversations in Exile: Russian Writers Abroad. Ed. John Glad. Durham, NC: Duke University Press, 1993.

Conversations with Derek Walcott. Ed. William Baer. Jackson: University Press of Mississippi, 1996.

Czesław Miłosz: In Memoriam. Ed. Joanna Gromek. Kraków: Znak, 2004.

Czyżewski, Krzysztof. "Linia powrotu" [The Line of Return]. *Tygodnik Powszechny,* August 22, 2004.

Derrida, Jacques. *Monolingualism of the Other; or, The Prosthesis of Origin.* Trans. Patrick Mensah. Stanford, CA: Stanford University Press, 1998.

———. *Politiques de l'amitié.* Paris: Galilée, 1994.

Fast, Piotr. "Josif Brodski a Polska" [Joseph Brodsky and Poland]. *Panorama Polska* (Edmonton, Ont.), no. 37 (November 1996): 4.

———. *Spotkania z Brodskim* [Encounters with Brodsky]. Wrocław: Wirydarz, 1996.

———, ed. *Poezja polska w Przekładach Josifa Brodskiego.* Katowice: Wydawnictwo Uniwersytetu Sląskiego, 2004, 138.

Fiut, Aleksander. *W stronę Miłosza* [Toward Miłosz]. Kraków: Wydawnictwo Literackie, 2003.

Gombrowicz, Witold. *Dziennik, 1961–1966* [Diaries, 1961–1966]. Paris: Instytut Literacki, 1982.

Gorczyńska, Renata. *Jestem z Wilna i inne adresy* [I am from Vilnius, and Other Addresses]. Kraków: Wydawnictwo Krakowskie, 2003.

Gross, Jan T. *Revolution from Abroad.* Princeton, NJ: Princeton University Press, 1988.

Gross, Jan T., and Irena Grudzinska Gross. "A Conversation with Tomas Venclova." *Aneks* 28 (1982): 123–53.

Gross, Irena Grudzinska. "Adam Mickiewicz: A European from Nowogrodek." *East European Politics and Society* 2 (Spring 1995): 295–316.

———. *The Scar of Revolution: Custine, Tocqueville, and the Romantic Imagination.* Berkeley: University of California Press, 1991.

Hartwig, Julia. "Najwieksze szczęście, największy ból" [The Greatest Happiness, the Greatest Pain]. Interview with Jarosław Mikołajewski. *Wysokie Obcasy,* March 26, 2005, 10.

Heaney, Seamus. "The Singer of Tales: On Joseph Brodsky." *New York Times Book Review,* March 3, 1996.

———. "What Passed at Colonus." *New York Review of Books,* October 7, 2004.

Herling-Grudziński, Gustaw. *Dziennik pisany nocą, 1997–1999* [Diary Written at Night, 1997–1999]. Warsaw: Czytelnik, 2000.

Hertz, Zygmunt. *Listy do Czesława Miłosza, 1952–1979* [Letters to Miłosz]. Ed. Renata Gorczyńska. Paris: Instytut Literacki, 1992.

Hofmann, Michael. "On Absenting Oneself: Joseph Brodsky's Modesty, Americanism, and Tenderness towards Things." *Times Literary Supplement*, January 10, 1997, 6–8.

Intellectuals and Social Change in Central and Eastern Europe. Proceedings of a conference at Rutgers University, April 1992. Ed. William Phillips. Special issue of *Partisan Review* 59, no. 4 (Fall 1992): 525–750.

International Czesław Miłosz Festival. Proceedings of festival at Claremont McKenna College. Special section of *Partisan Review* 66, no. 1 (1999): 9–152.

Iosif Brodskij. Ed. Victor Kulle. Bibliography of his publications in Russian. St. Petersburg: Russian National Library, 1999.

Iosif Brodskij: Un crocevia fra culture [Joseph Brodsky: A Crossroads of Cultures]. Ed. Alessandro Niero and Sergio Pescatori. Milan: MG Print on Demand, 2002.

Issatschenko, A. V. "Russian." In *The Slavic Literary Languages: Formation and Development,* ed. Alexander M. Schenker and Edward Stankiewicz, 126–27. New Haven: Yale Russian and East European Publications, 1980.

Janion, Maria. *Do Europy tak, ale z naszymi umarłymi* [To Europe, Yes, but with Our Dead]. Warsaw: Sic! 2000.

Josifas Brodskis: Vaizdas i jura [With the View of the Sea]. Ed. Lilija Tulyte and Konstantas Markevicius. Vilnius: Vyturys, 1999.

Karpiński, Wojciech. *Książki zbójeckie* [Dangerous Books]. Warsaw: Biblioteka Narodowa, 1996.

Karwowska, Bożena. *Miłosz i Brodski: Recepcja krytyczna twòrczości w krajach anglojęzycznych* [Miłosz and Brodsky: Critical Reception of Their Work in English-Language Countries]. Warsaw: IBL, 2000.

Kennan, George F. *Memoirs, 1925–1950.* Boston: Little, Brown, 1967.

Kimmelman, Michael. "The Undefeated." *New York Review of Books,* March 24, 2005.

Kiślak, Elżbieta. *Walka Jakuba z aniołem: Czesław Miłosz wobec romanty-czności* [Jacob's Fight with the Angel: Czesław Miłosz and Romanticism]. Warsaw: Prószyński, 2000.

Konwicki, Tadeusz. *Bohiń.* Warsaw: Czytelnik, 1987.

Kundera, Milan. "The Tragedy of Central Europe." *New York Review of Books,* April 26, 1984, 35–38.

———. "An Introduction to a Variation." *New York Times Book Review,* January 6, 1985, 1.

Labov, Jessie. "Reinventing Central Europe: *Cross-Currents* and the Émigré Writer in the 1980s." Ph.D. diss., Department of Comparative Literature, New York University, 2003.

Levine, Madeline G. "*Abecadło* i trzecia powieść Czesława Miłosza, jak dotąd nie napisana" [*ABC* and the Third Novel of Miłosz, So Far Unwritten]. In *Poznawanie Miłosza, Część Druga* [Understanding Miłosz, Part Two], ed. Aleksander Fiut, 305–12. Kraków: Wydawnictwo Literackie, 2001.

"Lisbon Conference on Literature: Central European and Russian Writers." About conference on May 7–8, 1988. Ed. Ladislav Matejka. *Cross Currents: A Yearbook of Central European Culture* 9 (1990): 75–124.

Logan, William. "The Poet of Exile." *New York Times Book Review,* April 8, 2007, 1, 8–9.

Loseff, Lev. *Iosif Brodskij: Opit Literaturnoy Biografii* [Joseph Brodsky: A Literary Biography]. Moscow: Mołodaja Gvardia, 2006.

——— [Losiev, Lev]. "O lubvi Ahmatovoj k 'Narodu'" [About Akhmatova's Love of "Narod"]. In *Iosif Brodskij: Un crocevia fra culture* [Joseph Brodsky: A Crossroads of Cultures], ed. Alessandro Niero and Sergio Pescatori, 159–81. Milan: MG Print on Demand, 2002.

Lotman, Mikhail. "On 'The Death of Zhukov.'" In *Joseph Brodsky: The Art of a Poem,* ed. Lev Loseff and Valentina Polukhina, 33–57. New York: St. Martin's Press, 1999.

Mandelstam, Nadezhda. *Mozart and Salieri.* Trans. Robert A. McLean. Ann Arbor, MI: Ardis, 1973.

Marinelli, Luigi. "Miłosz et l'autre Europe." Manuscript in possession of Irena Grudzinska Gross.

———. "Ricerca di una patria: L'Europa familiare di Miłosz fra Seteinai e la baia di San Francisco" [Search for a Homeland: Miłosz's Europe from Šeteinai to San Francisco Bay]. In *I Nobel letterari polacchi* [Polish Nobels in Literature], Convegno dedicato al contributo della letterature polacca alla cultura europea [proceedings from a conference dedicated to the contribution of Polish literature to European culture], 49–65. Milan: Mimep-Docete, 2005.

Matuszewski, Ryszard. *Alfabet: Wybór z pamięci 90-latka* [Alphabet: From the Memory of a Ninety-Year-Old]. Warsaw: Iskry, 2004.

Melnyczuk, Askold. "Killing the Common Moth." In *Seamus Heaney: A Celebration,* ed. Stratis Haviaras, 108—11. Cambridge, MA: Harvard Review Monograph, 1996.

Mendelson, Edward. *Later Auden.* New York: Farrar, Straus and Giroux, 2000.

Mickiewicz, Adam. *Forefathers' Eve.* In *Polish Romantic Drama: Three Plays in English Translation,* ed. Harold B. Segel. Ithaca, NY: Cornell University Press, 1977.

Molloy, Sylvia. "Bilingualism, Writing, and the Feeling of Not Quite Being There." In *Lives in Translation: Bilingual Writers on Identity and Creativity,* ed. Isabelle de Courtivron, 69–77. New York: Palgrave-Macmillan, 2003.

Nathan, Leonard. "On przynosi ratunek" [He Rescues Us]. *Tygodnik Powszechny,* June 9, 1996.

Nayman, Anatoly [Anatolij]. *Rasskazy o Annie Achmatowoj* [On Anna Akhmatova]. Moscow: Khudozhestvienna Literatura, 1989.

———. *Remembering Anna Akhmatova.* Trans. Wendy Rosslyn. Intro. Joseph Brodsky. New York: Henry Holt, 1991. [Translation of *Rasskazy o Annie Achmatowoj.*]

———. *Roman s Samovarom.* New York: Novyi Medved, 2006.

O Brodskim: Studia, szkice, refleksje [On Brodsky: Studies, Essays, Reflections]. Ed. Piotr Fast. Katowice: Śląsk, 1993.

Pilch, Jerzy. "Czesław Miłosz." *Polityka,* August 28, 2004.

Poezja polska w przekladach Josifa Brodskiego [Polish Poetry in Joseph Brodsky's Translations]. Comp. and ed. Piotr Fast. Katowice: Uniwersytet Śląski, 2004.

Polukhina, Valentina. *Joseph Brodsky: A Poet for Our Time.* Cambridge: Cambridge University Press, 1989.

———. *Brodsky through the Eyes of His Contemporaries.* London: Palgrave-Macmillan, 1992.

Pomorski, Adam. "Los i wola" [Fate and Will]. In *O Brodskim: Studia, szkice, refleksje* [On Brodsky: Studies, Essays, Reflections], ed. Piotr Fast, 37–78. Katowice: Śląsk, 1993.

The Power of Poetry: Joseph Brodsky and Derek Walcott in Discussion. Ed. Raoul Granqvist. Special issue of *Moderna Språk* 1 (1995).

Pyszny, Joanna. "Sprawa Miłosza, czyli poeta w czyścu" [L'Affaire Miłosz, or the Poet in Purgatory]. In *Poznanie Miłosza Drugie, 1980–1998* [Understanding Miłosz, 1980–1998], ed. Aleksander Fiut, 53–81. Kraków: Wydawnictwo Literackie, 1998.

Reeder, Roberta. *Anna Akhmatova: Poet and Prophet.* New York: St. Martin's Press, 1994.

Renata Gorczyńska Papers Relating to Czesław Miłosz. General Collection of Rare Books and Manuscripts, Beinecke Rare Book and Manuscript Library, Yale University.

Rey, Jean-Michel. "Sur Samuel Beckett." *Café Librairie* 1 (1983): 63–66.

Rice, James. Review of two books on Osip Mandelstam: *Osip Mandel'shtam i ego vremia,* comp. and preface Vadim Kreid [Kreyd] and Evgenii Necheporuk; and *Mandel'shtam i stalinskaia epokha: Ezopov iazyk w poezii Mandel'shtama 30-kh godov,* by Irina Mess-Beier [Mess-Baher]. *Slavic Review* (Summer 1998): 482–83.

"Robert Silvers Speaks with Czesław Miłosz and Joseph Brodsky." New York Institute for the Humanities, September 22, 1981. Brodsky Papers, General Collection of Rare Books and Manuscripts, Beinecke Rare Book and Manuscript Library, Yale University.

Sawicka, Elżbieta. *Przystanek Europa: Rozmowy nie tylko o literaturze* [The Europe Stop: Conversations Not Only about Literature]. Warsaw: Most, 1996.

Schell, Jonathan. "Paradise." *Granta* 21 (Spring 1987): 201–18.

Sharp, Ronald A. *Friendship and Literature: Spirit and Form.* Durham, NC: Duke University Press, 1986.

Shtern, Ludmilla. *Brodsky: A Personal Memoir.* Fort Worth, TX: Baskerville Publishers, 2004.

Sjöberg, Leif. "An Interview with Derek Walcott." In *Conversations with Derek Walcott,* ed. William Baer, 79–85. Jackson: University Press of Mississippi, 1996.

Slezkine, Yuri. *The Jewish Century.* Princeton, NJ: Princeton University Press, 2004.

Smith, Gerry. "A Song without Music." In *Joseph Brodsky: The Art of a Poem,* ed. Lev Loseff and Valentina Polukhina, 1–23. New York: St. Martin's Press, 1999.

Snyder, Timothy. Review of *Legends of Modernity,* by Czesław Miłosz. *The Nation,* January 9–16, 2006, 26–30.

Swir, Anna. *Talking to My Body.* Trans. Czesław Miłosz and Leonard Nathan. Port Townsend, WA: Copper Canyon Press, 1996.

——— [Swirszczyńska, Anna]. *Budowałam barykadę* [Building the Barricade]. Kraków: Wydawnictwo Literackie, 1974.

Szymak-Reiferowa, Jadwiga. *"Anno Domini* Josifa Brodskiego" [*Anno Domini* of Joseph Brodsky]. In *O Brodskim: Studia, szkice, refleksje* [On Brodsky: Studies, Essays, Reflections], ed. Piotr Fast, 119–32. Katowice: Śląsk, 1993.

———. *Czytając Brodskiego* [Reading Brodsky]. Kraków: Wydawnictwo Uniwersytetu Jagiellońskiego, 1998.

Tosza, Elżbieta. *Stan serca: Trzy dni z Josifem Brodskim* [The State of the Heart: Three Days with Joseph Brodsky]. Katowice: Książnica, 1993.

Venclova, Tomas. "Lithuanian Nocturne." In *Joseph Brodsky: The Art of a Poem,* ed. Lev Loseff and Valentina Polukhina, 107–49. New York: St. Martin's Press, 1999.

———. *Niezniszczalny rytm: Eseje o literaturze* [Indestructible Rhythm: Essays on Literature]. Sejny: Pogranicze and Fundacja Zeszytów Literackich, 2002.

―――. "Petersburskie spotkania: Achmatowa i Brodski" [Petersburg Encounters: Akhmatova and Brodsky]. *Zeszyty Literackie* 83 (2003): 166–80.

Volkov, Solomon. *Conversations with Joseph Brodsky.* Trans. Marian Schwartz. New York: Free Press, 1998.

Walcott, Derek. *Collected Poems, 1948–1984.* New York: Farrar, Straus and Giroux, 1986.

―――. "The Italian Eclogues." *New York Review of Books,* August 8, 1996.

Wieseltier, Leon. "Czesław Miłosz, 1911–2004." *New York Times Book Review,* December 12, 2004.

Weissbort, Daniel. *From Russian with Love: Joseph Brodsky in English.* London: Anvil Press, 2004.

―――. "Peter Viereck." *Modern Poetry in Translation,* no. 18 (2001): 236–40.

―――. "Something Like His Own Language: Brodsky in English." In Joseph Brodsky, *Collected Poems in English,* ed. Ann Kjellberg. Manchester, Eng.: Carcanet Press, 2001. Reprinted in *Iosif Brodskij: Un crocevia fra culture* [Joseph Brodsky: A Crossroads of Culture], ed. Alessandro Niero and Sergio Pescatori, 275–88. Milan: MG Print on Demand, 2002.

Weststeijn, Willem G. "The Thought of You Is Going Away . . ." In *Joseph Brodsky: The Art of a Poem,* ed. Lev Loseff and Valentina Polukhina, 177–90. New York: St. Martin's Press, 1999.

"Whether and How History Speaks." Transcript of a debate between Joseph Brodsky, Czesław Miłosz, and Peter Viereck, Mount Holyoke College, October 16, 1985. In possession of the author.

Witkowska, Alina. *Mickiewicz: Słowo i czyn* [Mickiewicz: Word and Deed]. Warsaw: PIW, 1975.

Woroszylski, Wiktor. Diary. In possession of the author.

Zagajewski, Adam. "Derek Walcott." *Zeszyty Literackie* 41 (1993): 59–63.

―――. "Miłosz: Rozum i róże" [Miłosz: Reason and Roses]. *Gazeta Wyborcza,* June 29, 2001.

————. "A Morning in Vicenza." Trans. Clare Cavanagh. *New Republic,* December 27, 1999.

————. "Przyszli tłumacze: Z Adamem Zagajewskim rozmawia Joanna Gromek" [Future Translators: Conversation with Joanna Gromek]. *Gazeta Wyborcza,* July 10, 2003.

Zaleski, Marek. *Zamiast: O twórczości Czesława Miłosza* [Instead: On the Work of Czesław Miłosz]. Kraków: Wydawnictwo Literackie, 2005.

Index